CAPITAL PUNISHMENT

A Reference Handbook

CAPITAL PUNISHMENT

A Reference Handbook

Michael Kronenwetter

CONTEMPORARY WORLD ISSUES

ABC-CLIO

Santa Barbara, California
Denver, Colorado
Oxford, England

Library of Congress Cataloging-in-Publication Data

Kronenwetter, Michael.
    Capital punishment : a reference handbook / Michael Kronenwetter.
      p. cm.—(Contemporary world issues)
    Includes bibliographical references and index.
    1. Capital punishment—United States. 2. Capital punishment.
  I. Title.   II. Series.
  HV8699.U5K76 1993   364.6'6—dc20

ISBN 0-87436-718-2

99 98 97 96 95   10 9 8 7 6 5 4 3

ABC-CLIO, Inc.
130 Cremona Drive, P.O. Box 1911
Santa Barbara, California 93116-1911

This book is printed on acid-free paper ⊖ .
Manufactured in the United States of America

From the beginning of our Nation, the punishment of death has stirred acute public controversy. Although pragmatic arguments for and against the punishment have been frequently advanced, this longstanding and heated controversy cannot be explained solely as the result of differences over the practical wisdom of a particular government policy. At bottom, the battle has been waged on moral grounds. The country has debated whether a society for which the dignity of the individual is the supreme value can, without a fundmental inconsistency, follow the practice of deliberately putting some of its members to death.

Supreme Court Justice William Brennan, in his concurring opinion in the case of Furman v. Georgia, *408 U.S. 238, 257 (1972).*

Contents

Preface

All punishment is based on the same simple proposition: there must be a penalty for wrongdoing.

In order for there to be punishment, there must be both a wrongdoer and an authority to inflict the penalty. In a family, punishment is usually handed out to offending children by their parents. In society at large, punishment is inflicted on those who break the law by the criminal justice system, made up of the police, the courts, and the prisons. In both cases, the message from the authority to the wrongdoer is clear. Wrongdoing has consequences. If you do something wrong, you will suffer for it. The more serious the offense, the more serious the penalty.

Capital punishment—or death—is generally considered the most terrible penalty society can inflict. This is not only because it is the most violent of all legal punishments, but because it is the most final and complete. Execution deprives its victims not only of their freedom, but of their very futures. Or, as Supreme Court Justice William Brennan wrote in his dissenting opinion in the case of *Gregg v. Georgia:* "Death for whatever crime and under all circumstances is truly an awesome punishment. The calculated killing of a human being by the state involves, by its very nature, a denial of the executed person's humanity. . . an executed person has indeed 'lost' the right to have rights."

In many ancient societies, death was imposed for all sorts of criminal and political offenses. In modern times, however, it is used more sparingly. Many modern nations don't use it at all. Those that do, including the United States, usually reserve it for those crimes the society considers most serious. If you offend society deeply enough, you die.

Because of its violence and finality, the death penalty is extremely controversial. The controversy is strongest in those societies that hold human life most sacred. Many nations—most of them either in the Western Hemisphere or in Europe—have totally abolished capital punishment. Others confine its use to the most hardened and brutal criminals. Still others allow for it in their laws but never—or almost never—actually impose it.

In the United States, use of the death penalty has been on the rise in recent decades, following a period during the late 1960s and early 1970s when there were no executions at all. Today 36 states make at least one crime punishable by death, as do the federal government and the United States military. Fourteen states and the District of Columbia have no death penalty.

Plan of the Book

This book begins with an overview of the entire subject of capital punishment, complete with a discussion of the many controversies that swirl around the practice. It goes on to provide a selection of valuable information relating to the death penalty, and suggestions for obtaining still further information on the subject.

Chapter 1 consists of a general introduction. It includes an explanation of the justifications most often put forward for the death penalty, as well as a brief history of the practice, giving special attention to its use in Britain and the United States. Chapter 2 explores the many criticisms—both practical and philosophical—often leveled at the death penalty, including claims that it is ineffective, unconstitutional, and immoral.

Chapter 3 presents a chronology of important developments, while Chapter 4 provides brief biographies of people, past and present, who have helped to form modern attitudes toward capital punishment. Chapter 5 presents a variety of significant facts and figures, many in the form of tables and graphs; as well as excerpts from important documents and key articles on the subject.

Chapter 6 presents a list of organizations that do work relating to the death penalty. Chapters 7 and 8 offer annotated bibliographies and resource lists. The book concludes with a glossary of terms frequently used in discussions of capital punishment.

Taken as a whole, it is hoped that this book will provide a useful resource for anyone interested in this ancient, but increasingly controversial, practice.

1

An Introduction to Capital Punishment

WHY CAPITAL PUNISHMENT? WHY DOES SOCIETY feel the need to take some of its criminals and kill them as punishment for their crimes?

On the face of it, killing criminals seems to be a brutal and uncivilized thing to do. Killing is, after all, a violent act, no matter how it is done, and no matter who carries it out. It is not as though we have nothing else to do with those Americans who break the rules of our society. Hundreds of thousands of them, in fact, are held for varying periods of time in the many jails and state and federal prisons that dot the national landscape. Some will be imprisoned for the rest of their lives. How can we, as a society, justify taking what amounts to only a handful of this multitude of prisoners and killing them?

As individuals, most of us instinctively shrink from the idea of taking the life of another human being. Killing is forbidden by every major religion, and murder is considered a crime in every civilized human society. How can the government of a civilized society claim the right to kill any of its citizens—and to kill them in the name of the very law that condemns murder?

In reality, the prohibition on killing has never been absolute—even many religions make exceptions. Despite the commandment "Thou shalt not kill," for example, most branches of the Jewish and Christian faiths accept at least the occasional need for war, as well as the right of an individual to kill in self-defense or to protect someone else from a murderous attack.

If anything, civil governments make even more exceptions than major religions. In time of war, soldiers are not only permitted to kill other human beings, they are required to do so. Many U.S. jurisdictions permit a citizen to kill not only in self-defense but (in some circumstances, at least) in defense of his or her property. Capital punishment, then, is only one of many exceptions that our society makes to the general prohibition against killing.

Still, the question remains. Why? Why does society kill? Why should society kill? Proponents of the death penalty make a number of arguments on its behalf, ranging from the practical, to the moral, to the philosophic.

"Uncontrollable Brutes"

Several of the reasons put forward for capital punishment have to do with the protection of society. Certain criminals must die, the defenders of the death penalty argue, so the rest of us can be safe (or, at least, safer).

How do the deaths of some criminals protect the rest of us? In several ways, according to the death penalty's proponents. On one level, the execution of dangerous criminals can be seen as a simple matter of self-defense, because, at the very least, death stops executed criminals from ever repeating their crimes. This is how Judge Alfred J. Talley of New York saw it in a famous debate with lawyer Clarence Darrow. "If I, as an individual, have the right to kill in self defense," asked Talley, "why has not the State, which is nothing more than an aggregation of individuals, the same right to defend itself against unjust aggression and unjust attack?"[1]

Some supporters of the death penalty argue that truly vicious criminals are like rabid animals that must be destroyed. There is no way to cure them of their disease, which makes them attack and kill others. Why not simply get rid of them before they kill or injure someone else? As the scientist Albert Einstein once suggested, "There is no reason why society should not rid itself of individuals proved socially harmful."[2]

Philosopher Jacques Barzun compares such criminals to wolves and calls for them to be dispatched by what he terms *judicial homicide:* "The uncontrollable brute whom I want put out of the way is not to be punished for his misdeeds, nor used as an example or a warning; he is to be killed for the protection of others. . . ."[3]

Even some of the "brutes" themselves agree with this prescription. Westley Allan Dodd, who was executed in 1993, asked for the state of Washington to kill him. Dodd's crimes had been especially horrible. He had raped and murdered three young boys, the youngest of whom was only four years old. He tortured one of the children for two days before killing him, keeping a diary of his atrocities, and taking pictures of the boys to keep with him afterwards. When he was arrested, he was in the process of kidnapping still another young victim from the bathroom of a movie theater. The actual details of the killings were so awful that some of the jurors who were forced to listen to them went for psychiatric counseling after the trial.[4]

Dodd asked to be put to death, insisting that only execution could stop him from continuing his murderous ways. If he were not executed, he told a judge, he would kill a guard in order to escape. Once free, he would seek out more young boys to kill. The state of Washington willingly granted his request, and he was hanged on 5 January 1993.

Dodd is a prime example of the kind of criminal Barzun wants destroyed. If the death penalty were limited only to those like him, however, it would almost never be applied. Obsessive killers like Dodd are rare. They make up a tiny fraction of the thousands of murderers convicted in the United States each year. Most fall into very different categories. A few are professional killers for hire. Many more commit murder in the process of committing a robbery or other crime. Some kill in the throes of a drug- or alcohol-induced fit. Perhaps the largest percentage of all kill in the heat of the moment, in a sudden burst of rage or jealousy. Still others act in desperation, like the battered wives and abused children who strike out in a final attempt to free themselves from a situation they can no longer endure.

Some murderers, like Dodd, may be determined to kill again and again, but most are not. Many are only as likely to kill again as the average citizen is to murder someone in the first place. It is no more necessary to execute them to keep them from repeating their crimes than it is to execute others who once turned violent without actually killing anybody. However, some supporters of capital punishment believe society is protected by executing any killer, believing that executions discourage other potential murderers from carrying out their crimes.

Deterrence

Robert E. Crowe, the Illinois state's attorney who demanded the death sentence for the infamous Chicago murderers Leopold and Loeb, was a great supporter of capital punishment. "I urge capital punishment for murder," he once explained, "not because I believe that society wishes to take the life of a murderer, but because society does not wish to lose its own. . . . It is the finality of the death penalty which instills fear in the heart of every murderer, and it is this fear of punishment which protects society."[5]

In other words, Crowe wanted Leopold and Loeb to die, not to protect society from them, but to protect society from others who might come after them. This is probably the most common of all the arguments made for the death penalty—the belief that the deaths of some criminals will deter others from committing similar crimes.

Many cold-blooded murderers plan their acts. This is particularly true of professional criminals, but it is often true of others as well, including spouses who kill each other for insurance money and enemies who kill out of hate or revenge. In making their plans, these potential killers must consider many different factors: How good is their plan? How likely are they to succeed in accomplishing what they set out to do? How likely are they to get caught? If they are caught, how likely is it that they will be convicted? If they are convicted, what will their punishment be?

One factor potential murderers should have to take into account, say proponents of the death penalty, is the likelihood—if not the certainty—that they will be killed if they get caught.

There is a great deal of debate over how powerful a deterrent capital punishment actually is. Most of us, however, have an instinctive feeling that the death penalty *must* deter, at least to some extent. Deterrence is, after all, one of the fundamental reasons for punishment of any kind. The harsher the punishment, the stronger the deterrent effect.

Since death is considered the harshest punishment available under the law, it seems logical that it must also be the most effective deterrent to crime. "No other punishment deters men so effectually from committing crimes as the punishment of death," remarked the English barrister James Stephen more than 125 years ago. "In any secondary punishment, however terrible, there is hope; but death is death; its terror cannot be described more forcibly."[6]

Another aspect of the deterrence argument applies to criminals who have already received the harshest punishment available in law short of death. They are the lifers, who have been condemned to spend the rest of their lives in jail.

Without the threat of execution to hold over these prisoners' heads, argue some prison officials, there is nothing to deter them from committing further terrible crimes while in prison. The dangers of this situation were pointed out by Professor Ernest van den Haag of New York University in an interview in 1976—a time when no death penalty had been carried out in the United States for several years. "The federal prisons now have custody of a man sentenced to life imprisonment who, since he has been in prison, has committed three more murders on three separate occasions— both of prison guards and inmates. There is no further punishment that he can receive. In effect, he has a license to murder."[7]

A Sense of Justice

The reasons for the death penalty discussed so far are essentially utilitarian. They assume the death penalty accomplishes something useful for society; that is, it protects society from criminals who might prey on it in the future if the death penalty is not there to stop them. However, not all the reasons for supporting capital punishment are utilitarian. For many people, support for the death penalty is not so much a practical decision as a gut instinct. It does not depend on logical arguments, but on a deep sense of justice—a sense that death is the only punishment truly fitting for crimes too monstrous to be dealt with in any other way.

As Professor Ernest van den Haag explains: "Our system of punishment is based not just on deterrence but also on what is called 'justice'—namely that we feel a man who has committed a crime must be punished in proportion to the seriousness of the crime. Since the crime that takes a life is irrevocable, so must be the punishment."[8] It was this sense that caused Judge Alfred J. Talley to refer to the death penalty as the very "symbol of justice."[9]

Lord Justice Denning, Master of the Rolls of the Court of Appeals in England, made the same point before a royal commission considering whether England should retain capital punishment some years ago: "It is a mistake to consider the objects of punishment as being deterrent or reformative or preventive and nothing else. . . . The truth is that some crimes are so outrageous that society insists on adequate punishment because the wrongdoer deserves it, irrespective of whether it is deterrent or not."[10]

The American judge Samuel Hand made a similar point almost 70 years earlier, tying it to the Judeo-Christian tradition of American law:

> In truth, there is inherent in all punishment for crime the idea of executing justice, of rewarding the offender according to his misdeeds. It is an idea entirely separate from and independent of any notion of prevention, even of public safety.
>
> "Vengeance is mine, and I will repay, saith the Lord," but vengeance—righteous vengeance—is the right and duty of the state. The state is, in this respect, the representative of the Divine Governor. To it, the sword of justice and retribution is delivered. By it, it must be wielded.
>
> Capital execution upon the deadly poisoner and the midnight assassin is not only necessary for the safety of society, it is the fit and deserved retribution of their crimes. By it alone is divine and human justice fulfilled.
>
> This is the crowning and all-sufficient ground for the destruction of the convicted murderer by the civil power.[11]

The death penalty has always been considered especially appropriate for the crime of murder. To many people, death seems the logical—and even the inevitable—consequence for that particular crime: the only fit retribution. Death is, after all, the only punishment that has the same remorseless finality as murder itself. As Shakespeare had a haunted man proclaim about the murder he had committed, "It will have blood, they say; blood will have blood."[12]

Some supporters of the death penalty believe that it is precisely this appropriateness that justifies capital punishment. The "real reason" for the death penalty, says Los Angeles County District Attorney Ira Reiner, is that "the overwhelming majority of [the American public] feels that it is the appropriate penalty for certain limited types of crimes." Those crimes, Reiner specifies, are "the most horrendous of the murder cases."[13]

Historically, the special connection between murder and capital punishment is emphasized by the fact that when states began cutting back on the use of the death penalty in the nineteenth century, most retained it for murder. Today, not only the United States but most other countries in the world that still use the death penalty continue to reserve it primarily for murderers.

Here is how a nineteenth-century judge expressed this peculiar appropriateness to a murderer he was sentencing to die:

> By our law, the crime of which you stand convicted is the only one that is punishable with death. Against the murderer, the law has attached the greatest penalty known to criminal jurisprudence. The universal opinion and sanction of all ages has induced our legislature to put this law upon the Statute book; and as life is the most sacred boon to man, it is only allowed to be taken for the highest offense which it is considered in the power of man to inflict upon his fellow-man, of this offense you stand convicted.[14]

This feeling is so strong in some judges in non-capital-punishment states that they hunger for the ability to impose death sentences. In 1992 one frustrated Wisconsin judge sentenced a 34-year-old man who had killed three people and wounded another with a machine gun to three life sentences for the killings, plus another 25 for attempted murder. Since people serving life sentences in Wisconsin eventually become technically eligible for parole, the judge set the killer's potential parole date as the year 2100.[15]

Keeping Order

In ancient times, individuals were expected to take their own revenge on those who had wronged them. If a man robbed or killed another person, or raped a woman, it was up to the victim or the victim's family to exact their price from the wrongdoer. Sometimes that price was paid in money, sometimes in blood.

This practice had some obvious flaws. One of the worst was that it left the weak at the mercy of the strong. Another was that it led to social disorder. One act of violence led to another. Families developed vendettas against one another, and violence multiplied over the generations.

Through the centuries, governments took over the job of exacting retribution from wrongdoers and carrying out society's ever-changing view of justice. Laws, police forces, courts, and prisons were developed to discover and punish criminals.

No legal system was ever perfect. Some punishments seemed much too harsh, others much too light. Some criminals escaped discovery and punishment altogether. By and large, however, people tended to agree that legal systems worked better than private vengeance ever did. Here in the United States, most people believed that the American legal system worked better than most.

There were times and places, however, when people believed the legal system had broken down. They lost faith in the law's version of justice and became dissatisfied with the way the government protected them. In times like these, people frequently took the law into their own hands.

In frontier days there were usually few sheriffs, judges, or other legal officials to deal out justice throughout a large territory. Some communities had no law enforcement officers at all. Not wanting to be at the mercy of toughs and criminals, local citizens formed vigilante groups, private organizations that became their own "law" and took it upon themselves to punish wrongdoers or to chase out of town people they considered dangerous.

In time virtually every American community of any size organized an official police force of some kind, and federal and state courts extended effective coverage over the entire country. Gradually the need for regular vigilante organizations disappeared. Even then, however, there were still individual cases in which outraged citizens became impatient with the law and took it upon themselves to punish criminals—or those they thought were criminals.

Occasional acts of vigilantism were common in parts of the United States in the late nineteenth century, continuing well into the twentieth. These were not acts of individual vengeance, but group actions carried out by self-righteous mobs. Minor criminals were daubed with hot tar, sprinkled with feathers, and escorted to the county line. Accused rapists or murderers were lynched. Lynchings of black men—sometimes men whose worst crime was showing disrespect to a white person—remained fairly common in the South into the 1930s. Individual cases continued to occur even into the 1950s and 1960s.

Vigilante lynchings are different from other murders because they are accepted—even condoned—by the community. Although many citizens personally disapprove of lynching, few want to see the killers punished. In some sense, the killers are seen as trying, however misguidedly, to uphold the community's sense of justice.

The need to control or end vigilantism is still another reason put forward for having the death penalty. In Colorado, for instance, capital punishment for murders was briefly abolished in 1897. Within a few years, Colorado mobs had lynched three accused criminals they believed were murderers. One victim, a black man, was horribly burned at the stake. The death penalty was quickly reinstated.[16]

U.S. Supreme Court Justice Potter Stewart recognized the lynching problem in his concurring opinion in the historic *Furman v. Georgia* decision in 1972. "The instinct for retribution is part of the nature of man," he wrote, "and channeling that instinct in the administration of criminal justice serves an important purpose in promoting the stability of a society governed by law. When people begin to believe that organized society is unwilling or unable to impose upon criminal offenders the punishment they 'deserve,' then there are sown the seeds of anarchy—of self-help, vigilante justice, and lynch law."[17]

Vigilante lynchings have been rare in recent decades, but the threat is always there. "Most people desire some sort of retribution," warns Richard Samp of the pro-capital-punishment public interest group, Washington Legal Foundation. If they don't get it from the criminal justice system, some, at least, will be tempted to take justice into their own hands. "[T]he one way we can prevent vigilantism," says Samp, is to give people "confidence that society is going to mete out justice to people who commit violent crime."[18] For the worst examples of premeditated first degree murder, Samp would argue, death is the only punishment potential vigilantes will accept as just.

This reason for the death penalty assumes that there is a fundamental difference between ordinary citizens killing criminals and the state doing the same thing. If the family of a murder victim hangs the killer from a tree, that is a lynching. If the state electrocutes the same killer, that is justice. The murderer is dead in either case, but in the first case, social order and the rule of law have broken down. In the second, insist the supporters of the death penalty, they have been reinforced.

The Origins of Capital Punishment

We know the death penalty was prescribed for various crimes in Babylon at least 3,700 years ago, and we can assume that it was used in many parts of the world long before that. Some ancient societies applied it sparingly, and only for the most terrible of crimes. Others imposed it even for minor offenses. Under Rome's law of the Twelve Tablets in the fifth century B.C., for example, death was the penalty for publishing "insulting songs" and disturbing the peace of the city at night.[19] Under Greece's Draconian legal code in the seventh century B.C., death was the punishment for *every* crime.

The Draconian Code was an exception, however. Death was rarely the only available punishment. Captured criminals who were not executed were often tortured or maimed. Many primitive societies did not have the death penalty at all, and many of those that did reserved it either for crimes against the ruler or religious crimes like blasphemy. Punishment for crimes committed against individuals—like murder, rape, and robbery—was rarely handed down by any legal authority. It was left up to the victims, or their families or clans, to exact the appropriate penalty or to carry out the appropriate revenge.[20]

Beginning in ancient times and continuing well into the twentieth century, executions were usually carried out in public. Execution grounds were set up in spacious town squares or jail yards—easily accessible places where there was plenty of room for crowds of spectators. Ordinary citizens were not only allowed but encouraged to watch wrongdoers pay for their crimes.

Public executions had benefits for everyone concerned. For surviving victims of the criminals, the executions provided the grim satisfaction of witnessing the final punishment of those who had wronged them. For the authorities, executions served as vivid demonstrations of their determination to protect the public safety. With criminals being dispatched before large crowds in the city square, who could doubt that the police and judges were doing their jobs?

Public executions actually helped authorities to do their jobs by serving as grisly object lessons for potential wrongdoers. What better way to strike fear into the hearts of those who might be tempted to take up a life of crime than to show them the fatal consequences if they did? In some places, corpses or body parts of executed criminals were displayed in public places. Bodies were left dangling from gibbets on hills outside of town. Decapitated heads were perched on stakes at the city gates.

For the spectators, meanwhile, the awful ceremonies served as a kind of spectacle—a rare opportunity to gather together and share the horror and excitement of watching other men and women die. In some times and places, executions were actually regarded as a form of public entertainment—a kind of blood sport. This was true, for example, in the days of the Roman Empire, when condemned criminals were forced to participate in battles to the death known as gladiatorial games.

Even the condemned criminals themselves had something to gain from having their deaths take place in public. It was one last chance to publicly proclaim their innocence, or to cry out their defiance of the society that was executing them. It was also an opportunity to win sympathy from the crowd. There was some honor to be gained by "dying well," and the authorities often complained that some execution victims were regarded as heroes by the crowds.

Class Distinctions

In many societies, the extent and nature of criminal punishment depended as much on the social standing of the criminal as on the nature of the crime. Commoners were executed more often than aristocrats and nobles, and for a wider variety of crimes. Minorities and foreigners were treated more harshly than members of the dominant group. In many European countries, from the seventh century on, clergymen could not even be tried, much less put to death, by civil authorities for ordinary crimes.

The method of execution varied as well. In general, the more socially privileged the criminal, the more merciful the form of execution. (An exception was sometimes made for nobles who committed treason.) As late as 1813, Jews, Christians, and members of other religious minorities who ran afoul of the law were still being impaled alive in at least one corner of the Ottoman Empire: stakes being driven up through their bodies with blows of a heavy mallet. Turks, on the other hand, were swiftly decapitated.[21]

The Death Penalty in England

The death penalty was used less commonly in England than in most European countries in the Middle Ages. During much of the eleventh century, in fact, it wasn't used at all. Neither King Canute (1016–1035) nor William the Conqueror (1066–1087) relied on the executioner to keep order in the kingdom. That didn't mean they dealt gently with criminals, however. Death penalty or no death penalty, it was a violent age. Torture was common, and many prisoners died while being tortured. However, there were few, if any, executions as such.

Later English rulers reimposed the death penalty, but for centuries British law remained merciful compared with the laws on the continent. During the late Middle Ages, at a time when several European countries continued to execute people for minor offenses, England primarily reserved the death penalty for such relatively serious crimes as murder, treason, rape, arson, and robbery. (Pickpockets and other petty thieves were still often executed, however.)

Hanging and beheading were the most common methods of execution in England, as they were in most European countries. As in Europe, beheading was usually reserved for members of the upper classes, while hanging was favored for other criminals. When there was a desire to make sure a traitor or other heinous criminal suffered as much as possible, he or she might be left to dangle for a while, choking at the end of a rope, before being taken down and gutted with a knife. Others were drawn and quartered.

The array of crimes punishable by death in England increased over the years, until by the early nineteenth century more than 200 different crimes had become capital offenses. Gypsies could be executed simply for overstaying their welcome in the country. Even the native born could be hung for stealing fish out of a pond, illegally hunting deer, or cutting down a growing tree.[22] Passing a single forged bank note could send a counterfeiter to the scaffold. Several women as well as men were executed for that crime. In the single year of 1820, some 46 people were hung for forgery.[23]

The Death Penalty in the American Colonies

English law provided the main model for the legal codes of Britain's American colonies. Even so, the colonies did not imitate the mother country's policies slavishly. In fact, each of the colonies had its own laws and its own list of crimes punishable by death. Even though they all flowed from a common legal tradition, there was a great range of difference among them.

On one end of the American spectrum were two colonies whose laws reflected the Quaker beliefs of their founders: William Penn's Pennsylvania, which prescribed the death penalty only for murder and treason, and West Jersey, which originally had no capital crimes at all. On the other end were colonies like Virginia, which imposed death even for petty crimes.

Most of the American colonies fell somewhere between these two extremes. While the laws were changeable, the average colony made roughly ten crimes subject to the death penalty at any given time. For example, at one time thirteen offenses were punishable by death in Massachusetts, at another, only nine.[24] Pennsylvania eventually went from its original two to fifteen.[25]

Murder was a capital crime in every colony at one time or another, as was treason or rebellion. Other crimes typically punishable by death were rape, robbery, arson, and perjury in a capital case. Some of the colonies also prescribed death for such sexual offenses as adultery, sodomy, and bestiality, as well as for such religious offenses as witchcraft or blasphemy (public disrespect for God). In Massachusetts, at one point, even cursing one's parents was a capital crime.[26]

The Death Penalty in the United States

In the wake of the American Revolution, the U.S. Constitution gave both the states and the federal government the right to set their own criminal penalties. The very first Congress of the United States passed federal laws making death the penalty for rape and murder, and each of the original states made several other crimes punishable by death as well.

The usual manner of execution in most states was hanging, although Native Americans and slaves were sometimes burned at the stake. In Louisiana, whose legal traditions were French instead of British, beheading was sometimes used, at least for slaves. As in most other parts of the world, executions in the early United States were public affairs, and the bodies of the executed were often put on display for days—and sometimes months—afterwards.

Although the death penalty was widely accepted throughout the early United States, it was not approved by everyone. The founders of the United States were profoundly influenced by the ideas of the European Enlightenment, and one of the most striking of those ideas was the belief that capital punishment might be abolished. This radical notion was proposed by an Italian named Cesare Beccaria in a landmark essay entitled *On Crimes and Punishment,* which was translated into English in 1767. The essay had already played an important part in leading Tuscany to abandon capital punishment, and it encouraged many thoughtful Americans to consider abandoning the practice here.

Some prominent founders of the United States, like Thomas Jefferson, had serious doubts about the death penalty and hoped to see its use severely limited in the new nation. Others—like Dr. Benjamin Rush, the Surgeon General of the American forces during the revolutionary war—called for it to be abolished altogether. So, although capital punishment was initially established in every state, it remained controversial, particularly among intellectuals.

There would be three great waves of anti-death-penalty sentiment in the first two centuries of the country's history. The first, which occurred in the mid-nineteenth century, led to important restrictions on the use of the death penalty in several northern states, while Michigan, Wisconsin, and Rhode Island abandoned the practice altogether. The movement for the abolition of the death penalty was led by many of the same reformers who called for the abolition of slavery. As slavery became a more and more important issue, the death penalty tended to recede into the background, until it all but disappeared in the smoke and blood of the Civil War. As historian David Brion Davis wrote, "Men's finer sensibilities, which had once been revolted by the execution of a fellow being, seemed hardened and blunted."[27]

The second wave of abolition rose up toward the end of the nineteenth century and continued until the country's entry into World War I. The state of Missouri and the territory of Puerto Rico both abolished the death penalty in 1917, but no other state or territory would abolish it for 40 years to come.

Opposition to the death penalty gathered strength again in the mid-twentieth century. Sympathy for the cause was fueled by the controversial executions of Willie Francis, Burton Abbott, Caryl Chessman, and Barbara Graham. What's more, powerful and popular movies about Chessman *(Cell 2455 Death Row)* and Graham *(I Want To Live!)* vividly portrayed both the sufferings of the condemned and the possibilities for error inherent in putting people to death. Once again, several states either abolished or restricted the use of the death penalty.

In 1972 abolitionists scored their greatest success ever. In the case of *Furman v. Georgia,* the U.S. Supreme Court declared that the death penalty, as then practiced, was "cruel and unusual" punishment under the Eighth Amendment and was therefore unconstitutional. For a time, it seemed the abolitionists had finally won, once and for all. However, many state legislatures scrambled to write new laws that the Court might consider constitutional, and four years later, in *Gregg v. Georgia,* the Court announced that several of those efforts had succeeded. Once again, the death penalty was considered constitutional in the United States, and it remains so today.

Conclusion

Capital punishment is a well-established element of the American criminal justice system. The great majority of states have capital punishment laws on their books, and 21 of them have actually carried out executions since 1976, when the Supreme Court ruled the death penalty constitutional.[28] What's more, public opinion poll after public opinion poll shows that the vast majority of Americans approve of the death penalty.

Still, capital punishment remains extremely controversial. It has been abandoned not only by 15 states but by the overwhelming majority of the western developed nations. In the following chapter, we will explore the objections abolitionists raise to the death penalty, and examine the arguments both for and against this most ancient form of criminal punishment.

NOTES

1. "Should Capital Punishment Be Retained?," *Congressional Digest* (August–September 1927): 231.

2. Albert Einstein, *Berliner Tageblatt,* quoted in *Congressional Digest,* 243.

3. "In Favor of Capital Punishment," *American Scholar* (Spring 1962). Reprinted in *Social Ethics: Morality and Social Policy,* Thomas A. Mappes and Jane S. Zembaty, eds. (New York: McGraw-Hill, 1977), 89.

4. "Washington Sex Offender Dies by Hanging," *Wausau Daily Herald*, 5 January 1993.

5. *Congressional Digest*, 228.

6. Quoted by Leonard A. Stevens in *Death Penalty: The Case of Life vs. Death in the United States* (New York: Coward, McCann & Geoghegan, 1978), 73.

7. "Bring Back the Death Penalty," *U.S. News & World Report* (April 1976). Reprinted in *The Death Penalty*, edited by Irwin Isenberg (New York: H. W. Wilson, 1977), 133.

8. Isenberg, 135.

9. *Congressional Digest*, 232.

10. Royal Commission on Capital Punishment, Minutes of Evidence (1 December 1949): 207.

11. Samuel Hand, "The Death Penalty," *North American Review* (December 1881): 549.

12. *MacBeth*, act 3, scene 4.

13. Interviewed on *Crossfire*, CNN Television Network, 20 April 1992.

14. Carrie Cropley, "The Case of John McCaffary," *Wisconsin Magazine of History* (Summer 1952): 284.

15. "Fits Crime," *Wausau Daily Herald*, 19 July 1992.

16. J. E. Cutler, "Capital Punishment and Lynching," *Annals* (May 1907): 184.

17. *Furman v. Georgia*, 408 U.S. 238 (1972).

18. Speaking on *Close-Up*, C-SPAN Television Network, 16 November 1992.

19. John Laurence, *A History of Capital Punishment* (New York: Citadel Press, 1960), 2.

20. "Capital Punishment," *International Encyclopedia of the Social Sciences*, vol. 2. David L. Sills, ed. (New York: The Macmillan Company & Free Press, 1968), 290.

21. Charles Lewis Meryon, "Execution by Impalement: Latakia, 1813," a contemporary account published in *Eyewitness to History*, John Carey, ed. (New York: Avon, 1987), 284.

22. Louis E. Lawes, quoted in *Congressional Digest*, 232.

23. Laurence, 14.

24. Philip English Mackey, *Voices Against Death* (New York: Burt Franklin & Company, 1976), xii.

25. Hugo Adam Bedau, *The Death Penalty in America*, rev. ed. (New York: Aldine, 1968), 6.

26. Mackey, xi.

27. David Brion Davis, "The Movement to Abolish Capital Punishment in America, 1787–1861," *American Historical Review* (October 1957): 46.

28. NAACP Legal Defense and Educational Fund, Execution Update (5 March 1993): 6.

2

Questions and Controversies

DISCUSSIONS OF THE DEATH PENALTY TEND to resolve themselves into debates between retentionists, who wish to see the death penalty retained, and abolitionists, who wish to see it abolished. This debate is a complicated one. Capital punishment is not merely—or even primarily—a legal question. It is a practical, philosophical, social, political, and moral question as well. Each of these elements of the issue has many ramifications, and each affects the others in a variety of ways.

For the sake of simplicity, we will sometimes talk about what abolitionists believe and what retentionists believe, as though everyone in each group thinks alike. In reality, of course, they do not. There is a wide range of belief and nuance within each group. Some people in each camp claim a religious foundation for their views, others approach capital punishment as a practical question, still others consider it a moral issue. Some on both sides focus primarily on questions of social justice, others on the requirements of law enforcement. Some are primarily concerned with the protection of society, others with legal technicalities, and so on.

Some retentionists would like to see capital punishment maintained, but used as little as possible. They favor reserving the death penalty for such specific and rare offenses as presidential assassination and treason in time of war. Others would like to see the use of the death penalty expanded: either by increasing the number of capital crimes or by actually executing a higher percentage of those convicted of the crimes already punishable by death.

In essence, the complex concerns raised by the death penalty can be boiled down into three very different questions.
The first is practical: *Is the death penalty useful?* Put another way, Does it help protect society?
The second is philosophical: *Is the death penalty morally acceptable?* Put another way, Is it right and just?
The third question is essentially political: *Should we, as a society, continue to execute people?*

In this chapter, we will explore the first two questions. It is hoped that this exploration will help readers answer the third question for themselves.

Practical Questions

Does the Death Penalty Really Deter Crime?

Traditionally, the notion of deterrence has been at the very center of the practical debate over the question of capital punishment. Other beliefs, instincts, and desires may run deeper as personal motives for favoring or opposing the death penalty, but the public argument over the death penalty inevitably returns to the question of deterrence.

Most of us assume that we execute murderers primarily because we believe it will discourage others from becoming murderers. Retentionists have long asserted the deterrent power of capital punishment as an obvious fact. "No other punishment deters men so effectually . . . as the punishment of death," insisted Sir James Stephen back in 1804. "This is one of those propositions which it is difficult to prove, simply because they are in themselves more obvious than any proof can make them. It is possible to display ingenuity in arguing against it, but that is all. The whole experience of mankind is in the other direction. The threat of instant death is the one to which resort has always been made when there was an absolute necessity for producing some result. . . ."[1]

Still, abolitionists believe that deterrence is little more than an assumption—and a naive assumption at that. "Cruelty and viciousness are not abolished by cruelty and viciousness," said publisher William Randolph Hearst, "not even by legalized cruelty and viciousness."[2]

The question is not whether the death penalty could ever be a deterrent to crime. Even the most confirmed abolitionist will admit that it could. If everyone caught littering the street were immediately hung from the nearest lamppost, most of us would be very careful about what we did with our Kleenexes and candy wrappers. The real question is how effective the death penalty can be as a deterrent to serious crimes like murder.

Littering is a casual offense. It is usually committed for no better reason than convenience. It's easier to toss a wrapper down in the street than to hang onto it until you come to a litter basket. With such a weak reason for breaking the law, virtually any severe penalty would be enough to convince most people to dispose of their trash more carefully. Murder, however, is rarely casual. It is often committed for the strongest, not the weakest, of motives — motives like passionate hatred, anger, or greed.

Abolitionists argue that most murders cannot be rationally deterred by *any* penalty, including death. They are crimes of passion, committed in moments of intense rage, frustration, hatred, or fear, when the killers aren't thinking clearly of the personal consequences of what they do. For people in such states, the death penalty cannot be a deterrent, because they don't even think about it.

Most other murderers — the ones who cold-bloodedly plan and carry out their crimes — think they are too clever to be caught. The death penalty cannot be a deterrent to them either, because they are convinced they will escape punishment of any kind. "The death penalty never once acted as a deterrent in all the jobs I carried out . . . and I have executed more people than anyone this century,"[3] declared Albert Pierrepoint, the legendary British executioner who became an opponent of capital punishment after his retirement in the 1950s.

Retentionists consider testimony like Pierrepoint's irrelevant. The threat of capital punishment obviously hasn't deterred those criminals who have committed capital crimes. No one expects the death penalty to deter every criminal and to prevent every terrible crime. It is enough, retentionists say, that it deters some criminals and prevents some crimes. Even that is difficult to prove with any certainty, however.

Supporters of capital punishment face an obvious problem when they try to prove that the death penalty actually deters. How can they establish that someone *would have* committed a crime if they had not been deterred by the existence of the death penalty? Historically, defenders of the death penalty have brushed aside such problems, relying on arguments based on common sense and anecdotes.

In the early 1970s, the Los Angeles Police Department reported interviews conducted with 99 criminals who had not carried lethal weapons in their crimes. According to the police, roughly half gave fear of the death penalty as the reason for their decision to reject weapons. The others claimed that it had had no effect on them, either because they weren't worried about it or because they would never have carried a deadly weapon anyhow.[4]

Abolitionists respond with their own anecdotal evidence. "On June 21, 1877," Professor George W. Kirchwey recounted, "ten men were hanged in Pennsylvania for murderous conspiracy. The *New York Herald* predicted the wholesome effect of this terrible lesson. 'We may be certain,' it said, 'that the pitiless severity of the law will deter the most wicked from anything like the imitation of these crimes.' And yet, the night after this large-scale execution two of the witnesses at the trial of these men had been murdered, and within two weeks five of the prosecutors had met the same fate."[5]

Abolitionists base most of their argument against deterrence on statistics. As long ago as 1919, American professor Raymond T. Bye used a statistical study to show that "there is no measurable relation between the existence or non-existence of capital punishment and the homicide rate."[6] That same conclusion has been reached by dozens of studies since. They have compared all sorts of statistical variations, including murder rates in states that have abolished the death penalty versus those in states that use it extensively; rates of serious crimes in countries that have the death penalty versus those that do not; and differences in the rates of capital crimes before and after the abolition or reinstatement of the death penalty in a particular state or nation.

After examining the statistical studies available in the 1950s, Thorsten Sellin issued a report for the American Law Institute concluding that capital punishment did little or nothing to deter crime.[7] A decade later the *International Encyclopedia of the Social Sciences* could still report that statistical studies "have in general failed to identify any meaningful correlation between the presence of the death penalty and rates of serious criminality."[8]

If the death penalty really does deter murderers, suggest the abolitionists, then societies that execute murderers should be relatively free of murder. Still, many of the most murder-ridden societies in history have practiced capital punishment. Even today, the four states that make the most use of the death penalty[9] are consistently among those with the highest murder rates. Texas, which has carried out more than one out of every four executions in the entire country since 1976, has one murder for every 6,385 residents. Florida has one per 9,952, Georgia one per 8,997, and Virginia one per 11,249. This compares to one per 20,383 and one per 43,750 in the non-capital-punishment states of Wisconsin and Minnesota.[10]

Retentionists argue that none of this statistical evidence proves that capital punishment never deters potential criminals. They point out that the murder rate in any given state depends on many things besides whether or not that state has capital punishment. They cite such factors as the proportion of urban residents in the state, the level of economic prosperity, and the social and racial makeup of the population. States like Texas and Florida, they say, would probably have even higher murder rates if they did not have the death penalty to keep things at least partly in check.

Retentionists do have some figures of their own. The most notable statistical study upholding the value of deterrence was conducted by an economist, Isaac Erlich, who examined the possible effects of capital punishment on murder rates in the United States in the mid-twentieth century. Erlich suggested that "an additional execution per year . . . may have resulted, on average, in seven or eight fewer murders."[11] Erlich's methods were scientifically controversial, however, particularly because his results contradicted the great majority of other work in the field. A board of experts commissioned by the National Academy of Sciences to examine Erlich's study in 1975 brushed it aside as offering "no useful evidence" on the deterrent effect of capital punishment.[12]

In addition to Erlich's study, retentionists point to events in the United States during the 1950s, 1960s, and 1970s. Throughout the late 1950s and early 1960s executions in the United States held fairly steady at between 40 and 65 each year. During that time, the number of murders in the United States remained fairly stable, too, at between 8,060 and 9,140. As the 1960s moved on, however, the number of executions dropped dramatically, until there were no executions at all during the nine years from 1968 until 1977. (The Supreme Court decision striking down the capital punishment statutes came in 1972, and the ruling allowing executions to resume came in 1976.) As executions dragged to a stop, murders soared, reaching a high of 20,600 in 1974.[13]

Proponents of deterrence take this as evidence that the threat of the death penalty *must* have deterred murders prior to 1968, since the number of murders rose so sharply when it was removed. Opponents of deterrence protest that there is no evidence the rise in murders had anything to do with the absence of the death penalty. They point out that homicides continued to rise even after the death penalty was restored in 1976 and have climbed since, although more slowly. Murders in the United States reached a new high—of 24,040—in 1991.[14] What's more, there was actually a sharp jump in murder rates in two states—Florida and Georgia— in the very next year after executions resumed in the wake of the *Gregg* decision.[15]

If retentionists cannot prove that capital punishment deters crime, abolitionists cannot prove that it doesn't. Even so, the bulk of the statistical evidence has convinced even some retentionists to abandon the deterrence argument. In his famous essay *In Favor of Capital Punishment*, Jacques Barzun conceded that he is "ready to believe the statistics tending to show that the prospect of his own death does not stop the murderer."[16] Murderers, Barzun points out, are often "blind egoists" who fully expect to get away with their crime, and could not really imagine their own deaths in any case. Barzun bases his defense of the death penalty on other arguments, relying primarily on the need to protect society from killers who are considered high risks for killing again.

Two very similar conclusions about deterrence were reached by Great Britain's Royal Commission on Capital Punishment in 1953 and by U.S. Supreme Court Justice Potter Stewart in 1976. After examining all the international evidence available—both from countries that had abandoned the death penalty and from those where it was still practiced—the Royal Commission concluded that "there is no clear evidence of any lasting increase" in murders resulting from abolition of the death penalty. What's more, "there are many offenders on whom the deterrent effect is limited and may often be negligible."[17] "Although some of the studies suggest the death penalty may not function as a significantly greater deterrent than lesser penalties," Stewart wrote, "there is no convincing empirical evidence either supporting or refuting this view."[18]

Might the Death Penalty Actually Encourage Murder?

"Of all the arguments against the death penalty," writes Dr. Louis Joylon West, Chairman of the Department of Psychiatry and Behavioral Sciences at the UCLA Medical Center, "there is one that is perhaps both least understood and most paradoxical: *Capital punishment breeds murder.*"[19] It does this, the abolitionists argue, in at least two ways.

Killing To Avoid Capture

The threat of capital punishment raises the stakes of getting caught. Anyone already subject to the death penalty has little to lose by killing again and again. Their potential sentence cannot be made any worse than it already is. This makes criminals who already face death for a previous crime more likely to kill in order to avoid being captured. In particular, it gives them more reason to silence any witnesses against them.

This is a particularly telling argument against making crimes other than murder punishable by death. When kidnapping is a capital crime, for example, kidnappers have little practical reason not to kill their victim. The same is true of rape and other possible capital crimes.

The Death Penalty as Suicide

Most criminals don't want to be caught. They want—and usually expect—to get away with their crimes. According to West and other leading psychiatrists, however, this is not true of all criminals. Some not only want to be caught, they want to be punished. Some even want to die, and for them the death penalty can become a kind of suicide.

Gary Gilmore was apparently one of these. Gilmore, the first criminal to be executed after the *Gregg* decision reinstated the death penalty in the mid-1970s, protested the legal efforts abolitionists made to save his life. He insisted the state *owed* him an execution. "I took 'em serious when they sentenced me to death," he once complained. "I thought you were supposed to take 'em serious. I didn't know it was a joke."[20]

Dr. John C. Woods, the chief of forensic psychiatry at Utah State Hospital, who examined Gilmore, was convinced that the killer sought his own death. "He took the steps necessary to turn the job of his own destruction over to someone else," Woods told an interviewer. "[T]hat's why he pulled two execution-style murders he was bound to be caught for. I think it's a legitimate question, based on this evidence and our knowledge of the individual, to ask if Gilmore would have killed if there was not a death penalty in Utah."[21]

In an article originally published in a psychiatric journal, Dr. West described several other cases of men who killed in hopes of getting the death penalty. Whether out of fear or for some other reason, they chose not to kill themselves but to let society do it for them. In one case West cites, a truck driver explained to police that he had killed a total stranger because he (the killer) was "tired of living." In another, a killer-to-be actually left a state that didn't have the death penalty in order to commit his crime in one that would execute him when he was caught.[22]

Days before his execution in 1992, an Illinois murderer named Lloyd Wayne Hampton explained that he had killed a 69-year-old man partly because "I had given up trying to make it. What was I going to do . . . ? I either had to put myself in a position of being killed by someone else or committing suicide. At that point, I had strong beliefs about not killing myself. . . . So I put myself in a position to have the state kill me."[23]

Summary

The death penalty probably does deter some potential criminals, as its supporters believe, and it probably does incite some others to commit crimes, as psychiatrists insist. Does it save more lives than it costs or does it put more lives in jeopardy than it saves? Although neither side in the death penalty debate is content with the answer, the reality seems to be that there is no way to tell. This being so, concerned citizens must decide for themselves where the greater danger lies.

Do We Need the Death Penalty To Stop Murderers from Killing Again?

Jacques Barzun is far from alone in favoring the death penalty as a way of protecting society from "uncontrollable brutes." One of the most elemental concerns people have about those who have already committed terrible crimes is the fear that they will commit more of them. People know that most murderers who are not executed eventually get out of prison, and they believe that these released killers are likely to kill again.

This belief is fostered by sensational news reports of those murderers who do kill again, as well as by politicians anxious to win votes off the public's natural fear of crime. In 1988, Democratic presidential candidate Michael Dukakis was badly damaged by television ads featuring the case of a convicted murderer named Willie Horton. Horton had been serving a life sentence in a Massachusetts prison during the time Dukakis was governor of the state. Released for short periods of time on a special program that allowed some Massachusetts prisoners a taste of freedom, Horton had committed another brutal murder. The publicity surrounding this case solidified a widespread belief that Dukakis was soft on criminals, and it may have intensified the hostility and distrust a frightened public already felt toward released murderers.

Despite the widespread public belief that murderers are likely to be recidivists (repeat criminals), the evidence suggests that murderers are relatively unlikely to kill again. A number of studies, both in the United States and elsewhere, indicate that apart from professional hit men and a small number of serial killers, most murderers are good risks never to repeat their crimes. The United Kingdom Royal Commission on Capital Punishment, which looked into recidivism rates among murderers in the United Kingdom and Europe, found almost no repeat offenders among released murderers.[24] An even more sweeping American study covered all the released murderers in 12 states from the turn of the century up to 1976. Of the 2,646 killers released from prison during that time for any reason, only 16 ever returned for committing another murder—barely more than one half of one percent.[25] Recidivism rates for most other serious crimes are much higher.

Even inside prisons, convicted murderers do not seem to be especially high risks to kill again.[26] Many murders do take place in prisons, but most are not committed by prisoners held for murder. None of the 16 California prisoners who committed murders in a two-year study period in the 1960s, for example, were serving a sentence for murder at the time.[27]

So far, even the most determined retentionists have not seriously suggested executing everyone who kills another human being. So the problem for those who want to protect society by eliminating truly dangerous murderers becomes identifying them. How do we tell Barzun's "uncontrollable brutes" from the great majority of murderers who are apparently no greater threat to kill again than are other members of society?

This is no easy task. At the time of his conviction for murder in the 1920s, Nathan Leopold would have seemed to be as much of a risk as any killer of the time. His crime had been a "thrill killing," denounced as cold-blooded and heartless by the prosecution. Leopold, himself, expressed no remorse. Released from prison many years later, Leopold led an apparently blameless life, even serving as a medical missionary in Puerto Rico.[28]

In some cases, however, the line seems easy to draw. There are even a few killers, like the child-murderer Westley Allan Dodd, who draw it for themselves. They declare themselves uncontrollable, and insist that the only way to stop them is to kill them. Even Dodd later changed his tune, however. In a final statement, delivered at the time of his execution, he announced that he had "found peace in the Lord, Jesus Christ."[29] Few psychologists believe it's possible to tell with certainty which killers will and will not kill again if eventually released.

What of serial killers who kill obsessively? Killers like Ted Bundy, John Wayne Gacy, Ed Gein, and Jeffrey Dahmer have already killed over and over again. It may not be certain that they will repeat their crimes if given a chance, but it's far from certain that they won't. Most of us would feel very uncomfortable if one of them were released and moved in next door to us.

Abolitionists point out that, despite the enormous publicity given to serial killers by the media, such people are actually very rare. One reason they get as much attention as they do is because they are so unusual. As horrible as their crimes are and as numerous as they sometimes seem to be, serial killings make up only a tiny fraction of the more than 20,000 murders committed in the United States in a typical year. If the people who commit them were the only people executed, we would probably have less than one execution in the United States per year.

Besides, abolitionists argue, history proves that there is no need to execute even relentless killers like these in order to keep them from repeating their crimes. Few if any serial killers, once caught, have ever killed again—mostly, of course, because they were successfully incarcerated. Of those mentioned above, only Bundy has been executed so far. Gacy is under sentence of death, while Gein was imprisoned for many years and then released. Dahmer is serving a life sentence in a state that does not have the death penalty. None of these men has been implicated in any killing since his conviction.

If the death penalty is really necessary to protect society from killers who have already been caught and convicted, it seems there should be some evidence of it. States that do not have capital punishment should have more problems with once-convicted murderers than death penalty states do, but there seems to be no evidence that this is so.

Does the Death Penalty Discourage Convictions?

Far from protecting society by eliminating dangerous criminals, abolitionists argue that the death penalty may actually protect some criminals by making juries reluctant to convict them. "The punishment of murder by death multiplies murders, from the difficulty it creates of convicting people who are guilty of it," wrote Dr. Benjamin Rush in 1798. "Humanity revolting at the idea of the severity and certainty of a capital punishment, often steps in, and collects such evidence in favour of a murderer, as screens him from death altogether, or palliates his crime into manslaughter."[30] In modern times, this reluctance has been translated into the American courts' recognition that "death is different." A variety of special procedures and legal technicalities kick into effect in capital cases. Designed to protect the rights of defendants whose lives are on the line, they make it more difficult to convict people accused of capital crimes. As we will see in the next section, these protections also add greatly to the expense of prosecuting cases involving the death penalty.

Even aside from the legal technicalities, capital punishment raises the stakes of a guilty verdict, and jurors know it. The knowledge that death may await the person they convict may well make some jurors more scrupulous than they would be otherwise, and therefore less willing to convict. This is, of course, not entirely a bad thing. Juries *should* be very certain of their facts before sending a defendant to the executioner.

If the shadow of the death penalty makes juries more reluctant to find defendants guilty, its absence may encourage them to convict. Three years after the death penalty was abolished in Minnesota, there was no significant change in the number of murders committed in the state. According to the Minnesota Governor A. O. Eberhart, however, there was an increase in the percentage of murder *convictions* "to the extent of approximately fifty percent."[31]

The Question of Expense

Among those applauding the January 1993 execution of Westley Allan Dodd was the popular evangelist minister, TV talk show host, and sometime presidential candidate Rev. Pat Robertson. He defended the execution partly on economic grounds. If Dodd had been allowed to live, he told the audience of his program, *The 700 Club,* the state of Washington would have had to support him in a costly prison cell for the rest of his life. "Why should the taxpayers have to pay [to support] this killer?," asked Robertson.[32]

The same question is frequently asked about other murderers as well. Why should honest citizens have to pay for the food and lodging of killers? Why not simply execute them and be done with them—and save a lot of money in the bargain? (The same question could also be asked about other criminals. Why should honest citizens pay to support rapists, thieves, or embezzlers?)

Many retentionists assume that it is cheaper to execute a criminal than to keep him or her in prison for life, or even for several years. How much does a bullet cost? How expensive can it be to build an electric chair, and to send a couple of thousands of volts of electricity through a criminal's body?

Ironically, cost is also important to the abolitionists, who claim that it actually costs more to execute criminals than to imprison them. They point out that the cost of maintaining capital punishment involves much more than the relatively minor cost of actually killing the condemned.

Death Is Expensive

Going for the death penalty doesn't just raise the stakes for the defendant whose life is on the line. It raises the financial stakes for the state as well. Simply charging a defendant with a capital crime escalates the costs of the trial. The Supreme Court insists that the awesome finality of the death penalty requires a "correspondingly greater degree of scrutiny of the capital sentencing determination."[33] This is why, for example, all but two capital punishment states provide for automatic review of all death sentences.[34]

As the American Civil Liberties Union Foundation of Northern California explains, the possibility of the death penalty raises the costs at every stage: "A capital case requires two trials (one to determine guilt and another to determine penalty), automatic state supreme court review, post-conviction proceedings, and Supreme Court appeals, all of which are extremely costly to the state both in terms of money and human resources. Jury selection and pretrial motions are also more lengthy in capital cases, and expert consultants such as psychiatrists often must be retained. The cost of maintaining death rows in state prisons, clemency hearings, and the execution itself must also be added to the price of executions."[35]

That price is very high. A one-time administrator of the California prisons has pointed out that "the actual cost of execution, the cost of operating the super-maximum security condemned unit, the years spent by some inmates in condemned status, and a pro-rata share of top-level prison officials' time spent in administering the units, add up to a cost substantially greater than the cost to retain them in prison the rest of their lives."[36]

A 1988 Kansas Legislative Research Department study found that trying a capital case cost the state over $116,000 more than holding a non-capital trial.[37] In the 1980s, the state of Florida spent six times more per person to execute a criminal than to maintain him or her in prison for life without parole.[38]

It has been estimated that Texas, which has executed more people than any other state since 1976, spent a whopping $183.2 million on expenses related to the death penalty in only six years.[39] "Whether you're for [the death penalty] or against it," declared Chief Criminal Judge James Ellis of Oregon (a state that has capital punishment but hasn't used it in recent years), "I think the fact is that Oregon simply can't afford it."[40] According to the *Sacramento Bee* newspaper, California would save $91 million a year by getting rid of the death penalty.[41]

The special costs of the death penalty hit the hardest on local governments, and hardest of all on the governments of small towns and counties that have relatively few resources. Ironically, for those who favor the death penalty on the grounds that it helps to maintain law and order, these costs often come out of state and local funds that would otherwise go to building jails and prisons and putting more police officers on the streets. This is one reason why prosecutors and other law enforcement officials are sometimes reluctant to file capital charges.

The Death Penalty Information Center points out that Florida recently had to reduce its Department of Corrections budget by $45 million, although the state had spent more than $57 million enforcing the death penalty in recent years. The result was that 18 convicted murderers were permanently removed from society by execution, but 3,000 other convicted criminals had to be released from prison early because Florida didn't have the money to keep them there.[42]

Cutting Costs?

A lot of the enormous cost of maintaining the death penalty could be saved if the legal system stopped treating death as "different"— if capital crime trials and appeals were conducted in the same way that ordinary criminal cases are. Accomplishing this, however, would take a massive transformation in American judicial philosophy. Critics of the way death penalty cases are treated now believe that judges bend over backwards to protect the rights of criminals. Whenever there is a doubt, critics charge, the courts tend to err on the side of the defendant. It is time, they say, for the courts to start erring on the side of society. They argue that many savings could be made if judges just took a less sympathetic attitude toward the rights of defendants.

The U.S. Supreme Court itself seems to be moving in that direction. Under Chief Justice William Rehnquist, the Court has been increasingly unsympathetic and even hostile to repeated appeals to the federal courts (habeas corpus appeals) from death row inmates. However, even while the Rehnquist Court has been eating away at certain of the special protections granted to capital defendants, it has not only reaffirmed but extended others.

It would probably be unrealistic—as well as unfair—to ask judges at any level to cut legal corners or to dispense with any presumed rights of defendants when lives are at stake. Judges, after all, are human beings too. They need to feel justified in what they do. Supreme Court Justice William O. Douglas spoke for many of his judicial colleagues when he wrote, in 1953, "As a justice it is also important that before we allow human lives to be snuffed out, we be sure—emphatically sure—that we act within the law. If we are not sure, there will be lingering doubts to plague the conscience after the event."[43]

Moral Issues

The Sanctity of Life

If deterrence is at the heart of the practical debate over the death penalty, the sanctity of human life is at the heart of the philosophical debate. Both sides claim to put a high value on human life, but their attitudes toward the death penalty reflect that value in opposite ways.

For many abolitionists, every person's life is equally sacred and no life should be taken unless absolutely necessary. They have an instinctive feeling, as Minnesota Congressman O. J. Kvale expressed it, that the death penalty "cheapens human life. And human life should be sacred."[44]

Most abolitionists accept the idea that it might be necessary to kill someone—for example, in battle, in self-defense, or to protect the life of another person. However, they do not accept the argument that it is necessary to kill convicted criminals who can be punished in other ways. The life of the murderer's victim is already lost and cannot be brought back by killing the murderer. Because they see no absolute need to take the life of a prisoner, who is already confined and controlled in jail, abolitionists believe it is wrong to do so.

Retentionists, on the other hand, are much more concerned with the sanctity of the victim's life than with the murderer's. They are impatient with arguments based on the value of the life of a killer. Theodore Roosevelt, who ordered men into battle as a colonel in the Spanish-American War, scoffed at the idea that a criminal's life was too precious to destroy. "[I]nasmuch as, without hesitation, I have again and again sent good and gallant and upright men to die, it seems to me the height of a folly both mischievous and mawkish to contend that criminals who have deserved death should nevertheless be allowed to shirk it. No brave and good man can properly shirk death and no criminal who has earned death should be allowed to shirk it."[45]

Other supporters of capital punishment turn the abolitionist's argument around. They insist that it is the sacredness of human life itself that demands the death penalty. "All religions that I'm aware of feel that human life is sacred," Professor Ernest van den Haag told an interviewer, "and that its sacredness must be enforced by depriving of life anyone who deprives another person of life."[46] Van den Haag was overstating his point. Some religions disapprove of the death penalty. Still, he was stating a widely held retentionist belief that instead of cheapening human life, the death penalty affirms its worth.

For those who agree with van den Haag, the execution of a killer is the ultimate proof of the value society puts on the life of the killer's victim. It is not the death penalty but the failure to impose it that "demeans the value of innocent human life," insists

Paul Kamenar of the Washington Legal Foundation.[47] For Kamenar, unwillingness to execute a vicious murderer puts a higher value on the murderer's life than the victim's.

Economist and philosopher John Stuart Mill made a similar, but more complicated, point to the British Parliament over a century ago. "Much has been said of the sanctity of human life, and the absurdity of supposing that we can teach respect for life by ourselves destroying it. But I am surprised at the employment of this argument. . . . It is not human life only, not human life as such, that ought to be sacred to us, but human feelings. The human capacity of suffering is what we should cause to be respected, not the mere capacity of existing. And we may imagine somebody asking how we can teach people not to inflict suffering by ourselves inflicting it? But to this I should answer—all of us would answer—that to deter by suffering from inflicting suffering is not only possible, but the very purpose of penal justice. Does fining a criminal show want of respect for property, or imprisoning him, for personal freedom? Just as unreasonable is it to think that to take the life of a man who has taken that of another is to show want of regard for human life. We show, on the contrary, most emphatically our regard for it, by the adoption of a rule that he who violates that right in another forfeits it for himself, and that while no other crime that he can commit deprives him of his life, this shall."[48]

Is Death the Ultimate Punishment?

Most people assume that death is the worst possible punishment a civilized society can impose. As James Stephen wrote nearly two centuries ago, "In any secondary punishment, however terrible, there is hope; but death is death; its terrors cannot be described more forcibly."[49]

Not everyone agrees, however. Some believe that life imprisonment, far from being a mercy, is often a more terrible penalty than a relatively swift and painless execution. As philosopher John Stuart Mill rhetorically asked the British Parliament in 1868, "What comparison can there really be, in point of severity, between consigning a man to the short pang of a rapid death, and immuring him in a living tomb, there to linger out what may be a long life in the hardest and most monotonous toil, without any of its alleviations or rewards—debarred from all pleasant sights and sounds, and cut off from all earthly hope, except a slight mitigation of bodily restraint, or a small improvement of diet?"[50]

The father of Westley Allan Dodd's four-year-old victim insisted that his desire to see Dodd die was not based on the belief that this was the most terrible punishment that Dodd could suffer, only the most final. "If justice were to be served in a vindictive way," he told a reporter, "I'd want him to spend . . . his life in jail. That's the cruel and unusual punishment in this case."[51]

Some criminals seem to agree. As we have already seen, Gary Gilmore and Lloyd Wayne Hampton not only preferred death but virtually demanded it. Charles Bryant, whose death sentence for aggravated rape was overturned in Louisiana, explained that if given a choice between death and life imprisonment, he would choose death. "Even if they could fry me tomorrow," he said, "that would be preferable to spending the rest of my life here [in Angola State Prison]. This isn't living. It's just existing."[52]

The Gilmores, Hamptons, and Bryants are exceptions, however. Most condemned criminals battle to the end to have their death sentences overturned.

Private Vengeance and Public Retribution

Every murder has many victims besides the person whose life is ended. Family members—children, parents, husbands, wives— and everyone else who loved or valued the murdered person are all victims too. So, in another way, are the family members and others who love and value the murderer. In a sense, the entire society, and everyone in it, is a victim.

Whenever a great wrong has been done, people feel the need to do something that puts the wrong right. Murder is a great wrong that can never actually be put right, in the sense that the life, once taken, can never be restored. Even if the wrong cannot be righted, though, it can at least be avenged. For many people, the death of the wrongdoer seems the only medicine that can possibly heal the wound that has been inflicted on society.

For most supporters of capital punishment, the desire for retribution is an impersonal thing—a judgment about what is best for society. For those who knew and loved the murdered person, however, the wound is an intensely personal one. Their need for healing is not abstract, but real and specific.

Family members and other close survivors often look forward to the deaths of those who victimized their loved ones. Some even ask to attend the execution so that they can have the satisfaction of watching the killer die. Some have a hunger for revenge. Others deny this motive. They simply hope the execution of the murderer will somehow help them close the chapter on their tragedy and get on with their lives. As we have seen, the father of a young boy who was tortured and then murdered by Westley Allan Dodd was impatient for the execution of his son's killer because he believed it would help end the continuing stress on his family.[53] "I'm not vengeful," declared the widow of a policeman explaining her wish to see the death penalty inflicted on his murderer, "but I feel it's scriptural." The policeman's daughter, who, like her mother, did not ask to attend the execution, still expected it to bring "a lot of relief. . . . I feel," she added, "like Daddy will finally be put to rest."[54]

Even opponents of capital punishment can understand and sympathize with the pain that causes many loved ones of murder victims to call for the death of the killer. In some ancient societies, it was left to the families of the dead person to exact a price for the wrong that had been done to them—whether that price was an economic penalty or "a life for a life." Punishment by the state is, in an essential way, a substitute for personal vengeance. It was meant not only to replace it, but to supersede it.

There is a real question, then, whether the personal feelings of those close to the murdered person have any place in the legal proceedings that decide the killer's fate. One view is that they don't belong in that process at all. Judges and juries are there to inflict punishment, not to satisfy anyone's desire for revenge. "Punishment as retribution has been condemned by scholars for centuries," wrote Thurgood Marshall in his opinion in the *Furman* case, "and the Eighth Amendment was adopted to prevent punishment from being synonymous with vengeance."[55] An opposing view is that the pain and trouble a murder causes to other individuals is a valid aggravating circumstance that should be taken into account when determining the seriousness of the crime.

Even some retentionists make a distinction between society's desire for retribution and the individual citizen's demand for vengeance. The damage done to society and the damage done to individual survivors are very different things: just as public outrage and personal anguish are distinct. However understandable the feelings of individual survivors may be, many people believe they should not be allowed to influence death penalty sentencing.

In June 1991, however, the U.S. Supreme Court declared that "victim impact" evidence could be allowed in the penalty phase of a capital trial.[56] Juries can now take the suffering of the victim's family into account when deciding whether to inflict the death penalty. In effect, this means they can take the family's desire for revenge into account as well.

Opponents of victim impact evidence argue that it inevitably leads to increased hostility and prejudice against the defendant. They also complain that it leads juries to put a higher value on the lives of certain victims than others, assuring that the deaths of victims with many loving friends and family members will be considered more terrible—and so more deserving of the death penalty—than those of victims who died friendless.

Some abolitionists argue that if the feelings of the *victim's* family deserve to be taken into account, so do those of the *defendant's* family. Shouldn't the jury hear from them as well? Shouldn't the jury consider the agony they will suffer if their loved one is executed? Aren't they just as innocent and just as deserving of consideration as the friends and relatives of the victim?

Not all close survivors of murder victims desire the killer's death. Some actively call for mercy, although often only after the trial is over and the defendant has already been sentenced to die. The Franciscan Sisters of Mary Immaculate, of Amarillo, Texas, appealed for mercy on behalf of Johnny Frank Garrett, who had raped and murdered an elderly member of their order, Sister Tadea Benz. The nuns issued a statement protesting Garrett's death sentence long after the brutal murder, as his execution day approached. "[W]e are still convinced, ten years later, that faithfulness to Jesus Christ and to our founder, St. Francis, requires of us that we forgive Johnny Frank Garrett. . . . [A]s the family of Sister Tadea Benz we respectfully submit that justice would not be served by executing [him]. . . ." they pleaded.[57] The sisters went on to ask the Texas State Board of Pardons and the Governor to commute Garrett's sentence to life imprisonment. They refused, however, and Johnny Frank Garrett was executed in February 1992.[58]

If the use of victim impact evidence harks back to the ancient tradition of family vengeance, then the wishes of survivors should be considered whatever they may be. While it is true that in some ancient cultures the family members were free to destroy the killer who had wronged their relative, they were equally free to let the killer live. In modern times, however, juries, judges, governors, and pardons boards seem to be more influenced by relatives' calls for death than by their calls for leniency. It is as though the desire for vengeance is somehow more understandable, and easier to sympathize with, than the desire for mercy.

In any event, many abolitionists and retentionists alike are uncomfortable about the state basing decisions of who should die on the personal wishes of individuals. Even for an expansionist like Paul Kamenar of the Washington Legal Foundation, the anger and anguish of family members is not the main point. "What's at work here is not personal feelings of vengeance that may come up in some cases," he declares. "What's important is that there's a societal interest of retribution, which is a collective self-expression of society's revulsion about the heinousness of the crime that was committed."[59]

Fairness

Abolitionists complain that the death penalty is all but totally reserved for those members of society who are already the weakest and most disadvantaged: the social outcasts, the unpopular minorities, and the poor. There is no question that the death penalty falls unequally on different groups within society, although retentionists insist that this has more to do with the different behaviors of these different groups than with any built-in bias of the criminal justice system.

The Indigent

"Execution," remarked Clinton Duffy, an ex-warden of San Quentin prison, is a "privilege of the poor."[60] On the other side of the social coin, as Supreme Court Justice William O. Douglas once pointed out, "One searches our chronicles in vain for the execution of any member of the affluent strata of this society."[61]

There may be many reasons why the death penalty is imposed primarily on poor and lower class defendants. One reason, at least, is glaringly obvious. They can't afford good lawyers.

Under the American legal system, a death sentence is never inevitable, even for defendants convicted of the most terrible of crimes. Therefore, what happens in the preparation of a case, at trial, and on appeal is vital. The better the case is handled, the lower the risk the defendant will be put to death. A good, experienced lawyer improves the defendant's chances at every stage of the process. This means that, all else being equal, the better the lawyer, the better the defendant's chances of escaping execution.

Indigent (poor) defendants simply cannot afford to hire the best lawyers, particularly in the most important early stages of their cases. Once a person has already been sentenced to death, he or she may receive the help of competent pro bono attorneys who donate their services because they are opposed to capital punishment. However, in the crucial earlier stages of the case—when the decisions of guilt or innocence, life or death are being made—the poor defendant is often virtually alone. According to Amnesty International, the lawyer for one poor defendant in Louisiana apparently spent only eight hours preparing his case. The lawyer for another was working on 300 other cases simultaneously. Not surprisingly, both these defendants were executed. What's more, "a recent study found that capital defendants in Texas with court-appointed lawyers were more than twice as likely to receive a death sentence" as those who were able to hire their own lawyers.[62] It's hardly surprising, then, that the poor have always made up the majority of inhabitants on American death rows.

Race

Historically, says John Healey of Amnesty International, the death penalty "has been primarily used against the black community [and] primarily in the South."[63] Slaves could be executed for many more crimes than their masters, and, even after slavery was abolished, African Americans continued to be executed at a much higher rate than other Americans until late in the twentieth century.

African Americans made up more than half of all the people executed from 1930 (when the government started keeping records) until 1972, although they made up little more than 10 percent of the population during that time. When the Supreme Court authorized new executions in 1976, it assumed that the new laws passed since 1972 had corrected the problem. In fact, the proportion of black defendants sentenced to death has dropped dramatically. As of April 1991, the NAACP Legal Defense Fund knew of 966 black convicts awaiting execution, compared to 1,243 whites.[64] This means that black people are no longer a majority on the nation's death rows, although they still make up a much higher percentage of death row residents than of the population at large.

Despite this apparent improvement, abolitionists insist that the application of the death penalty is still heavily influenced by race—often not the race of the defendant, but the race of the victim. In the words of Henry Schwarzchild, of the American Civil Liberties Union (ACLU) Capital Punishment Project, "We reserve the death penalty in this country essentially only for people who kill whites, irrespective of their own race."[65]

Schwarzchild was exaggerating, but there was some truth in what he said. Of the 14 people (all male) executed in 1991, for instance, only three (one of whom was white) died for killing black people. The other 11 had killed whites.[66] This proportion of black victim cases (21 percent) may seem reasonable, until it's remembered that roughly as many blacks as whites are murdered each year.

In the 1980s, Professor David C. Baldus made an extensive study of more than 2,000 murders that had occurred in Georgia in the previous decades. Even allowing for 230 separate nonracial factors, the study concluded that the race of both victim and defendant helped determine whether the defendant would be condemned to death or receive a lighter sentence. Baldus's study didn't claim that race was always decisive. In the case of the most atrocious murders, defendants tended to be sentenced to death regardless of their race or that of the victim. Similarly, in cases where the mitigating circumstances clearly overwhelmed the aggravating circumstances, the defendants almost always escaped death. In less obvious cases, however, death was imposed in 34 percent of those involving white victims, but only 14 percent of those in which the victims were black—a disparity of more than 2 to 1. If the other, nonracial factors were ignored, the difference was 11 to 1.[67]

The Baldus study was an important piece of evidence in a 1987 appeal to the U.S. Supreme Court in which a black Georgia defendant, Warren McCleskey, argued that his death sentence had been influenced by his race and the race of his white victim. Despite accepting the validity of Baldus's figures, the Court rejected McCleskey's appeal.

The majority of justices were clearly worried that accepting McCleskey's statistical claim might lead to the abolition of the death penalty altogether. It might even lead to unanswerable questions about jury decisions in other kinds of cases as well. If the Court accepted the Baldus study as proof that Georgia law and practice were biased, it might have to accept other "claims based on unexplained discrepancies that correlate to membership in other minority groups, and even to gender. Similarly, since McCleskey's claim relates to the race of his victim, other claims could apply with equally logical force to statistical disparities that correlate with the race or sex of other actors in the criminal justice system, such as defense attorneys or judges."[68]

In a strong dissent, Justice Harry Blackmun complained that the decision "seems to give a new meaning to our recognition that death is different. Rather than requiring 'a correspondingly greater degree of scrutiny of the capital sentencing determination,' the Court relies on the very fact that this is a case involving capital punishment to apply a *lesser* standard of scrutiny under the Equal Protection Clause."[69]

An equally distressed Justice William Brennan complained that the Court's unwillingness to accept the Baldus study's evidence as "sufficient is based in part on the fear that recognition of McCleskey's claim would open the door to all aspects of criminal sentencing. Taken on its face," Brennan continued, "such a statement seems to suggest a fear of too much justice."[70]

For abolitionists like Brennan, the central fact of racial discrimination in sentencing is clear and unmistakable. "At some point in this case," he wrote in his dissent, "Warren McCleskey doubtless asked his lawyer whether a jury was likely to sentence him to die. A candid reply to this question would have been disturbing. First, counsel would have to tell McCleskey that few of the details of the crime or of McCleskey's past criminal conduct were more important than the fact that his victim was white."[71]

Brennan's concerns were confirmed by a 1990 report from the U.S. government's General Accounting Office (G.A.O.). Evaluating 28 different studies of death penalty sentencing, the G.A.O. determined that there have, in fact, been "racial disparities in the charging, sentencing, and imposition of the death penalty after *Furman*."[72] One reason seems to be that prosecutors tend to seek the death penalty more often against black defendants, and particularly against black defendants accused of killing white people.

Retentionists argue that many of the supposed disparities are more apparent than real. Those that do exist, they argue, are coincidental, caused by factors other than racism. They point to conditions of poverty, drugs, and social unrest that make crimes of violence more common in black neighborhoods than in most other places. What's more, says George C. Smith of the Washington Legal Foundation, "Felony murders—those committed in the course of a rape or a robbery—are the chief crimes eligible for capital punishment under the post-*Furman* statutes. The available data demonstrates that whites constitute between 77 percent and 89 percent of rape and robbery victims. It follows inescapably that whites would represent a comparable percentage of murder victims killed during a rape or robbery. In other words, the seemingly disproportionate number of capital sentences involving white victims is nothing more than a statistical proxy for the established facts that murders of whites are more likely to be felony murders involving robbery or rape—i.e., capital murders."[73]

Abolitionists respond that, although murder in the course of rape or robbery may be the "chief crimes" that result in death penalties, they are not the only ones. What's more, the disproportionate percentage of murderers executed for killing whites cannot be explained by the numbers of white versus black murder victims. Those numbers are roughly equal. Yet, as of 1985 (the year the figures Smith cites were published), 89 percent of all those who had been executed since the *Gregg* decision had murdered whites.[74]

Ultimately, abolitionists argue, it makes little difference whether racism is the direct cause of disparities in death penalty sentencing or not. No matter what the cause may be, racial discrimination is the result—and racial discrimination is simply unacceptable in such a highly multi-racial society as ours.

Underrepresented Groups

Application of the death penalty does not seem to discriminate against all minorities. If the poor and the black are drastically overrepresented on death row, certain other groups are drastically underrepresented. Hispanics, for example, make up only about 7.3 percent of those sentenced to death, although they constitute about 9 percent of the population. Even more striking, Native Americans, Asian Americans, and Pacific Islanders make up roughly 3.7 percent of the population, but only 1.6 percent of the residents of death rows.[75]

Women of all races are by far the most underrepresented group of all. Although they make up over 51 percent of the American population—and roughly 14 percent of those convicted of homicide,[76] they make up less than 2 percent of the 4,329 people sentenced to death since 1973.[77] In all that time, only one woman has actually been executed.

Summary

Retentionists contend that some disparities are probably inevitable. People from different groups tend to commit different kinds and numbers of crimes. It follows that a higher proportion of criminals from those groups that tend to commit the most deplorable crimes will inevitably be subject to the death penalty.

Abolitionists respond that these differences are not coincidental. They stem from and reflect a variety of prejudices and hostilities at every stage of the criminal justice process. This seems fundamentally unjust. If the death penalty has any legitimacy at all, they argue, it must be applied equally and fairly ac ss the social spectrum.

Lack of Consistency

Both opponents and supporters of capital punishment complain about the capricious way in which death sentences seem to be imposed and carried out. Only a small minority of those who commit capital crimes are sentenced to death for them, and only a tiny minority of that minority are ever actually executed. Even comparing only similar murders, committed by members of a single racial and economic group, the death penalty is still being applied inconsistently in the United States today. This is an old problem, and one that is getting worse. In the two decades before the *Furman* decision halted executions in 1972, only about 20 percent of the people sentenced to die were ever actually executed.[78] In the time since the *Gregg* decision allowed them to resume, the rate has dropped to under 4 percent.[79]

Some of this inconsistency is built into the American judicial system, with its 50 state and two federal (civilian and military) jurisdictions. Some of these 52 jurisdictions have capital punishment, others do not. Some, like Texas and Florida, use the death penalty relatively frequently, others rarely if at all. Even within a single jurisdiction, people who commit virtually identical crimes receive death or prison terms unpredictably. Even criminals who commit the very same crime may receive different punishments. Charles Brooks was executed for murder in Texas in 1982, while his accomplice received 40 years in prison, even though it had never been established which of them had actually killed the victim.[80]

Some inconsistency is even deliberate. "Discretion in the criminal justice system is unavoidable," writes Hugo Adam Bedau. "Society clearly wishes to mitigate the harshness of capital punishment by allowing mercy for some persons. But when discretion is used, as it always has been, to mark for death the poor, the friendless, the uneducated, the members of racial minorities, the despised, then discretion becomes injustice." Ironically, it is the desire for mercy in principle that often leads to discrimination in practice. Consequently, argues Bedau, "Thoughtful citizens, who in contemplating capital punishment in the abstract might support it, must condemn it in actual practice."[81]

In order for any punishment to be truly just, say the critics, it must be dispatched in a fair and even-handed manner. The more severe the punishment, the greater the need to apply it consistently. If the great majority of those who theoretically deserve to die are spared, then it seems manifestly unjust that a handful of others are not. This unfairness is made worse, the opponents of capital punishment say, by the fact that the small number of those who are actually forced to suffer the ultimate penalty are so often black, poor, or mentally ill.

Supporters of capital punishment have other objections to the haphazard way it is administered. They complain that inconsistency undermines death's value as a deterrent. They insist that the key to making capital punishment a truly effective deterrent is making sure that it is carried out swiftly and certainly—if not in every case, at least in most of them. That is far from true today.

If the execution rate is a mere 4 percent for those actually sentenced to die, it is practically insignificant for those who *might* have been sentenced to die had they been caught and effectively prosecuted. Richard Samp, of Washington Legal Foundation, puts the odds at 1,000 to 1 that someone who commits a capital crime will be executed for it. This troubles retentionists because, says Samp, "We have so few executions that it really is not possible to say definitively that the death penalty is a deterrent."[82] How could such long odds be expected to deter anyone?

In theory, at least, one solution to the unfairness of executing only a handful of the people liable to the death penalty would be to execute many more of them. However, applying the death penalty to everyone already condemned would mean proceeding with thousands of executions. Opponents of capital punishment view the idea of wholesale executions with horror. "If we kill everybody on death row," argues John Healey, "we'll kill more people than Khomeini did when he took over Iran."[83] To do this, Healey warns, would mean losing for the United States all claim to moral leadership in the eyes of the other nations of the world. (Healey has some knowledge of the way the United States is regarded by other nations, having once served as director of the Peace Corps.)

Most observers doubt that such an unprecedented slaughter will ever happen. Even in the past, when executions were much more common in the United States than they have been in recent decades, only a relatively small proportion of first degree murderers were ever executed. "People say that capital punishment might deter if it were enforced," wrote Warden Lawes of Sing Sing Prison almost three-quarters of a century ago, when executions were more common than they have been in recent decades. "The point is that until the characteristics of mankind change, it will never be enforced. . . . Capital punishment has never been and can never be anything but an uncertainty."[84]

Charles L. Black, Jr., the author of an important book on the administration of the death penalty, agrees. No matter how the laws are written, says Black, "No society is going to kill everybody who meets certain preset verbal requirements, put on the statute books without awareness or coverage of the infinity of special factors the real world can produce."[85]

Discretion in death penalty sentencing may lead to discrimination in many cases; but removing discretion would lead to a kind of ruthlessness totally outside the British and American tradition. Ever since colonial days, the death penalty's bark has always been worse than its bite. The laws of the colonies that prescribed death for a wide variety of offenses were often ignored or softened by judges and juries alike. As Philip Mackey has written, "[D]espite the severity of colonial criminal laws and practices, there is evidence of an underlying leniency toward criminals in American society of the mid-nineteenth century."[86]

Although historically many countries have been more relentless in applying the death penalty than the United States, none has ever executed everyone guilty of murder, regardless of the circumstances of the case, without review and without opportunity for a condemned person to appeal. It is hardly likely that the United States will prove to be the first.

Even some supporters of the death penalty caution against applying the death penalty too widely. As attorney Howard Friedman warned other supporters of capital punishment, "An indiscriminate application of the death penalty will ultimately result in such public revulsion that [the death penalty] will not survive."[87]

Shame and Excitement—the Public's Response

Most ordinary citizens can no longer attend executions in the United States. Although a handful of press and public witnesses are permitted, and even required by law, they are limited to a small number of people who are well screened in advance. Sketch artists are allowed in some jurisdictions, although photographs are forbidden. This means that the only visual records we have of modern executions are drawings.

Some critics suggest that the official fog cast over the actual event is a sign that society feels a sense of shame about holding executions at all. If we are really at ease with the practice of executing criminals, and even proud of it, why do we refuse to look at it directly? Why don't we let the whole country see exactly what we do to those whom we decide must die?

As far back as 1872, the famous newspaper editor Horace Greeley commented on the growing trend in some states of holding executions away from the public eye. "When I see any business or vocation sneaking and skulking in dark lanes and little by-streets which elude observation, I conclude that those who follow such business feel at least doubtful of its utility and beneficence. They may argue that it is a 'necessary evil,' but they can hardly put faith in their own logic."[88]

Modern critics of the death penalty suggest that conducting executions behind the closed doors of prisons is not only cowardly, it is hypocritical. On the one hand, we claim to need executions to frighten potential criminals out of committing terrible crimes. On the other hand, we protect the same potential criminals—along with the rest of us—from witnessing the very events whose horrors are supposed to frighten them.

In 1962, author William Styron suggested that if society were really serious about deterrence, executions would be held on television. "Until by legislative mandate, all executions are carried on the television networks of the states involved (they could be sponsored by the gas and electric companies), in a dramatic fashion which will enable the entire population—men, women, and all the children over the age of five—to watch the final agonies of those condemned, even the suggestion that we inflict the death penalty to deter people from crime is a farcical one."[89]

Some abolitionists support the idea of making executions public again because they believe it would arouse revulsion against the death penalty. If large numbers of citizens had to face the reality of putting their fellow citizens to death, they say, the public would soon clamor for an end to capital punishment once and for all.

Historically, there is some reason to believe that some people would be appalled. Certainly many witnesses of past public executions were repulsed by what they saw. Eighteenth-century author James Boswell was so overcome by the "gloomy terrors" he felt after witnessing a man being hanged in London in 1763 that he didn't dare to sleep alone that night.[90] Nearly a century later, another famous author, William Makepiece Thackery, reported that the sight of an execution "left on my mind an extraordinary feeling of terror and shame. It seems to me that I have been abetting an act of frightful wickedness and violence. . . . "[91]

Reactions like these were far from universal, however. In fact, a great many people enjoyed attending executions in the days when they were public. In ancient Rome executions were considered to be public entertainments. In revolutionary France, executions became a kind of patriotic celebration. One revolutionary wrote to his brother, "What pleasure you would have experienced if, the day before yesterday, you had seen national justice meted out to two hundred and nine villains. What majesty! What imposing tone! How completely edifying."[92]

In less revolutionary times and places, the public was usually less triumphant, but often equally entertained. Thackery reported that a crowd of 40,000 Londoners attending an execution were apparently thrilled to "give up their natural quiet night's rest, in order to partake of this hideous debauchery . . . more exciting than sleep, or than wine, or the last new ballet, or any other amusement they can have. . . . "[93] Charles Dickens described the crowd attending a public execution in Rome as "resign[ing] all thoughts of business, for the moment, and abandoning themselves wholly to pleasure," as they jockeyed for good positions in the throng. After the young man's severed head was displayed for all to see, Dickens continued, "Nobody cared, or was at all affected. There was no manifestation of disgust, or pity, or indignation, or sorrow."[94]

Would it be any different today? We might like to think that civilization has passed beyond the point where we would eagerly gather together to watch fellow human beings be killed, but there is little evidence that we really have.

The idea of televising executions may have seemed a little farfetched when Styron proposed it in 1962, but it is a real possibility today. Public television station KQED-TV in San Francisco unsuccessfully sued to be allowed to televise the execution of Robert Alton Harris in 1991. An anti-capital-punishment group in California, Death Penalty Focus, passed a resolution supporting the idea, "providing the condemned agrees," in the belief that "faced with the grisly horror of watching an individual put to death—the people of California will be moved to abolish executions."[95]

It is not at all clear that this assumption is correct. If the past is any guide, in fact, it is probably wrong. Accounts of the crowds at executions, from different countries at different historical periods, are surprisingly similar. While some spectators were sickened by what they saw, others were titillated, and the crowds kept coming back for more. In the end, it was not public indignation but the squeamishness of politicians that drove executions behind closed doors.

The Risk of Mistake

No issue is more troubling to abolitionists and retentionists alike than the possibility that the state might execute an innocent person. This possibility alone is frightening enough to convince some people that capital punishment should be abolished. Retentionists argue, however, that capital punishment saves lives as well as takes them, and that some risk that an innocent life may inadvertently be lost is worth taking in order to save many others.

There is no serious question that the risk exists. As Supreme Court Justice William O. Douglas once wrote: "[O]ur system of criminal justice does not work with the efficiency of a machine— errors are made, and innocent as well as guilty people are sometimes punished. . . . [T]he sad truth is that a cog in the machine often slips; memories fail; mistaken identifications are made; those who wield the power of life and death itself—the police officer, the witness, the prosecutor, the juror, and even the judge—become overzealous. . . . "[96] Judges know this, and juries know this, too. Even the most confirmed defenders of the death penalty know it.

In 1987 Hugo Adam Bedau and Michael L. Radelet published the results of a study in which they named 350 people they said had probably been wrongfully convicted of capital crimes between 1900 and 1987.[97] Although the authors are both abolitionists, they have solid reputations for integrity. For the most part, the cases they reported involved prisoners who either had been pardoned or had their convictions overturned because of the presentation of new evidence. As we have already seen, however, once a person is convicted, his or her guilt is accepted as legal fact. It is extremely hard, after that, for a defendant to get a court to consider new evidence. We can only guess at the number of innocent people who may have been actually executed before new evidence could surface or be heard.

Some retentionists might try to take comfort from the Bedau-Radelet study, arguing that most of the cases involved defendants who were not, after all, executed. The system may have made some mistakes, but ultimately, it seems, the system worked. According to Diann Rust-Tierney, director of the Capital Punishment Project of the ACLU, however, it is not always the system that works. She cites several "recent examples of people who were on death row in Georgia [and] Texas who were released—who were found to be innocent—not by the normal [legal] process but by some chance."[98]

One of the lucky ones was Randall Dale Adams, who was convicted and sentenced to death for killing a Dallas policeman in 1976. His sentence was commuted to life imprisonment three days before he was due to die. Years later, a former private investigator who had turned filmmaker made a documentary movie about Adams' case, alleging that Adams had been convicted on perjured evidence, encouraged by the prosecution in the case. The film, *The Thin Blue Line*, got enough attention to reopen the case. After reviewing the evidence, a Texas appeals court judge ruled that the prosecution "had been guilty of suppressing evidence favorable to the accused, deceiving the trial court . . . and knowingly using perjured testimony."[99] Adams was eventually cleared and released in 1989.

Although he admits the theoretical possibility that an innocent person might be executed, Richard Samp of the Washington Legal Foundation insists, "I don't think anybody seriously contends that anybody who's been executed in the past fifteen years in this country had any legitimate claim of innocence."[100]

The American Civil Liberties Union and others concerned with the rights of criminal defendants disagree. They point to a number of recent cases in which they claim serious doubts exist about the guilt of those who were executed. Among them was the case of Willie Darden, who was on death row in the Florida State Prison at Starke so long before being executed in 1988 that he was known as the Dean of Death Row. "If ever a man received an unfair trial," declared Supreme Court Justice Harry Blackmun, "Darden did."[101]

Safeguards are built into the system to assure that miscarriages of justice never result in the execution of an innocent person. Perhaps the most important is the right of convicted prisoners to make habeas corpus appeals to the federal courts, but, as we have also seen, these safeguards are far from foolproof, and the Supreme Court itself has been eating away at the right to habeas corpus in recent years. It has become harder and harder for those convicted of a capital crime to get a chance for a new trial.

After adding to the protections against wrongful conviction in capital cases in the wake of the *Gregg* decision, the U.S. Supreme Court has proceeded to crack down on what Chief Justice William Rehnquist and some other justices consider unnecessary delays and frivolous appeals. Beginning more than a decade ago, the Court has done what it can to speed up appeal processes in death penalty cases. In the process, the Court has launched what three of its own justices have attacked as an "unjustifiable assault on the Great Writ [of habeas corpus]."[102]

The Court has undercut the same Eighth and Fourteenth Amendment protections it has upheld by refusing to consider possibly valid claims of constitutional violations on the grounds that the defendant has raised them improperly, or too late in the appeals process, or has simply come to the Court too often.[103] In addition, the Court has denied poor death row inmates free legal assistance to prepare their appeals.[104]

The Court's impatience with death sentence appeals was exhibited most dramatically in the 1992 case of Roger Keith Coleman, whose otherwise valid appeal was turned down on the grounds that Coleman's attorney had been a day late in filing a petition in the state court of Virginia. In Coleman's case, the Supreme Court virtually ordered the lower courts to stop granting stays and to proceed with his execution.[105]

In January 1993, the Court made what may be its most controversial procedural death penalty ruling yet. By a vote of 6 to 3, it refused to block the execution of Leonel Herrera, who was scheduled to die for killing a Texas policeman in 1981, despite new evidence that it was someone else, and not Leonel, who had committed the murder. Three of the judges who voted against Herrera believed that his new evidence was not persuasive enough to warrant a hearing. The other three concurring justices, however, indicated that it didn't matter how persuasive the evidence was. Innocence was no reason for the court to step in to stop the execution so late in the process. In effect, they were saying it is not unconstitutional in the United States to execute an innocent person. This so outraged Justice Harry Blackmun that he spoke from the bench to emphasize his dissent. "Execution of a person who can show that he is innocent," protested Blackmun, "comes perilously close to simple murder."[106]

As long as there is a death penalty, it is clear that some risk of executing innocent people will continue to exist. It is also clear that the risk is a limited one. The real question becomes, is any risk worth taking?

Confirmed opponents of the death penalty argue that it is not. Any risk that the state might kill an innocent man or woman is far too high. Defenders of the death penalty respond that the possibility that an innocent person might die is no reason to abandon capital punishment altogether. Taken to its extremes, they say, the potential for injustice could be used as an argument against any kind of punishment at all. There is always some chance that an innocent person might be convicted of any crime by mistake.

Abolitionists insist, however, that the death penalty is fundamentally different from all other punishments. As Diann Rust-Tierney puts it, "[T]he death penalty, unlike other punishments, does not give us a chance to correct mistakes."[107] Other injustices can be alleviated. If they cannot always be set right, they can at least be amended. Society can at least try to make up for its error. If it is found that a prisoner serving a life sentence was not guilty after all, he can be released. His reputation can be restored. Apologies can be made. If the injustice was gross enough, money can be paid to him to make up for the shame and suffering he endured. Once a person has been executed, though, there is nothing society can do to make up for its mistake.

Clemency—the Potential for Mercy

Rejecting Herrera's appeal, the Court advised that if he really were innocent, the proper place for him to seek help was no longer the courts but the executive authorities of his own state. Rather than seeking a new trial at this late stage in the process, he should appeal for clemency.

Clemency is the traditional last resort, not only for wrongly convicted defendants, but for those seeking some special mercy on humanitarian grounds. In most states, the governor has the power to pardon and release a convicted criminal, or to commute (reduce) his or her sentence from death to some lesser punishment. In some states, as in Texas, that power is at least partly vested in a state board or agency.

Even if all else fails and the judicial system makes a terrible mistake, the defenders of the death penalty comfort themselves with the thought that the mistake is correctable by political authorities. The governor or pardons board is there to step in and set things right before it is too late. Even while reinstating the death penalty in *Gregg*, the Supreme Court emphasized the need to keep open the possibility of executive clemency. Not to provide that potential remedy, the Court declared, "would be totally alien to our notions of criminal justice."[108]

The last-minute phone call from the governor is more than a staple of dramatic movies and television comedy routines. It actually happens. As far back as 1824, the hanging of four white men for the murder of several Native Americans in Indiana was interrupted by the governor's arrival on horseback, come to spare the youngest of the four.[109] Unfortunately, the correction may not always come in time. In 1957, for example, California Governor Goodwin J. Knight's phone call to the San Quentin gas chamber came just moments too late to save convicted murderer Burton Abbott.[110]

Death penalty opponents argue that clemency is a very thin reed on which to risk an innocent person's life. Governors are political officeholders, and the public that elects them favors the death penalty. Many if not most governors are reluctant to grant clemency because they fear being considered soft on crime. Far from being eager to exercise clemency, some governors get elected by emphasizing their eagerness to sign as many death warrants as possible. As one observer put it, the central issue in the 1990 race for governor of Texas between the Republican Clayton Williams and Democrat Ann Richards was "Who can kill the most Texans?"[111]

The reluctance to grant clemency is so great that the practice is extremely rare. During the 1980s, only 23 clemencies were granted in the entire United States, for an average of less than two and a half per year. That compares to a total of 2,724 death sentences handed down during that time, or just under 275 per year. In 1991, however, the number of clemencies rose to ten, thanks to eight granted in Ohio alone. (Legal challenges have been launched to seven of the Ohio clemencies, however.)[112]

"Cruel and Unusual Punishment"

In *Gregg*, the U.S. Supreme Court ruled that capital punishment, as such, does not violate the Eighth Amendment's ban on cruel and unusual punishments. However, are some methods of execution so painful or so liable to go wrong that they violate modern standards of decency and humanity? This possibility was raised by U.S. Supreme Court Justice Stanley Reed, who declared in his opinion in a 1947 case that "[t]he traditional humanity of modern Anglo-American law forbids the infliction of unnecessary pain in the execution of the death sentence."[113]

Even the most fervent supporters of capital punishment would balk at drawing and quartering criminals, burning them at the stake, or boiling them in oil; yet, all of these methods have been common in some countries in the past. What about the methods used in the United States today—lethal injection, electrocution, gas, hanging, and the firing squad? Each was originally proposed as being more humane than the methods used before it. Each has been hailed as quick and virtually painless by its defenders. However, each has also been protested as cruel and unusual.

Clearly, none of these methods is foolproof. Electrocution may or may not be relatively painless when death is virtually immediate; but several electrocutions in the 1980s—in at least three different states—required more than one charge to kill, and at least one victim took ten minutes to die.[114]

Opponents of the gas chamber argue that it is "excruciatingly painful and slow."[115] One expert compared the experience of being asphyxiated by cyanide gas to the "pain felt by a person during a massive heart attack."[116] When James Autry was executed in Texas in 1984, *Newsweek* magazine reported that he "took at least ten minutes to die and throughout much of that time was conscious, moving about and complaining of pain."[117]

Some of the worst problems have occurred with the most modern and most frequent method of execution in the United States—lethal injection. In 1985 a Texas executioner spent 40 minutes poking the victim 23 separate times before finding a vein that could be used to insert the needle.[118] Arkansas authorities took a full hour trying to insert the needle in the arm of Rickey Ray Rector in 1992. In desperation, they even dug into his arm with a scalpel searching for a usable vein. Even after they were successful, and the first of the solutions began entering Rector's bloodstream, the massive prisoner took 19 minutes to die.[119]

Ironically, the two oldest methods of execution may still be the most efficient. British hangman Albert Pierrepoint once pronounced a modern hanging "the fastest and quickest method in the world bar nothing. It is quicker than shooting, and cleaner."[120] In fact, most recent hangings have gone fairly smoothly. There have been no recent problems with executions by firing squad, either, although they rarely occur in the United States today.

So far, at least, the U.S. Supreme Court has rejected the argument that any current methods are "cruel and unusual."

For most retentionists and many abolitionists as well, debates over the relative cruelty of this method versus that method are irrelevant. For supporters of the death penalty, they are red herrings that abolitionists try to throw in the way of particular executions, while defenders of the death penalty insist that abolitionists who complain about particular methods of execution are hypocrites. Abolitionists, they say, will never admit that any form of execution is *not* cruel and unusual. Whichever form of execution is threatened will always be the one they complain is unusually cruel. If the condemned prisoner is about to be hung, then hanging is barbaric compared to electrocution. When he or she is about to be electrocuted, electrocution is excessively painful compared to lethal injection. When lethal injection is the method in question, it becomes a torturous experiment compared to the time-tested practice of hanging, and so on.

Some retentionists argue that it doesn't really matter whether particular methods of execution are painful or not. So what if it hurts? Why shouldn't vicious criminals sentenced to death suffer some moments of pain for the atrocities they have committed? George C. Smith of the Washington Legal Foundation insists that "[t]here is no suggestion in the [Eighth] Amendment or in its historical context that the government is required to make the punishments for crime as painless and inoffensive as possible. Pain and discomfort are an inherent and necessary aspect of legal punishment for crime. Were this not so, the deterrent value of punishment would be drastically undercut."[121] Even those retentionists who prefer executions to be as painless as possible accept the idea that some pain is probably inevitable. However unfortunate it may be, argues Paul Kamenar of the Washington Legal Foundation, condemned criminals "are not entitled to die with no pain whatsoever."[122]

Some abolitionists agree that debates over execution methods are irrelevant. They believe, along with Supreme Court Justice Brennan, that "arguments about the 'humanity' and 'dignity' of any method of officially sponsored execution are a constitutional contradiction in terms."[123] Whatever the method, they believe execution is a form of torture. "The whole process, not just what happens in the death chamber, is torturous," insists the Reverend Joe Engle. "Imagine someone placing you in a large closet, telling you how you're going to be killed in a few years . . . taking you out to kill you . . . stopping . . . finally one day slaughtering you."[124] If that is not torture, abolitionists ask, what is?

The Brutalizing Effects of Capital Punishment

"A government that persists in retaining these horrible punishments," wrote nineteenth-century English philosopher Jeremy Bentham, "can only assign one reason in justification of their conduct: that they have already so degraded and brutalized the habits of the people, that they cannot be restrained by any moderate punishments."[125] Louis E. Lawes, who presided over many executions as the warden of Sing Sing Prison, agrees. "Executions, like war, brutalize men," wrote Lawes. "[T]he more that take place, the greater the number there is to execute."[126] "It is the deed that teaches, not the name we give it," echoed George Bernard Shaw in his play *Man and Superman*. "Murder and capital punishment are not opposites that cancel one another, but similars that breed their kind."

If Bentham, Lawes, and Shaw were miraculously brought back to life, they would not be surprised to learn that the United States—the only one of the five largest western nations that has the death penalty for ordinary crimes—has a much higher murder rate than any of the others. There are roughly three times as many murders in the United States each year as in Canada, France, Germany, and the United Kingdom combined, although those four countries together have almost as many people.[127] Nor would they be surprised that the localities that produce the most executions are consistently among those with the highest murder rates. Texas has executed more people since 1977 than any other state, as we have seen. Still, despite the supposed deterrent effect of the death penalty, three Texas cities—Houston, Dallas, and Fort Worth—have murder rates among the top 25 in the country.[128]

On the other side of the coin is New York City, located in a state that does not have the death penalty. Despite its reputation for violent crime, New York is not even among the top 25 cities in regard to the murder rate. What's more, while the murder rate in most large American cities (including the three Texas cities named above) went up in 1991, New York City's rate actually went down.[129]

Abolitionists would say this all demonstrates something Bentham wrote nearly 200 years ago: "[T]he most savage banditti are always to be found under laws the most severe, and it is no more than what might be expected. The fate with which they are threatened hardens them to the suffering of others as well as their own. They know that they can expect no lenity, and they consider their acts of cruelty as retaliations."[130]

Retentionists argue that the high execution rates in the United States as a whole, and in Texas in particular, are the results of the high murder rates—not the other way around. Abolitionists respond that they are not making a which-came-first argument. Their point is that the two forms of death tend to go together.

Whether or not capital punishment is brutalizing to society, it is certainly a burden on those who have to carry it out. "Execution is an abominable thing," declared Canon Popot, a French priest and prison chaplain who comforted 79 condemned prisoners in their last moments, "a vast comedy in which everyone lies, hides his feelings, and is deeply ashamed."[131]

Those who do not become brutalized themselves often join the abolitionist cause. Historically, many prominent opponents of capital punishment came from the ranks of prison wardens, executioners, and others who have assisted in the application of the death penalty. Among them were Lewis E. Lawes and Thomas Mott Osborne, both of whom served as wardens of Sing Sing, and Clinton Duffy, the legendary warden of San Quentin. In Britain, even Albert Pierrepoint, who bragged of being the most prolific executioner in modern British history, eventually became convinced that the death penalty was a mistake.

"Why, then, execution?" asked Tom Teepen, writing about the execution of the vicious child-killer Westley Allan Dodd. "Because," he answered, "killing him felt good—so much so a crowd outside the prison partied raucously, chanting and firing Roman candles. At the end, we are reduced to holding that it is all right to execute just because the killing is, well, satisfying. Shouldn't it give us pause, at least, that Westley Dodd would understand?"[132]

Executing the Incompetent

Even many retentionists are troubled by executions of those who are not fully responsible for their actions: the mentally ill, the retarded, and young people under the age of 18.

The Mentally Ill

There has always been a reluctance to execute those criminals most laypeople would consider lunatics, no matter how horrible their crimes. This tradition remains alive in American law today. Insanity is, in and of itself, a defense against a criminal charge, even a charge of murder. In most jurisdictions, defendants so ill at the time of the crime that they were unable to understand the nature and consequences of their actions will be found innocent "by reason of insanity."

Innocent, in such cases, is a technical term. Those found innocent for this reason can still find themselves confined for long periods of time. Those who are considered threats to repeat their atrocities are usually committed to an institution for the dangerously insane, where their imprisonment often lasts longer than an ordinary prison sentence for the same crime. Even so, this technicality angers many members of the public, who find it absurd that someone who has clearly committed a terrible act can be found innocent.

When it comes to capital punishment, the defendant's mental condition at the time of the crime is not the only issue. Even a defendant who was legally sane when he or she committed a crime cannot be executed for it if he or she is found to be insane at the time set for execution.[133] In theory, then, no one who is insane should ever be executed in the United States. That is the theory, but the reality is something different. Legal insanity is more a legal technicality than a medical diagnosis. A number of people have been executed despite being what any layman would consider raving lunatics. Amnesty International claims that at least three such people were executed during the 1980s alone.[134] Other abolitionists would argue that this is a very conservative estimate.

One of these people was Morris Mason, a black man who had raped and murdered a white woman in Virginia. He was executed in 1985, at the age of 32, even though he had been diagnosed as a paranoid schizophrenic three different times, by three different state mental institutions. (Schizophrenia is considered the most extreme class of mental illness; schizophrenics often find it impossible to distinguish between reality and fantasy.) In addition, Mason was severely mentally retarded, and was an active drug addict and alcoholic as well. He had specifically asked for help dealing with his mental conditions at least twice in the days leading up to his fatal crime.

Despite all of the above, Mason was unable to plead insanity at his trial because he had no money to pay for psychiatrists to examine him and testify on his behalf. He could only plead guilty and rely on the mercy of court. The court, however, showed no mercy and he was sentenced to death.[135]

Not long before Mason's execution, the U.S. Supreme Court ruled that states had to provide psychiatric help to indigent defendants in cases where the court is convinced that sanity is a real issue. The Court's ruling might have helped Mason if it had been made earlier, but the Court refused to apply it to cases, like Mason's, in which verdicts had already been reached.

The 1985 decision should help mentally ill defendants in the future, but the fact that it will be easier for them to plead insanity is no guarantee that their pleas will succeed. The definition of legal insanity remains imprecise and extremely difficult to meet, and juries are notoriously wary of insanity pleas. It is also no guarantee that, once found guilty, they will not be sentenced to death, and executed.

The Young

The United States is one of very few countries that execute people for crimes committed when they were under 18 years of age. Indeed, 18 seems to be the closest thing there is to an internationally accepted minimum age for the imposition of capital punishment. More than 70 countries have laws setting 18 as the minimum, several others have signed treaties agreeing not to execute people below that age. Most of the countries that have no formal age restriction have refrained from executing people under 18 in practice. According to Amnesty International, the only countries known to have executed people under 18 in recent years are Iran, Iraq, Bangladesh, Pakistan, and the United States.[136]

By doing so, the United States violates at least two international agreements: The International Covenant on Civil and Political Rights and the American Convention on Human Rights. The United States actually signed both these agreements, although it has not ratified either of them.[137]

A number of prominent American organizations—not all of them total abolitionists—have come out against the execution of juveniles.[138] Organizations like the American Bar Association's House of Delegates, the National PTA, the American Society for Adolescent Psychiatry, and the Child Welfare League of America make two main arguments: first, that adolescents are not fully responsible for their actions, and second, that they are peculiarly subject to reform and rehabilitation. What's more, juvenile offenders often commit their crimes under the influence of adult criminals. To punish adolescents equally with—or, in some cases, even more harshly than—the older offenders seems unfair and excessive.

Nonetheless, since 1972 over 90 young people have received death sentences for crimes committed when they were under 18. The youngest was 14 at the time of the crime, and the oldest 17. Four had been executed by the beginning of 1991.

The U.S. Supreme Court has ruled that the youth "of a minor is itself a relevant mitigating factor of great weight" when deciding whether to impose the death penalty.[139] However, it remains just one mitigating factor to be weighed with others against whatever aggravating factors there may be. Despite the Court's ruling, evidence suggests that, in some cases, at least, judges and juries have largely discounted age as a factor.

In 1988 the Supreme Court overturned the death sentence of a young man who had been sentenced to death in Oklahoma for taking part in a murder when he was 15. Four of the nine justices ruled that the execution of a 15-year-old was cruel and unusual punishment, but Justice Sandra Day O'Connor, who provided the fifth vote to overturn, gave a different reason. She ruled that the Oklahoma law was too vague because it set no specific minimum age for receiving the death penalty. This, she argued, violated the need to take special care in imposing the death penalty.[140] The ruling was taken by some to mean that 16 was now, in effect, the minimum constitutional age for imposing the death penalty. That hasn't stopped Alabama and Florida from sentencing young men to death for murders committed when they were 15 (the Florida sentence came as recently as 1991). Like the Oklahoma law, the Alabama law has no minimum age limit.

The laws of ten states and the federal government specify 18-at-the-time-of-the-offense as the youngest at which a defendant may be sentenced to death. Sixteen states specify some lower specific age, ranging as low as 14. In Montana, defendants theoretically can be tried as adults and sentenced to death as young as 10. It is extremely unlikely, however, that such a sentence would be upheld. Nine of the death penalty states set no minimum age, despite Justice O'Connor's attack on the vagueness of the Oklahoma law.

Although American public opinion favors retaining the death penalty in general, it opposes executing those under 18.[141] Nonetheless, there is no sign that those states that still execute juveniles intend to bring the United States in line with most of the world by eliminating the practice any time soon.

The Retarded

Some condemned criminals who are no longer children in a physical or chronological sense are still children mentally and emotionally. Their mental retardation—even severe mental retardation—is not necessarily considered a disqualification for execution.

Some death row inmates are so retarded they are virtually unable to understand their situation. "Am I going with you?" one asked hopefully when a visitor rose to leave after interviewing him.[142] Another, who was scheduled to die on a Friday evening, put aside the dessert he was given along with his traditional last meal, intending to eat it later. "[He] thinks he'll be back in his cell on Saturday morning," his lawyer explained.[143]

Both of these men were considered competent enough to be executed. This means that they were presumed to be competent to aid their attorneys in preparing their defense and appeals. James Bowden was considered competent too. Although he was 33 years old chronologically when he was executed in Georgia in 1986, he was estimated to have a mental age of about 12.

Shortly before Bowden's execution, a state-hired psychiatrist gave him a three-hour test to determine how retarded he actually was. It determined that he had an IQ of 65—35 points below that of the average adult. The Georgia Board of Pardons and Paroles decided this score was too high to keep him from execution. One member of the board remarked that he would have needed a score lower than 45 to do it. "Ultimately," the *Atlanta Constitution* editorialized in disgust, "the difference between life and death for James Bowden boiled down to a few numbers . . . toted up by state-paid professionals. . . . If anyone doubts the role of brutal whimsy as states apply the death penalty, this wretched tale offers convincing proof."[144]

If Bowden's IQ test proved nothing else, it proved that he was not smart enough to cheat on the test and fail it badly enough to save his life. It is not unusual, however ironic, for death row residents to try their hardest to do well on such tests.

Judeo-Christian Religious Beliefs

The Capitall Lawes of New-England, established in the Massachusetts Bay Colony in 1636, cited specific Old Testament passages as authority for each of the 13 separate crimes it made punishable by death.[145] The American political debate over the death penalty has been entangled with religious beliefs—and particularly with Judeo-Christian religious beliefs—ever since. Many abolitionist and retentionist leaders alike have testified that their positions on the death penalty flow from their religious beliefs.

Both supporters and opponents of the death penalty quote biblical passages to defend their views. God, as described in the Old Testament, meted out death to those who offended him in the form of plagues, wars, and natural disasters. Religious supporters of the death penalty look to society to follow his prescription, "Whoso sheddeth man's blood, by man shall his blood be shed."[146] They point to a number of other biblical passages as well, which seem to mandate death for 15 different offenses, including not only murder, but witchcraft, working on the Sabbath day, and having sexual relations with animals, among others.

Most religiously motivated retentionists acknowledge that not all the offenses proclaimed to deserve death in the Old Testament ought to be capital offenses today. They insist, however, that such passages make it clear that the Judeo-Christian God favors the practice of putting at least some kinds of evildoers to death.

Religious abolitionists, on the other hand, argue that "Whoso sheddeth man's blood, by man shall his blood be shed," is not a command to execute evildoers, but a warning to the evildoers to reform. They take comfort in the commandment, "Thou shalt not kill," and note that, in the case of the first act of murder recorded in the Bible, God himself refused to condemn the killer to death. After Cain killed Abel, God not only declined to kill Cain in return, but put a mark on him as a warning to others not to harm him.

For the most part, however, Christian abolitionists look to the New Testament for support, while defenders of capital punishment look to the Old Testament, pointing to prescriptions of "an eye for an eye, and a tooth for a tooth." Opponents like Thomas Mott Osborne respond by pointing out that Jesus Christ specifically rejected that formula in the Sermon on the Mount.[147]

What's more, Christian abolitionists point out, on the only occasion the Bible reports Christ as being present at an execution (other than his own), he put a stop to it. When a crowd was about to stone an adulterous woman to death, as prescribed by law, Jesus turned them away, admonishing them that only someone "who is without sin among you," should cast the first stone.[148]

Abolitionists dispute Ernest van den Haag's statement that "All religions that I'm aware of feel that human life is sacred, and that its sacredness must be enforced by depriving of life anyone who deprives another person of life."[149] They point out that religious pacifists like the Quakers have historically opposed the taking of any human life, even that of the most vicious criminals. According to Amnesty International USA, "the leading bodies of at least 20 major religious denominations in the USA have passed resolutions opposing the death penalty on religious, moral, humanitarian, and social grounds."[150] It is true, however, that many traditional American Protestant sects and ministers do strongly support the death penalty, and others do not oppose it.

Internationally, though, the highest authorities of the two worldwide faiths with the most influence on American attitudes, Judaism and Roman Catholicism, have never officially condemned capital punishment. At times some have seemed to support it.

On the other hand, neither the major rabbinical organizations nor recent Popes have been vocal supporters of the practice. Rabbi Israel J. Kazis of Massachusetts has argued that "to understand the Jewish attitude toward capital punishment," it is necessary to look beyond the many death penalty prescriptions in the Bible. "It is quite clear that the many restrictions and provisions imposed by the Rabbis made it very difficult to inflict capital punishment," writes Kazis. "[I]t is reasonable to maintain that [the Rabbis] did not look with favor upon capital punishment."[151] In 1969 Roman Catholic authorities removed the Vatican from the capital punishment provisions of the Italian criminal code.[152] What's more, several Catholic bishops have spoken out opposing the death penalty. Visiting death row at California's San Quentin prison in 1987,

Mother Teresa warned the world to "[r]emember, what you do to these men, you do to God."[153]

Ultimately religious belief is a matter of faith, and the faiths of individuals and churches differ greatly. There is no single Jewish, Protestant, or Catholic position on the death penalty. As one professor of Christian ethics has explained, "all the above viewpoints will be found among thoughtful and conscientious Christians of every denomination."[154] The same could be said of many other religious faiths.

The Political Question

Once all of the practical and moral arguments have been explored, the political question remains. Should we continue to execute people in the United States? For some of us, a particular moral or practical argument may be decisive. If I believe that it is always wrong to kill, then I must be against the death penalty. If I believe that fundamental justice demands a life for a life, then I must favor it.

For many people, if not most, the answer is not that clear-cut. They find themselves undecided, sympathetic to some arguments on each side of the issue, but not absolutely persuaded by any of them. They would like to see the death penalty abolished, but wonder if it is really right—or safe—to do so. For these people, an important consideration is what we can do instead. Is there an equally effective alternative or combination of alternatives to retaining the death penalty?

Put this way, the answer depends on what you consider the purpose of the death penalty to be. If the purpose of capital punishment is simply retribution—an eye for an eye—then no other penalty seems to fit the crime so well. If, however, you believe the real purpose of capital punishment is to protect society from criminals, then it is reasonable to consider alternatives like those discussed below.

Life Imprisonment

Polls indicate that if there were no death penalty, the alternative the public would most prefer would be sentences of life imprisonment.

without possibility of parole. Such sentences promise to remove the dangerous criminal from society permanently, and are arguably as effective a deterrent as the death penalty itself. A poll conducted in Florida in the 1980s indicated that 84 percent of Floridians favored the death penalty over the alternatives then being practiced, but 70 percent said they would support sentencing murderers to a lifetime of prison labor instead, if the money they earned went to the family members of their victims.[155] In a sense, this would hark back to the ancient practice of family members demanding financial penalties from those who killed their relatives.

Many members of the public mistrust life sentences, however, knowing that in many jurisdictions even prisoners sentenced to life eventually become eligible for parole. This is not true everywhere, however, and even where it is, not all lifers who become eligible for parole receive it. Many lifers do, in fact, die in prison.

In defense of parole, abolitionists point out that some criminals do reform. What's more, it is generally true that there is less and less need to protect society against particular individuals as time goes by. For whatever reason, criminals seem to become less violent as they get older. Murder, in particular, seems to be a young person's crime. There are relatively few middle-aged murderers, and almost no elderly ones. Almost 52 percent of the people on the nation's death rows at the end of 1990 had been between the ages of 20 and 30 when they were sentenced to death. Only 0.5 percent were 60 or older.[156]

Although most abolitionists would prefer to keep the possibility of parole open even for lifers, many would gladly surrender the possibility of eventual release in return for an end to capital punishment. For this reason, they join in efforts to pass "life means life" bills that assure that defendants who receive life sentences will never get out of prison.

Among prison officials, there is a certain amount of wariness about combining "life means life" laws with the abolition of capital punishment. The hope that prisoners might eventually be released if they maintain a record of good behavior can be a powerful motivation for them to behave themselves. Prisoners who know they will never get out, but cannot be executed, have little to lose and no incentive to behave. For this reason, some prison officials believe that "life means life" should be accompanied by a potential death sentence for those who commit murder while in captivity.

Rehabilitation

For some abolitionists, the most promising alternative to death is rehabilitation. For many people, and for Christians in particular, there is a special attraction in the idea of redemption, even aside from the social benefits of turning a destructive criminal into a reliable and productive member of society.

Thomas Mott Osborne reported a conversation he had with a 20-year-old condemned prisoner. The young man told Warden Osborne he was "sorry to go" without "the chance to do enough good in the world to balance the harm I've done." Osborne was moved by the doomed man's complaint. "He had the right idea," said Osborne. "The only way to balance a debit is by a credit. Resist not evil, but overcome evil with good. Balance wrong by right. Give the man a chance to redeem himself after his sin by doing good to make things balance. That can be done, even in prison."[157]

Some retentionists consider rehabilitation an unacceptable option to retribution. "If rehabilitation were our aim," admits the pro-death-penalty psychologist Ernest van den Haag, "most murderers could be released. Quite often, they are 'rehabilitated' by the very murder they committed. They are unlikely to commit other crimes." That is not the real point, though, he argues. "We punish [murderers] not for what they may or may not do in the future but for what they have done," he insists.[158]

Retentionists add that rehabilitation is only a hope, not a plan of action, and a hope, they say, is not enough on which to base a criminal justice system. "Nobody knows how to rehabilitate," insists van den Haag. "There seems to be little difference in the behavior of people who have been subjected to rehabilitation programs compared to those who have not been. The recidivism rate is about the same."[159] That being so, it is always a risk to release a once-vicious criminal, no matter how rehabilitated he or she might seem.

Abolitionists respond that rehabilitation does not necessarily mean release. While it might be preferable to release those who are truly reformed, if there is any doubt they can continue to be confined. As Warden Osborne has pointed out, it is possible for a criminal to do good "to make things balance . . . even in prison."

Improved Law Enforcement

Most ordinary citizens favor the death penalty primarily because they believe it protects them from violent criminals. Abolitionists argue that it does a very poor job of that—a fact they claim is demonstrated by the high murder rates in many capital punishment states.

Even some law enforcement officials who have no moral objection to the death penalty believe that there are more effective ways of maintaining law and order. They argue that society would be safer if it took the enormous resources spent maintaining a capital punishment system and put more police on the nation's streets and more judges in the nation's courtrooms. According to a past president of a prosecutors' association in Massachusetts, most district attorneys in that state oppose reinstating the death penalty there. These district attorneys are neither soft on crime nor sympathetic to violent criminals. They simply believe that the state's resources are more efficiently spent on prosecutions and prison cells.[160]

Norman Kinne, the district attorney of Dallas County, Texas, agrees. "Even though I'm a firm believer in the death penalty," says Kinne, "I also understand what the cost is. If you can be satisfied with putting a person in the penitentiary for the rest of his life . . . I think maybe we have to be satisfied with that as opposed to spending $1 million to try and get them executed. . . ."[161]

Summary

Are there alternatives to the death penalty? Certainly there are. After all, the United States didn't even have capital punishment for a decade. Several states do not have it now, and most of those that do use it sparingly, if at all. Ultimately, then, the real question is not if we *need* the death penalty. Capital punishment is not the core of our criminal justice system. It is only one aspect of it—and a minor aspect at that. As we have seen, only a small percentage of murderers are sentenced to death, and only a small percentage of those are executed. The real question is whether we insist on keeping the death penalty even though we don't need it—whether, in Norman Kinne's words, we can be satisfied without it.

Notes

1. *1953 Report.* Great Britain, Royal Commission on Capital Punishment, 1949–1953 (London: H. M. Stationary Office, 1953), 19.

2. "Should Capital Punishment Be Retained?" *Congressional Digest* (August–September 1927): 243.

3. "British Hangman Albert Pierrepoint," *Chicago Tribune*, 13 July 1992.

4. Frank Carrington, "Inconclusive Evidence Does Not Invalidate Deterrence," in *The Death Penalty: Opposing Viewpoints*, David L. Bender and Bruno Leone, eds. (St. Paul: Greenhaven, 1986), 124–125.

5. *Congressional Digest*, 228.

6. *Congressional Digest*, 242.

7. Thorsten Sellin, *The Death Penalty: A Report for the Model Penal Code Project of the American Law Institute* (Philadelphia: American Law Institute, 1959).

8. David L. Sills, ed., "Capital Punishment," *International Encyclopedia of the Social Sciences* (New York: The Macmillan Company & Free Press, 1968), 293.

9. Amnesty International, *The United States of America Death Penalty Developments in 1991* (New York: Amnesty International, February 1992), 5.

10. The murder rates quoted here are based on 1990 census figures compared to 1991 murders as reported by the Senate Judiciary Committee and reported on a chart, "Slayings Set Record in '91; No End in Sight," by Tom Squitieri, *USA Today*, 7 January 1992.

11. Isaac Erlich, "The Deterrent Effect of Capital Punishment: A Question of Life and Death," *American Economic Review* (June 1975): 398–414.

12. Alfred Blumstein and Jacqueline Cohen, eds., *Deterrence and Incapacitation: Estimating the Effects of Criminal Sanctions on Crime Rates* (Washington, D.C.: National Academy of Science, 1978), 62.

13. The figures in this paragraph are taken from "The Death Penalty Deters Murder," by Karl Spence, in Bender and Leone, 99–100.

14. Squitieri.

15. Amnesty International, *United States of America, The Death Penalty: Briefing* (New York: Amnesty International, October 1987), 18.

16. Barzun, *The Death Penalty in America*, 156.

17. *1953 Report*, 274.

18. *Gregg v. Georgia*, 428 U.S. 153, 96 S.Ct. 2909 (1976).

19. Louis Joylon West, M.D., "Psychiatric Reflections on the Death Penalty," *American Journal of Orthopsychiatry* (Vol. 45, No. 4) as reprinted in Bender and Leone, 102.

20. *American Justice*, Nugus/Martin Productions, 1992.

21. Jon Nordheimer, "Gilmore Is Executed," *New York Times*, 18 January 1977.

22. Bender and Leone, 101–106.

23. Rob Karwath, "Death—His Own—Was Killer's Goal," *Chicago Tribune*, 7 November 1992.

24. Amnesty International, *When the State Kills . . . The Death Penalty: A Human Rights Issue* (London: Amnesty International, 1989), 15.

25. *Briefing*, 19.

26. Sellin, 70–72.

27. *Briefing,* 16.

28. See Nathan Leopold's *Life Plus 99 Years* (Garden City, NY: Doubleday, 1958).

29. "Washington Sex Offender Dies by Hanging," AP news story, *Wausau Daily Herald,* 5 January 1993.

30. From Benjamin Rush's "An Enquiry into the Consistency of the Punishment of Murder by Death, with Reason and Revelation," reprinted in Philip English Mackey's *Voices against Death* (New York: Burt Franklin, 1976), 4.

31. *Congressional Digest,* 243.

32. *The 700 Club,* CBN Television Network, 5 January 1993.

33. *California v. Ramos,* 463 U.S. 992, 998–999 (1983).

34. U.S. Department of Justice, "Capital Punishment 1990," Bureau of Justice Statistics Bulletin, 7.

35. "Misconceptions About the Cost of the Death Penalty" (San Francisco: American Civil Liberties Union Foundation, October 1992), unnumbered.

36. Richard McGee, *Federal Probation,* quoted by Hugo Adam Bedau, "The Case Against the Death Penalty" (New York: American Civil Liberties Union, 1984), 22.

37. D. Von Drehle, "Bottom Line: Life in Prison One-Sixth as Expensive," *The Miami Herald,* 10 July 1988.

38. Ibid.

39. *Millions Misspent* (Death Penalty Information Center, Washington, D.C., October 1992), 4. For more on Texas, see D. Grothaus, "Death, Dollars, and Scales of Justice," *The Houston Post,* 7 December 1986.

40. J. Painter, "Death Penalty Seen as Too Costly for Oregon's Pocketbook," *The Oregonian,* 7 July 1987.

41. "Misconceptions. . . ."

42. *Millions Misspent,* 6.

43. Ira Gray and Moira Stanley, *A Punishment in Search of a Crime* (New York: Avon, 1989), 323.

44. *Congressional Digest,* 227.

45. Ibid., 243.

46. Ernest van den Haag, "Bring Back the Death Penalty?" *U.S. News & World Report* (26 April 1976), as reprinted in *The Death Penalty,* Irwin Isenberg, ed. (New York: H. W. Wilson, 1977), 135.

47. Interviewed on C-SPAN, 21 April 1992.

48. Bender and Leone, 34.

49. *1953 Report,* as quoted by Justice Thurgood Marshall, in *Furman.*

50. John Stuart Mill, *Hansard's Parliamentary Debate,* Third Series, 21 April 1868, as reprinted in Bender and Leone, 31.

51. Deeann Glamser, "The Spectacle of Death on the Gallows," *USA Today,* 4 January 1993.

52. "Death Row Interviews," *U.S. News & World Report* (12 July 1976), reprinted in Isenberg, 46.

53. Glamser.

54. Marshall Frady, "Death in Arkansas," *The New Yorker* (22 February 1993): 122.

55. *Furman v. Georgia,* 408 U.S. 238 (1972).

56. *Payne v. Tennessee,* 501 U.S.—, 115 L Ed 2d 720, 111 S Ct. 2597 (1991).

57. Amnesty International, *The United States of America: The Death Penalty and Juvenile Offenders* (New York: Amnesty International, October 1991), 24–25.

58. *Death Penalty Developments,* 30–31.

59. Interviewed on the C-SPAN Television Network, 21 April 1992.

60. Bedau, "The Case Against the Death Penalty," 13.

61. Ibid., 13.

62. *Briefing,* 6.

63. Healey, "Close-up," C-SPAN, 16 November 1993.

64. "Death Row, USA," NAACP Legal Defense Fund information bulletin (24 April 1991): unnumbered.

65. Henry Schwarzchild of the ACLU Capital Punishment Project, appearing on "Crossfire," CNN, 20 April 1992.

66. *Death Penalty Developments,* 5.

67. *McCleskey v. Kemp* (dissent of Justice Brennan).

68. Ibid., (majority opinion).

69. Ibid., (Blackmun dissent).

70. Ibid., (Brennan dissent).

71. Ibid.

72. See "Death Penalty Sentencing: Research Indicates Pattern of Racial Disparities; Report to Senate and House Committee on the Judiciary." 26 February 1990 (Washington, D.C.: Government Accounting Office, 1990).

73. George C. Smith, *Capital Punishment 1986: Last Lines of Defense* (Washington, DC: Washington Legal Foundation, 1986), 14.

74. *Briefing,* 8.

75. Figures on death row populations, as of the end of 1990, are taken from "Capital Punishment 1990"; U.S. population figures are from Bureau of the Census reports, 1990 census.

76. Bedau, "The Case Against the Death Penalty," 13.

77. See Victor L. Streib's *Capital Punishment for Female Offenders,* 5 March 1991, 1–2.

78. *Gregg v. Georgia.*

79. "Capital Punishment 1990," 12.

80. Ibid., 2.

81. Bedau, "The Case Against the Death Penalty," 15.

82. *Close-Up,* C-CPAN Television Network, 16 November 1992.

83. Ibid.

84. *Congressional Digest,* 232.

85. Charles L. Black, *Capital Punishment: The Inevitability of Caprice and Mistake* (1982), quoted by Bedau in "The Case Against the Death Penalty," 15.

86. Mackey, xiii.

87. Appearing on *Nightline,* ABC-Television, 15 April 1992.

88. Horace Greeley, *Hints Toward Reforms in Lectures, Addresses, and Other Writings* (New York: Harper & Brothers, 1850). Reprinted in Bender and Leone, 42.

89. William Styron, "The Death-in-Life of Benjamin Reid," *Esquire* (February 1962). Reprinted in Mackey, 260.

90. James Boswell, *Boswell's London Journal, 1762–1763,* the Yale Editions of the Private Papers of James Boswell (New York: McGraw-Hill, 1950), 253.

91. William Makepiece Thackeray, "Going To See a Man Hanged," *Fraser's Magazine* (August 1840): 156.

92. Simon Schama, *Citizens* (New York: Knopf, 1989), 783.

93. Thackery, 156.

94. Charles Dickens, *Pictures from Italy, 1846,* reprinted in *Eyewitness to History* (New York: Avon, 1987), 315–316.

95. "Capital Report," March/April 1991, #18, National Legal Aid & Defender Association, 2.

96. Quoted by Justice Marshall, *Furman,* concurring opinion.

97. Hugo Adam Bedau and Michael L. Radelet, "Miscarriages of Justice in Potentially Capital Cases," *Stanford Law Review* (November 1987): 21–179.

98. Interviewed on the C-SPAN Television Network, 21 April 1992.

99. James N. Baker and Frank Girney, Jr., "A Movie for the Defense," *Newsweek* (13 March 1989): 27.

100. *Close-Up,* C-CPAN Television Network, 16 November 1992.

101. Gray and Stanley, 188.

102. *McCleskey v. Zant,* 111 S.Ct. 1454 (1991).

103. *Dugger v. Adams;* also *McCleskey v. Zant.*

104. *Murray v. Giarratano,* 492 U.S. 1 (1989).

105. *Coleman v. Thompson.*

106. Dennis Cauchon, "Court: Late Evidence May Not Halt Execution," *USA Today,* 26 January 1993.

107. Diann Rust-Tierney, Director of the ACLU's Capital Punishment Project, C-SPAN, 21 April 1992.

108. *Gregg v. Georgia,* 428 U.S. 153 (1976).

109. Jessamyn West, *The Massacre at Fall Creek* (New York: Harcourt Brace Jovanovich, 1975), 313.

110. Joyce, 162.

111. *Millions Misspent*, 13.

112. *Death Penalty Developments*, 27.

113. *Louisiana ex rel. Francis v. Resweber*, 329 U.S. 459 (1947).

114. *When the State Kills . . .* , 58.

115. Rust-Tierney.

116. Declaration of Richard J. Traystman, Ph.D., "Exhibits in Support of Motion for Temporary Restraining Order in No. 92-70237 (ND Cal.)," quoted by Justice Stevens in his dissent in *Gomez v. District Court For N.D. of California*, 112 S.Ct. 1652 (1992).

117. *When the State Kills . . .* , 59.

118. Ibid., 59.

119. Marshall Frady, "Death in Arkansas," *New Yorker* (22 February 1993): 131.

120. "Pierrepoint."

121. Smith, 30.

122. *Today*, NBC-TV, 5 January 1993.

123. Smith, 31.

124. Maria Goodavage, "Death Penalty Cruelty Debated," *USA Today*, 20 April 1992.

125. Jeremy Bentham, *The Opinions of Different Authors on the Punishment of Death* (1809), quoted in Bender and Leone, 26.

126. *Congressional Digest*, 232.

127. Squitieri.

128. *Millions Misspent*, 9.

129. Ibid., 8–9.

130. Bender and Leone, 26.

131. Joyce, 93.

132. Tom Teepen, "Even Dodd No Case for Executions," *Atlanta Journal/Atlanta Constitution* (10 January 1993).

133. *Ford v. Wainwright*, 477 U.S. 339 (1986).

134. *When the State Kills . . .* , 299.

135. *Briefing*, 11–12.

136. *When the State Kills . . .* , 38.

137. *Juvenile Offenders*, 1.

138. Ibid., 74.

139. *Eddings v. Oklahoma*, 455 U.S. 104 (1982).

140. *Thompson v. Oklahoma,* 487 U.S. 815 (1988).

141. *Juvenile Offenders,* 77.

142. Healey.

143. Frady, 105.

144. Editorial, *Atlanta Constitution* (1 July 1986).

145. Bedau, *The Death Penalty in America,* 5.

146. Genesis 9:6.

147. *Congressional Digest,* 228 (citing Matthew, 38−39).

148. John 8:7.

149. Ernest van den Haag, "Bring Back the Death Penalty?" *U.S. News & World Report* (26 April 1976), reprinted in *The Death Penalty,* Irwin Isenberg, ed. (New York: H. W. Wilson, 1977), 135.

150. *Briefing,* 19.

151. Israel J. Kazis, "Judaism and the Death Penalty," a pamphlet reprinted in Bedau, *The Death Penalty in America,* 171–175.

152. *When the State Kills . . . ,* 230.

153. Gray and Stanley, 93.

154. Charles S. Milligan, "A Protestant's View of the Death Penalty," reprinted from *Social Action* (April 1961) with additions and revisions in Bedau, *The Death Penalty in America,* 175.

155. *Briefing,* 19.

156. "Capital Punishment 1990," 8.

157. *Congressional Digest,* 227.

158. Ernest van Haag and John P. Conrad, *The Death Penalty: A Debate* (New York: Plenum, 1983), 261.

159. Ibid.

160. *Millions Misspent,* 8−9.

161. Ibid., 6.

3

Chronology

18th century B.C.	The Code of King Hammurabi of Babylon prescribes the death penalty for 25 different crimes. Interestingly, murder is not among them.
16th century B.C.	The Assyrian Laws of this period contain references to death as a punishment.
	The first death sentence of which a record survives is handed down in Egypt. There have almost certainly been many others before this, not only in Egypt but elsewhere, but no record of them exists. The wrongdoer in this case is obliged to kill himself, a common requirement in many societies when the condemned is a member of the nobility. Members of the lower classes, on the other hand, are dispatched by government officials or mercenaries.
14th century B.C.	The Hittite Code contains references to the death penalty.
7th century B.C.	The legal code designed by Dracon of Athens (known as the Draconian Code) makes death the punishment for every crime.
5th century B.C.	The Roman Law of the Twelve Tablets calls for the death penalty for several crimes. Like many criminal codes elsewhere in the world, it makes several distinctions by social station: prescribing death for certain offenses only when

5th century B.C. *(cont.)*   they are committed against freemen, for instance, or only when they are committed by slaves.

In Britain, executions are being carried out for a variety of offenses.

c. 399 B.C.   The Greek philosopher Socrates is required to drink poison for the offenses of heresy and corruption of the young.

c. A.D. 29   In the most infamous execution in history, Jesus Christ, the founder of Christianity who is revered by his followers as the son of God, is crucified on a hill outside Jerusalem.

c. 315   The Emperor Constantine abolishes crucifixion in the Roman Empire.

438   The Code of Theodosius makes more than 80 crimes punishable by death.

1500   Only eight crimes are officially punishable by death in England. They are murder, treason (treachery against the state), petty treason (murder of a husband by his wife), larceny, robbery, burglary, rape, and arson.

1509–1547   Despite the relatively small number of crimes punishable by death, the reign of Henry VIII may be the bloodiest in English history. Estimates of the number of Englishmen and women executed by the oft-married monarch range as high as 72,000.

1608   In the first known execution in British America, George Kendall, an ex-councillor of the colony of Virginia, is executed for supposedly plotting to betray the British colony to the Spanish.

1612   Under its governor, Sir Thomas Dale, Virginia institutes the most unrelenting criminal code in any of the American colonies. Known as the Divine, Moral, and Martial Laws, it prescribes death even for such relatively minor offenses as trading with the Indians, killing chickens, and stealing grapes.

1619   The so-called Divine Laws are softened because it has become clear to Virginia officials that fear of the executioner is making potential colonists reluctant to settle in Virginia.

1636   The Capitall Lawes of New-England go into effect in the Massachussetts Bay Colony. Among the crimes made punishable by death are murder, witchcraft, sodomy, adultery, blasphemy, idolatry, assault in sudden anger, rape, statutory rape, manstealing, perjury (in a capital trial), and rebellion.

1665   New York colony institutes the so-called Duke's Laws, which make death the penalty for a wide variety of crimes, including sodomy and denial of the true God.

1682   William Penn's Great Act makes only two crimes—treason and murder—punishable by death in Pennsylvania. West Jersey soon passes a similar law. These two colonies, both settled by Quakers, are the most lenient of England's American colonies. Most of the others prescribe death for at least 11 or 12 separate crimes.

1689   The English Parliament adopts a Bill of Rights, which among other provisions forbids cruel and unusual punishments.

1747   9 April. Simon, the Lord of Lovat, is the last person executed by decapitation in England.

1754   Russia abandons death as a penalty for ordinary criminal offenses, including murder. It retains capital punishment for use against political criminals, however.

1756   Pennsylvania, once the most lenient of the American colonies, now mandates the death penalty for 14 different crimes.

1764   Cesare Beccaria's *Essay on Crimes and Punishments* is published in Italy. It calls for an end to capital punishment.

1767   Beccaria's *Essay on Crimes and Punishments,* which is already having a great impact in intellectual circles in Europe, is translated into English and begins to influence American abolitionists.[1]

1776   At the outbreak of the American Revolution, every colony except Rhode Island makes at least ten crimes punishable by death.

1777   A group of reformers led by Thomas Jefferson proposes abolishing capital punishment in Virginia, except for treason and murder. The exception for treason is somewhat ironic, considering that the reformers are engaged in what England regards as treason against the mother country.

1785   A bill to abolish capital punishment is defeated by a single vote in the Virginia legislature.

1787   9 March. Speaking in the home of Benjamin Franklin, Dr. Benjamin Rush delivers an address in which he opposes capital punishment. It is the first time a prominent American has publicly called for total abolition of the death penalty.

1789   Dr. Joseph-Ignace Guillotin proposes using a beheading machine (later called a "guillotine") for all executions in France. The idea of executing nobles and peasants by the same method is a truly radical notion. It is the democratic ideal of the French Revolution taken to the extreme and applied to the death penalty itself. Even the revolutionary National Assembly is reluctant to go this far.

1790   The first Congress to meet after adoption of the U.S. Constitution passes laws prescribing death by hanging as the punishment for the crimes of rape and first degree murder.

1791   The first nine amendments to the Constitution of the United States, known collectively as the American Bill of Rights, come into effect. Although none of them is primarily concerned with the death penalty, the Eighth prohibits cruel and unusual punishments and the Fifth forbids the government to deprive anyone of life without due process of law.

1792   25 April. A highwayman named Nicolas Pelletier becomes the first victim of the new French guillotine.

             21 August. Louis Collot d'Angremont, the secretary of the administration of the National Guard of France, becomes the first political victim of the guillotine. D'Angremont is

executed for his supposed involvement in a royalist plot. Although first proposed to the National Assembly by two prominent doctors, Joseph-Ignace Guillotin and Antoine Louis, as a more humane method of execution, it is fast becoming the most feared symbol of the revolutionary Terror that is sweeping France.

1793 "An Enquiry into How Far the Punishment of Death Is Necessary in Pennsylvania," by Pennsylvania Attorney General William Bradford, finds no strong evidence to support the need for a death penalty. Bradford, who will later become attorney general of the United States, recommends abandoning capital punishment for all crimes except murder and treason, at least until the question can be studied further.

1794 27 April. Pennsylvania becomes the first American state to abandon the death penalty for all crimes except murder in the "first degree." This is the first time that murder has been defined in terms of different degrees, subject to different punishments.

1812 Sixteen slaves who had participated in a slave rebellion are beheaded in New Orleans.

1820 At this time, roughly 200 crimes are punishable by death in England. They include stealing fish and cutting down a growing tree.

1824 Three white men are hanged for the murder of nine Native Americans at Fall Creek, Indiana. Three of the victims were women, two were children. So far as is known, this is the first time in American history that a white person is executed for the murder of an Indian.

Two other white men are involved in the incident, known as the Massacre at Fall Creek. One has already fled to escape prosecution. The other, who is hardly more than a boy, is also sentenced to die, but he is saved from death when James Brown Ray, the governor of Indiana, arrives at the execution site on horseback and pardons him.

1830 One thousand English bankers present a petition to the British Parliament requesting it to remove death as the punishment for forgery. The bankers argue that the death penalty is actually encouraging counterfeiting by making

1830
(cont.)

jurors reluctant to convict forgers. Jurors don't want to be a party to executing a man for such a relatively minor and nonviolent crime.

1833

Edward Livingston's "Introductory Report to the System of Penal Law Prepared for the State of Louisiana" calls for an end to capital punishment in that state.[2] Livingston is a native of New York State who has become a well-respected lawyer in New Orleans. The Louisiana legislature had commissioned him to suggest penal reforms for Louisiana, and Livingston made the abolition of the death penalty the heart of his proposal. Although the legislature rejects his recommendation to do away with capital punishment, Livingston's ideas are widely discussed, not only in the United States but in Europe as well.

1834

Pennsylvania becomes the first of the United States to ban public executions. Some other states, including New York, have already stopped conducting executions in public, although it remains legal to do so there. In most states, however, executions are still watched by large and often rowdy crowds.

1835

Over 10,000 people flood the streets of the state capital of Maine, jockeying for position to witness what is only the second execution in state history. Fights break out, and the police have to step in to prevent what threatens to become a riot.

1837

Tennessee gives juries the option of imposing lesser sentences than death for capital crimes. Until now, death has been mandatory (required) in all states for anyone convicted of any crime that carries the death penalty.

Still shocked by the near riot that took place at an execution two years before, the Maine legislature passes what comes to be known as the Maine Law. The measure requires the governor to wait for one full year after a person is convicted of a capital crime before signing the death warrant. It is intended to make governors think twice before ordering executions.

1844

By almost two to one, New Hampshire's voters turn down a referendum calling for an end to the death penalty.

1845 Reformers from several states meet in Philadelphia to establish a national organization to fight the death penalty. The new body is to be known as the American Society for the Abolition of Capital Punishment. Its first president is the Vice President of the United States, George Mifflin Dallas.

1846 Michigan becomes the first state to formally abolish capital punishment, except for the crime of treason against the state.

1848 November. In France, the constitution of the newly established Second Republic outlaws the death penalty for political crimes.

1852 Rhode Island abolishes the death penalty.

1853 Wisconsin abolishes the death penalty.

1862 The U.S. Congress provides an optional punishment for treason. Previously death has been the only punishment for this crime. From now on, however, treason will be punishable either by death or by a term in prison of at least five years, plus a fine of at least $10,000.

The nation of Greece abolishes the death penalty for criminal offenses.

26 December. Thirty-eight Native Americans are hanged at one time in what may be the largest mass execution in U.S. history.

1863 Colombia becomes the first nation in the Western Hemisphere to abolish the death penalty for criminal offenses.

1868 The Fourteenth Amendment to the Constitution of the United States extends the Fifth Amendment's protections to cover the states, forbidding them to "deprive any person of life, liberty, or property, without due process of law; nor to deny to any person within its jurisdiction the equal protection of the laws."

1870 The Netherlands abolishes the death penalty.

1872 Iowa abolishes the death penalty.

1874   Executioner William Marwood introduces the "long drop" to England. When done right, this method of hanging, in which the victim is dropped at the end of a long rope, kills instantaneously of a broken neck. Before this, most hanging victims had been left to choke to death slowly, dangling at the end of short ropes.

1875   The U.S. Congress amends the federal capital punishment laws of 1790 to give federal juries the option of convicting criminals of rape or first degree murder "without capital punishment." These new crime categories are subject to a penalty of either death or life imprisonment as the juries wish.

1876   The state of Maine abolishes the death penalty.

In Europe, Portugal abolishes the death penalty for ordinary crimes.

1878   Iowa becomes the first state to reinstitute the death penalty after once abandoning it.

1879   The U.S. Supreme Court decides *(Wilkerson v. Utah)* that a sentence of public execution against a murderer named Wilkerson does not violate the Eighth Amendment rule against cruel and unusual punishment. It is the first time the Court has ruled on the question of how the Eighth Amendment applies to a capital case. For the next century and more, the legal debate over the death penalty will center on this amendment.

1883   Maine reinstates the death penalty, which it had abolished only seven years before.

1887   Changing its mind once again, Maine abolishes the death penalty for the second time in 11 years.

11 November. Four men convicted of taking part in a bombing that killed seven Chicago policemen and wounded over 60 more during a labor rally in Haymarket Square the year before are hung in Illinois. A fifth man, who had also been sentenced to die, blew himself up in prison. Many if not most observers were convinced that the men, who were known as the Haymarket anarchists, had been railroaded.

1889	1 January. New York becomes the first state to adopt the electric chair as its method of execution.
1890	The U.S. Supreme Court rules *(In re Kemmler)* that "the punishment of death is not cruel within the meaning of that word as used in the Constitution." As used in the Eighth Amendment, says the Court, the term "implies . . . something inhuman and barbarous, something more than the mere extinguishment of life." The case involves the first use of electrocution as a method of execution.
	6 August. William Kemmler, whose case prompted an important U.S. Supreme Court decision on the meaning of "cruel and unusual punishment" becomes the first criminal to die in an electric chair. The event takes place in Auburn Prison at Auburn, New York.
1895	The American Federation of Labor adopts a resolution calling for the abolition of capital punishment, which it terms "a revolting practice."[3]
1897	The number of federal crimes punishable by death is dropped from 60 to only three: treason, murder, and rape. Of these, only treason carries a mandatory (required) death sentence. In effect, this brings the federal laws more in line with the laws of most states.
	Colorado abolishes the death penalty.
	Ecuador abolishes the death penalty. It had already abandoned capital punishment for political crimes in 1852.
1901	Alarmed by a rash of lynchings in the wake of the state's abolition of the death penalty in 1897, Colorado reinstitutes the death penalty.
1903	Panama abolishes the death penalty.
1905	Norway becomes the first European nation in the twentieth century to abolish capital punishment for ordinary crimes.
1907	Kansas, which has not actually carried out an execution for 35 years, formally abolishes capital punishment.

1910   The Supreme Court holds *(Weems v. United States)* that the meaning of "cruel and unusual punishment" may change over the years, due to an "enlightened" public opinion.

The criminal laws of the federal government are revised and reassembled under the title of the United States Criminal Code. Among other provisions, the code defines murder, as well as the distinction between murder in the first and second degrees.

Section 275 provides that "[e]very person guilty of murder in the first degree shall suffer death." Section 278 similarly provides that "[w]hosoever shall commit the crime of rape shall suffer death." Once again, however, juries are given the option of qualifying their verdict with the words "without capital punishment," thereby prescribing a penalty of life imprisonment instead of death.

Section 323 provides that "[t]he manner of inflicting punishment of death shall be by hanging."

1911   Minnesota abolishes the death penalty.

1913   The state of Washington abolishes the death penalty.

1914   Oregon abolishes the death penalty.

1915   North Dakota and South Dakota abolish the death penalty. Tennessee also abandons it, except for the crime of rape.

19 November. Joe Hill, a Swedish immigrant and labor organizer for the I.W.W. (Industrial Workers of the World), is executed by a Utah firing squad. Hill was convicted of armed robbery in a trial that many observers believed to be tainted by antilabor prejudice. As he goes to his death, Hill is regarded as a dangerous radical by the state of Utah, but as a martyred hero by the American labor movement.

1916   By a margin of only 252 in a statewide referendum, Arizona votes to abolish the death penalty.

1917   The first of the Mexican states abolishes the death penalty for ordinary criminal offenses.

The wave of abolition in the United States, which has seen six states abolish or seriously restrict the use of the death penalty in the previous ten years, may be reaching its limit. Both Missouri and Puerto Rico abandon capital punishment in this year, but South Dakota reintroduces it, and Tennessee, which had abolished it (except for rape) the year before, begins imposing it for other crimes once again.

1918   After only two years of abolition, Arizona reinstates the death penalty.

1919   Puerto Rico, Washington, and Missouri all reintroduce the death penalty. The wave of abolition is definitely rolling back.

1920   Following the lead of the neighboring state of Washington the year before, Oregon reinstates the death penalty.

1921   Nevada becomes the first state to adopt gas as a means of execution. Officials believe that gas poisoning will be more certain than the traditional methods of execution, with less chance that something will go wrong or the victim will suffer unnecessary pain.

Sweden abolishes the death penalty for ordinary crimes, retaining it only for certain offenses during wartime.

1924   8 February. In Nevada, a gang murderer named Gee Jon becomes the first person executed by cyanide gas. Gas was introduced as a humanitarian measure that would hopefully spare the victim not only the pain inflicted by previous methods, but the agony of the long countdown to the moment of execution as well. The state did not intend to let the condemned person know when he was actually scheduled to die, but simply to pump cyanide fumes into the cell while the prisoner was asleep. It turned out, however, that technical problems made this impossible, and so a special chamber was built, in which Jon's execution is carried out.

10 September. Judge John R. Caverly, Chief Justice of the Criminal Court of Cook County, sentences Nathan Leopold, Jr., and Richard Loeb to life plus 99 years in prison. Both defendants had pleaded guilty to the kidnapping and murder of a fourteen-year-old boy named Bobby Franks.

1924
(*cont.*)

The case has aroused an enormous amount of hostility against the young defendants. Not only are they wealthy and Jewish in a working class city with a large anti-Semitic population, they are rumored to be homosexual. Their defense attorney, Clarence Darrow, has placed their fate solely in the hands of Judge Caverly, making an impassioned plea that amounts to an attack on the death penalty itself.

The judge's decision not to condemn the young killers to death is considered a victory by opponents of the death penalty, but it outrages millions of other Americans who believe the boys got off because of their families' wealth.

23 September. In the wake of the controversial Leopold and Loeb verdict, the New York League for Public Discussion sponsors a debate, "Is Capital Punishment a Wise Policy?," at New York's Metropolitan Opera House. Speaking in favor of the death penalty is a prominent New York judge, Alfred J. Talley, who has publicly attacked the verdict. Opposed is Clarence Darrow himself.

1925

Lewis E. Lawes, Clarence Darrow, and others found the American League to Abolish Capital Punishment. The League, which for several decades is the most influential anti-death-penalty organization in the United States, attracts the support of such notable abolitionists as Kathleen Norris and Hugo Adam Bedau.

1927

22 August. Despite worldwide protests, two Italian immigrants to the United States, Nicola Sacco and Bartolomeo Vanzetti, are executed in the electric chair at the prison in Charleston, Massachussetts. They have been condemned for the killing of a guard and a paymaster during a robbery in Braintree, Massachussetts, seven years before. To the last, the men claim to be innocent of the crime, and thousands—if not millions—of people around the world believe them. (Doubts about the case still remain in the 1990s.)

1928

Iceland abandons the death penalty.

1929

Puerto Rico abolishes the death penalty for the second time.

1930

21 February. Mrs. Eva Dugan becomes the first woman ever executed by the state of Arizona. The execution does

not go well. The hangman misjudges the drop, and Mrs. Dugan's head is ripped from her body.

1935   Kansas reinstates the death penalty.

1936   August. An estimated 20,000 Kentuckians gather to watch a hanging at Owensboro, Kentucky.

1938   13 June. A rapist named Harold B. Van Venison is hanged in a Kentucky county jail yard. It is the last public hanging to take place in the United States.

1942   With World War II raging all around, the neutral nation of Switzerland abolishes the death penalty for ordinary crimes.

1944   Italy abolishes the death penalty for all crimes except military offenses during wartime.

1945   The death penalty is suspended in England and the rest of the United Kingdom.

1946   The Brazilian constitution bans the death penalty, except for military crimes in wartime.

1947   The appeal of a young black murderer named Willie Francis *(State ex rel. Francis v. Resweber)* is turned down by the U.S. Supreme Court, and Francis is executed by the state of Louisiana. The appeal had been made on the ground that Louisiana had already tried to electrocute him once before, and failed, causing him unacceptable pain and suffering in the process. The portable electrocution equipment used in the state's first attempt the year before had failed. Francis, who was then only 17, had described his first experience with the chair as "plumb miserable. I felt a burning in my head and my left leg, and I jumped against the straps."[4] To put him through such a horrible experience again, Francis argued, would surely be cruel and unusual punishment.

Although the Court agrees that there should be no "unnecessary pain" involved in an execution, the Court turns down the appeal. The majority of the justices hold that Louisiana acted in good faith in the first execution attempt, and therefore should be allowed to go ahead with the second. "The cruelty against which the Constitution

1947
(cont.)

protects a convicted man is cruelty inherent in the method of punishment," explains the Court, "not the necessary suffering involved in any method employed to extinguish life humanely."

1949

West Germany abolishes the death penalty for all crimes.

1953

19 June. In one of the most controversial executions in U.S. history, Ethel and Julius Rosenberg are electrocuted for turning over information on atomic weapons to the Soviet Union. It is the first time any American civilian is executed for espionage, as well as the first time a married couple has been executed together.

The press and the government blame the Rosenbergs for enabling America's cold war enemy, the Soviet Union, to build atomic weapons. In sentencing the Rosenbergs to death, the trial judge even blamed them for the "communist aggression in Korea, with the resultant casualties exceeding 50,000." What's more, he suggested, "millions more of innocent people may pay the price of your treason."[5]

Millions of terrified Americans welcome the verdict. Many others, however, feel the Rosenbergs are the victims of an irrational anticommunist hysteria. Even as the switch is thrown, some 2,000 sympathizers gather in New York's Union Square to protest their deaths.

1954

The still young nation of Israel abolishes the death penalty for ordinary crimes. It is retained for treason, as well as for crimes against the Jewish people, crimes against humanity, war crimes, and genocide.

1957

Alaska, Hawaii, and the Virgin Islands all abolish capital punishment. It is the first time in 40 years that any American jurisdiction has abandoned the death penalty.

15 March. Burton Abbott, who has been sentenced to die for the kidnap and murder of a 14-year-old girl, is brought to the gas chamber in California's San Quentin prison. It is shortly after 11 o'clock in the morning as Abbott is strapped into one of the two chairs in the small green chamber.

Abbott has steadfastly protested his innocence, but, so far, all his appeals for a new trial have been denied. His last hope is to receive a stay of execution from California's governor, Goodwin J. Knight. Knight has, in fact, decided to grant him that stay, but word has not yet reached the prison.

At 11:18, cyanide pellets are dropped into the acid bath that will release the deadly gas into the chamber. At 11:20, the phone call arrives from the governor. Abbott may well still be alive, although probably already gravely injured from the fumes. Even so, the warden decides it would be too dangerous for anyone to enter the room to rescue him. The execution continues.[6]

News of the botched reprieve helps reignite opposition to the death penalty.

1958 The United States Supreme Court rules (*Trop v. Dulles*) that the death penalty remains constitutional. In doing so, however, it declares that the standard for what is and what is not cruel and unusual punishment is subject to change, since the Eighth Amendment "must draw its meaning from the evolving standards of decency that mark the progress of a maturing society."

Delaware abolishes the death penalty.

20 February. Nathan Leopold, sentenced to life plus 99 years in prison for his part in the 1924 murder of Bobby Franks, receives parole.

1959 At the 1959 Academy Awards ceremony in Hollywood, Susan Hayward receives the Best Actress Award for her portrayal of condemned murderess Barbara Graham in *I Want To Live!* The movie, which came out the year before, shocks audiences with its graphic depiction of the procedures leading up to the doomed woman's execution in the San Quentin gas chamber. It also raises questions in many people's minds about the justice of Graham's death sentence.

1960 2 May. Convicted kidnapper Caryl Chessman is put to death in the gas chamber at San Quentin prison in California. Chessman has fought to evade this moment since his death sentence was first imposed on 25 June 1948. In the 12 long years he has spent on San Quentin's death row, he has written several books that have won support for his cause from around the world. Eight previous dates have been set for his execution, but each time he has won a stay from the courts. A ninth stay has actually been granted, but the call ordering the warden to halt the execution arrives some 15 seconds too late.

1961   December. Alarmed by a brutal murder in the state, the Delaware legislature reinstitutes the death penalty less than three years after abolishing it.

1962   After studying the available evidence, the United Nations issues its first report on the deterrent value of the death penalty. Entitled *Capital Punishment,* it concludes that removal of the death penalty from a particular crime "has never been followed by a notable rise" in the number of such crimes.[7]

1963   The U.S. Supreme Court decides not to consider the case of a man condemned to death for rape in Alabama *(Rudolph v. Alabama).* Justice Arthur Goldberg, however, urges the Court to take the case in order to examine whether the death penalty is still constitutional for crimes that do not take or endanger anyone's life. Goldberg's argument is credited with beginning a process that will result in the overturning of all the existing death penalty laws a decade later.[8]

The state of Michigan abandons the death penalty for treason.

1964   Oregon abolishes the death penalty again. This is the second time it has abandoned it, having done so in 1914, only to reintroduce it in 1920.

1965   West Virginia abolishes capital punishment, as does Iowa, which had previously abolished it for six years beginning in 1872.

Vermont and New York abandon the death penalty for most crimes.

The British House of Commons launches a five-year experiment, during which capital punishment will be suspended in the United Kingdom.

1967   Class action suits brought by the National Association for the Advancement of Colored People's Legal Defense Fund help persuade many states to call off proposed executions until certain legal issues surrounding the death penalty are resolved.

1968 This marks the first year in U.S. history in which no one is executed.

The United States Supreme Court rules against using the death penalty as a club to force defendants to plead guilty, overturning a law that provides a maximum penalty of death for a defendant who pleads innocent to a capital crime and is convicted, but only a maximum of life imprisonment for one who pleads guilty *(United States v. Jackson)*. The law is designed to encourage guilty people to admit their guilt and avoid long and costly trials, but its effect, the Court declares, is to "discourage the Fifth Amendment right not to plead guilty, and to deter exercise of the Sixth Amendment right to demand a jury trial." The Court rules that laws designed to "chill the assertion of constitutional right by penalizing those who choose to exercise them" are unconstitutional.

By an overwhelming 1,159,348 to 730,649, Massachussetts voters pass a referendum to retain the death penalty.

1969 The Abolition of the Death Penalty Act passes the British Parliament. It renews the general abolition of the death penalty established on an experimental basis in 1965, and makes it permanent. Death is retained as a possible punishment for treason, piracy, and certain military crimes, however.

1970 Illinois voters turn down a proposal to abolish the death penalty by a vote of almost two to one: 1,218,791 to 676,302.

The U.S. Supreme Court refuses to consider the claim of an Arkansas rapist that his death sentence was unduly influenced by the fact that he is black *(Maxwell v. Bishop)*. The condemned prisoner presented a study showing that a black man convicted of raping a white woman in Arkansas is more than three and a half times as likely to receive a death sentence as someone convicted of raping a member of their own race. The Court is unwilling to examine what seems to be a purely statistical claim of racial discrimination in death sentencing. It does, however, vacate the sentence on other grounds.

December. A United States Court of Appeals rules that a law calling for the death penalty in cases of rape in which

1970
(cont.)

there has been no threat to the life of the victim is cruel and unusual punishment. This is the first time an appeals court has ever ruled a death penalty unconstitutional under the Eighth Amendment.

1971

The U.S. Supreme Court rules *(McGautha v. California)* that a jury is free to sentence a defendant to death even when the judge fails to present legal guidelines for imposing the death penalty. Lawyers for a man condemned by a jury that had received no guidance from the trial judge argue that it is unconstitutional to allow juries to set their own conditions for who would live and who would die. The Court, however, disagrees, ruling that there is no need for trial judges to spell out any standards for juries to use in making their decision. Justice Harlan even goes so far as to suggest that it may be "beyond present human ability" to design such guidelines.

January. The National Commission on the Reform of Federal Criminal Laws recommends that the federal government remove the death penalty from all federal statutes.

1972

29 June. In by far its most important death penalty ruling to date *(Furman v. Georgia)*, the U.S. Supreme Court declares that the death penalty—as currently administered in the United States—is cruel and unusual punishment under the Eighth Amendment. In doing so, it overturns all the death sentences in effect in the United States, and throws out all current state and federal laws prescribing the death penalty.

The ruling actually involves three different cases, and three different condemned prisoners, all of whom are African American. One, William Furman, had been convicted of murder, the others of rape.

The vote of the justices is 5 to 4, but each of the five who make up the majority give somewhat different reasons for their decision. All agree, however, that the death penalty has been unfairly and arbitrarily applied.

Although hundreds of death sentences have been passed, there has not been an actual execution in the United States since 1967.

**1972–
1976**

State legislatures around the country work to frame new capital punishment statutes they hope will meet the objections the Supreme Court raised in *Furman* to the old laws.

1973

The death penalty is abolished for ordinary crimes in most of Australia. It is retained, however, in the state of New South Wales and elsewhere for the crimes of treason and piracy.

Kansas and the District of Columbia abolish the death penalty.

1976

Portugal totally abolishes capital punishment, while Canada ends the practice except for certain military offenses in wartime.

2 July. On the most significant day in the legal history of capital punishment since 19 June 1972, the U.S. Supreme Court hands down several death penalty decisions. The most important, *Gregg v. Georgia,* declares that death is not necessarily a cruel and unusual punishment under the Eighth Amendment after all.

Troy Gregg was convicted of armed robbery and murder under a Georgia capital punishment law that had been written after the Supreme Court's 1972 *Furman* decision. After examining the procedures set by that law to determine when a murderer should be sentenced to death in Georgia, the Court determines that the new law does not violate the Eighth Amendment. Georgia may proceed to execute Troy Gregg.

This is the first time that the Supreme Court has approved a death penalty since the *Furman* decision struck down all the capital punishment laws that then existed in 1972.

2 July. Several other important capital punishment cases are handed down on the same day as the *Gregg* decision. Together, they are the Court's effort to clarify what amounts to a new constitutional standard in applying the death penalty.

In *Jurek v. Texas,* the Court affirms the death sentence of Jerry Lane Jurek, who was convicted of strangling a ten-year-old girl after trying to rape her. The Texas statute under which Jurek is sentenced to die requires the jury to answer yes to at least two of a list of specific questions establishing aggravating circumstances. This the jury

1976
(cont.)

has done. The Court rules that this law, like the Georgia law, meets the new constitutional standard.

In *Proffitt v. Florida,* the Court affirms a Florida death sentence imposed after a judge found four aggravating circumstances.

Along with the *Gregg* decision, these cases mean that executions, which had been halted in the United States since 1967, can now begin again.

13 December. The United States Supreme Court agrees that a condemned prisoner in Utah, Gary Gilmore, is competent to decide not to appeal his death sentence. Gilmore's mother, Bessie, has appealed to have the sentence vacated on her son's behalf, but Gilmore himself has insisted that he wants to have it carried out. Three justices dissent from the Court's ruling, arguing that the Court should first decide whether Utah's new death penalty law is constitutional.

1977

Oklahoma becomes the first state to adopt lethal injection as a means of execution.

The U.S. Supreme Court forbids the imposition of the death penalty for the crime of rape. The case *(Coker v. Georgia)* involves a convicted rapist, murderer, and kidnapper who committed another rape while an escapee from a Georgia prison. Before overturning Coker's death sentence, the Court examines the usual practice of courts and juries in rape cases and finds that death is rarely prescribed for this crime. Partly as a result of this finding, the Court declares: "We have concluded that a sentence of death is grossly disproportionate for the crime of rape and is therefore forbidden by the Eighth Amendment as cruel and unusual punishment."

The Court also rules *(Dobbert v. Florida)* that Florida may execute John Dobbert, Jr., for the torture murders of two of his own children, even though the capital punishment law in effect in Florida at the time of the killings was unconstitutional. By the time Dobbert actually came to trial, a new and constitutional death penalty law was in effect. Ordinarily, people cannot be tried and punished under laws passed after the crime of which they are accused. In this case, however, the Court rules that Dobbert has no valid complaint. Both the old, unconstitutional law and the new law under which he was tried provided for capital punishment. Therefore, Dobbert had "fair warning" that he would be liable to the death penalty if he committed such a crime. What's more, the law in effect at the time of his trial actually gave him more safeguards than he would have had under the old law, not less.

17 January. Gary Mark Gilmore is executed by firing squad in Utah. It is the first execution permitted by the Supreme Court since the *Furman* decision in 1972, and the first actually carried out anywhere in the United States since 1967.

Gilmore's execution is unusual in other ways as well. For one thing, it is remarkably quick by modern standards, coming less than four months after Gilmore's murder conviction on 7 October 1976. Also, unlike most condemned criminals, Gilmore has not only refused to appeal his death sentence in the federal courts, but has pleaded for the death sentence to be carried out.

There have been no executions in Utah for so long that there is no place set aside for them. Gilmore is taken to a prison warehouse where a makeshift execution chamber was set up. "Let's do it," he says before being shot to death by a four-man firing squad.[9]

1978 The U.S. Supreme Court (*Lockett v. Ohio*) strikes down Ohio's capital punishment statute because it does not permit juries to consider the defendant's character, record, or even the circumstances of the case as mitigating factors in the sentencing phase of the trial. In essence, the Court rules that lawyers for the defendant must be allowed to present virtually *any* mitigating factors they wish during the sentencing phase of a capital trial.

Denmark abolishes capital punishment for all offenses. Spain abolishes it as well, except for military crimes in time of war.

1979 Brazil, Fiji, and Peru abolish the death penalty for ordinary crimes, while Norway, Nicaragua, and Luxembourg abolish it altogether.

25 May. John A. Spenkelink is executed in the electric chair at the Florida State Prison at Starke. It is the first time since 1972 that a death sentence has been enforced in

1979
(*cont.*)

the United States over the legal appeals of the condemned criminal.

1980

The U.S. Supreme Court (*Beck v. Alabama*) rules that juries inclined to convict in a capital case must be allowed to consider the alternative of convicting on any lesser included offense that is not subject to the death penalty.

1981

September. Ninety-nine years after the execution of Nicolas Pelletier, France retires the guillotine and abolishes the death penalty.

The U.S. Supreme Court (*Bullington v. Missouri*) rules that the prosecution cannot ask for a second death sentence in the case of a defendant who has won a new trial after already being convicted and sentenced to death for the same crime.

1982

The last Mexican state abolishes the death penalty for ordinary crimes. It has now been abandoned throughout Mexico, except for military crimes and treason.

The Netherlands, which had abolished the death penalty in 1870 but reinstituted it in the wake of World War II, abolishes it again.

July. The Supreme Court approves streamlined procedures for federal appeals courts to use in handling habeas corpus proceedings in capital cases. Under the new guidelines, processes that used to take weeks or even months can now be rushed through in days or hours. Defense attorneys protest that the new procedures drastically reduce the amount of time and consideration such appeals will receive.[10]

2 July. The United States Supreme Court (*Endmund v. Florida*) overturns the death sentence of a man who was convicted of the robbery and murder of an elderly couple in Florida. Endmund had not directly participated in the murders himself, but had only driven the getaway car. This was enough, under Florida law, to make him a "constructive aider and abettor" in the killings, and so liable to the death penalty. However, a majority of five of the Supreme Court justices rule that this is not enough to subject him to the death penalty, since they find Endmund had no intent to kill.

27 July. The Human Rights Committee of the United Nations issues a commentary on the International Covenant on Civil and Political Rights, declaring that, while "parties [to the Covenant] are not obliged to abolish the death penalty totally, they are obliged to limit its use, and, in particular, to abolish it for other than the 'most serious crimes.' "[11]

7 December. Charlie Brooks, Jr., becomes the first person executed by lethal injection. The execution takes place in the Texas Penitentiary at Huntsville, with both pro- and anti-capital-punishment demonstrators gathered outside.

The deadly solution is a mixture of sodium thiopental, pavulon, and potassium chloride. Although a doctor who works for the Texas prison system is present, both the mixing of the drugs and the injection itself are done by nonphysicians. Even so, the use of a traditionally medical procedure to kill raises concerns about medical ethics.

1984

Velma Barfield is executed by the state of North Carolina. She is the only woman executed in the United States since executions were resumed in 1977.

The nation of Argentina, the Australian state of Western Australia, and the American state of Massachussetts all abolish the death penalty.

1985

The Australian state of New South Wales abolishes the death penalty for piracy, treason, and arson at military and naval establishments—the last offense still punishable by death there. New South Wales had been the only Australian jurisdiction that still had the death penalty for any crime.

February. The U.S. Supreme Court rules that states must provide financial assistance to pay for psychiatric help in preparing the defense of indigent defendants who wish to plead insanity as a defense. Prior to this ruling, defendants who couldn't pay for psychiatrists to examine them and testify on their behalf had little or no chance to convince a judge or jury that they were legally insane. The ruling, however, will not be retroactive, even in capital cases. That is, the executions of indigent defendants who have already been convicted and sentenced to death without the benefit of psychiatric help in preparing their defense can go ahead.

1985
(cont.)

September. Charles Rumbaugh is executed in Texas, becoming the first person in more than 20 years to be executed in the United States for a crime committed when he was under 18. Rumbaugh had killed a man during a robbery more than ten years before, when he was 17.

November. President Ronald Reagan signs the Department of Defense Authorization Act of 1986. Among its provisions is an amendment to the U.S. Code of Military Justice that permits the death penalty for members of the U.S. military who commit espionage in peacetime. Until now, the code had only prescribed the death penalty for murder and for military crimes committed while the country was at war.

1986

April. The United States Supreme Court establishes new standards granting defendants a better opportunity to challenge the exclusion of people of their own race from juries *(Batson v. Kentucky)*.

May. By a vote of 6 to 3, the U.S. Supreme Court upholds the practice of "death-qualifying" juries *(Lockhart v. McCree)*. Ardia McCree had appealed his Arkansas murder conviction on the grounds that the prosecutors had excluded potential jurors who had admitted that they were opposed to the death penalty. McCree's lawyers presented several studies they claimed showed that death qualified juries, like McCree's, are more likely to convict, and so argued that McCree had not received a fair trial. The Arkansas Court of Appeals agreed, and voted to overturn McCree's conviction. Writing for the Supreme Court majority, Justice William Rehnquist admits that death qualified juries are "somewhat more conviction-prone," but insists that there is no constitutional requirement that a jury have a mix of opinions on the question of capital punishment.

In a strongly dissenting opinion, Justice Thurgood Marshall objects that the ruling means "[t]he State's mere announcement that it intends to seek the death penalty . . . [will] give the prosecution license to empanel a jury especially likely to return that very verdict." That is because, in Marshall's view, death-qualified jurors are less likely to be concerned with the defendant's rights and with "the danger of erroneous convictions" than other jurors would be.

June. The U.S. Supreme Court *(Ford v. Wainwright)* rules that the state of Florida cannot execute an insane convict, Alvin Ford. A 33-year-old black man, Ford had murdered a Florida police officer in 1974. The question before the Court did not involve Ford's sanity when he committed the crime, or at the time of his trial. During his years in prison, however, his mental condition had reached the point where a psychiatrist determined that he had "at best, only minimal contact with the events of the external world." The Court's ruling means that states cannot execute prisoners who are legally insane at the time of their scheduled execution, regardless of whether they were sane at the time of their crimes.

1987

Haiti, the Philippines, Liechtenstein, and the German Democratic Republic all abolish capital punishment.

In the United States, the Supreme Court upholds the death sentence of a black man named Warren McCleskey for the murder of a white policeman *(McCleskey v. Kemp)*. The vote is 5 to 4. McCleskey had argued that the Georgia jury that sentenced him to die had been unfairly influenced both by his own race and by the race of his victim.

In support of his argument, McCleskey's lawyers had presented a major statistical study showing that, in Georgia, murderers whose victims are white receive death sentences four times as often as those whose victims are black. This is true even when the murderers are white. Black murderers whose victims are white are condemned to death even more often.

Speaking for the majority of the Court, Justice Powell agrees that the study shows a clear "discrepancy that appears to correlate with race." Even so the Court will not assume that racism is the reason for the imbalance. Before it would overturn McCleskey's sentence, says Powell, the Court would need proof that the particular jury that had sentenced him had been influenced by race, and it had received no such proof.

The four dissenters (who include Justices Stevens and Blackmun, as well as the two longtime foes of capital punishment, Brennan and Marshall) argue that it is not necessary for a defendant to show specific prejudice on his own jury. The pattern showing the taint of racism on death sentences in Georgia is obvious.

1987
(cont.)

The *McCleskey* decision comes as a great blow, not only to abolitionists, but to civil rights campaigners across the country.

In *Booth v. Maryland,* the Court rules that victim impact evidence may not be used in the sentencing phase of a trial that decides whether or not the death penalty will be imposed.

1988

April. Georgia bans the use of the death penalty against defendants whom the jury has found "guilty but mentally retarded."[12] No other state has such a law.

June. The U.S. Supreme Court *(Thompson v. Oklahoma)* overturns the death sentence given to William Wayne Thompson by the state of Oklahoma for his part in the murder of his former brother-in-law. Thompson's sentence had been appealed on the grounds that it would be cruel and unusual punishment to execute him because he had been only 15 years old when he committed the crime. Although five of the nine Supreme Court justices vote to vacate the sentence, only four do so on those grounds. Justice Sandra Day O'Connor finds the sentence inappropriate because the Oklahoma statute sets no minimum age whatsoever. The divided ruling still leaves open the question of whether or not 15 is constitutionally too young to be sentenced to death.

1989

It is an important year for death penalty cases in the Supreme Court. In *South Carolina v. Gathers,* the Court expands its 1987 ruling in *Booth v. Maryland* by declaring it unconstitutional under the Eighth Amendment for prosecutors to praise the murder victim's character when trying to persuade jurors to impose the death penalty on a killer.

Gathers is an effort to protect the rights of a defendant in a capital trial, but in several other important cases, the Court continues to move away from the concerns it had expressed in 1972 in *Furman.* Taken together, these cases have the effect of drastically limiting the avenues of appeal available to condemned prisoners. In the eyes of abolitionists, the Court is rapidly stripping away the safeguards that protect prisoners from being put to death unfairly. In the eyes of pro-capital-punishment forces, on the other hand, the Court is merely limiting the ability of guilty criminals to delay their moment of reckoning by abusing legal technicalities.

28 February. In an important procedural case *(Dugger v. Adams)*, the Court turns down an appeal on behalf of a Florida defendant who argues that the judge at his trial had misinformed the jury about its role in sentencing. A federal district court had already ruled that the judge's mistake did violate the Eighth Amendment. In any case, the Supreme Court rules that it is too late for the defendant to raise the claim in federal court because he had failed to raise it in an earlier state court proceeding in which it would have been in order. In essence, the court seems to be saying that unless a constitutional claim is raised at the earliest opportunity, the defendant loses the right to raise it ever.

May. The United Nations Economic and Social Council passes a resolution recommending the abolition of the death penalty for mentally retarded people or others with severely "limited mental competence."[13]

23 June. The Court turns down a class action suit *(Murray v. Giarratano)* filed on behalf of impoverished residents of Virginia's death row who claim a constitutional right to free counsel to help them with appeals.

26 June. The Court declares *(Penry v. Lynaugh)* that it is not unconstitutional to impose the death penalty on a mentally retarded person. The case involves an adult murderer named Johnny Paul Penry, who has an IQ between 50 and 63, the ability to learn of a typical 6½-year-old child, and the social maturity of a 10-year-old. The Court does rule, however, that juries need to be instructed that they can consider mental retardation as a mitigating factor when deciding whether to impose the death penalty. Since Penry's jury had not been so informed, Penry's death sentence is overturned. Nonetheless, the Court's decision clears the way for states to execute other retarded criminals.

26 June. Ruling in the cases of two young men *(Stanford v. Kentucky* and *Wilkins v. Missouri)* convicted of brutal murders committed when they were 16 and 17 years old, the Supreme Court rules that their proposed executions are not cruel and unusual punishment despite their youth.

Lawyers for the defendants had argued that the community's "standards of decency" had evolved to the point

1989
(cont.)

where the execution of people that young was no longer acceptable. Writing for the majority, however, Justice Antonin Scalia disagrees. Among other things, he points out that most states that have capital punishment permit it to be applied to 16-year-olds.

13 July. The Indiana Supreme Court sets aside the death sentence of a young woman named Paula Cooper. Cooper, who was 16 at the time she was sentenced in 1986, was only 15 when she and other girls killed a 78-year-old woman with a knife. The court rules that death would be a disproportionate punishment, considering her youth at the time of the crime.

1990

15 December. By a vote of 59 to 26, the General Assembly of the United Nations adopts the Second Optional Protocol to the International Convenant on Civil and Political Rights. It calls on all member nations to take steps toward abolishing the death penalty. Forty-eight nations abstain from the vote.[14]

1991

April. Ray Copeland is sentenced to death in Missouri for a murder committed when he was 71 years old. He is the only person in the United States to be given a death sentence for a crime committed after the age of 70.

16 April. The U.S. Supreme Court sets strict new limits on the right of condemned prisoners to appeal their sentences more than once to the federal courts. The case *(McCleskey v. Zant)* involves a new appeal by the same Warren McCleskey whose claim that his death sentence had been influenced by race was turned down by the Court in 1987 *(McCleskey v. Kemp)*.

In effect, the Court is severely limiting the right of the writ of habeas corpus, which historically has protected citizens from acts of injustice by the government by allowing them to challenge the constitutionality of those acts in federal court. In the future, the Court rules, a prisoner can no longer file more than one habeas corpus petition unless exceptional circumstances require it. Any constitutional issue not raised in the initial writ cannot be raised in a later one. In order to have another writ considered, the prisoner must be able to show both that there was a good reason the issue or issues contained in it weren't raised before, and that he or she has suffered "actual prejudice" from the claimed abuse of constitutional rights.

Three justices (Marshall, Blackmun, and Stevens) file an angry dissent in which they attack the decision as an "unjustifiable assault on the Great Writ."

May. David Chandler becomes the first person sentenced to death under the only current federal law that meets the safeguards required by the 1972 Supreme Court decision striking down all the then existing capital punishment laws. It is the 1988 Anti–Drug Abuse Act, which makes participation in a murder either committed by or solicited by large-scale drug dealers a federal crime punishable by death.

June. Reversing its recent policy, the U.S. Supreme Court rules *(Payne v. Tennessee)* that juries can take into account the character of the victim and the impact on the victim's family when deciding whether to sentence a killer to death.

24 June. The U.S. Supreme Court refuses to consider an appeal from convicted murderer Roger Keith Coleman on the grounds that his attorney had been a day late in filing a petition in the state court of Virginia. The Court rules *(Coleman v. Thompson)* that failure to file an appeal at the proper time in a state court rules out any future consideration of the appeal in federal court. The 6 to 3 vote is a reversal of a policy established by the Court back in 1963, and is one more in a series of recent rulings that limits the right of habeas corpus.

30 June. The Canadian Parliament votes 148 to 127 against reintroduction of the death penalty, which has been outlawed in Canada since 1976. The vote is something of a surprise, since the Progressive Conservative Party had been elected with a large parliamentary majority in 1984 partly on the promise that it would bring the issue to a new vote.

6 September. Donald Gaskins is executed in South Carolina's electric chair for the 1982 contract murder of a fellow prison inmate. Gaskins, who had previously been convicted of killing nine white people, is the first white man executed in the United States for killing a single black person since 1944.

25 September. The state of Georgia electrocutes Warren McCleskey. McCleskey's conviction had been the basis for

1991
(*cont.*)

two appeals that had reached the U.S. Supreme Court, resulting in two landmark death penalty decisions— *McCleskey v. Kemp* (1987) and *McCleskey v. Zant* (1991). Both appeals had been rejected.

October. By a vote of 4 to 3, the Supreme Court of Canada rules that accused kidnapper, rapist, and murderer Charles Ng and convicted murderer Joseph Kindler can be extradited to the United States.

The ruling is controversial because Kindler is already under a sentence of death in Pennsylvania, and Ng is accused of several murders in California, a death penalty state. Previously Canada, which has abolished its own death penalty, has refused to extradite people to countries where they were liable to be put to death. Kindler's and Ng's lawyers argued that their clients should not be extradited unless the Canadian government first got assurances that their lives would be spared. Apparently not wanting Canada to become a refuge for fugitives from foreign death sentences, the Canadian justice department refuses to ask for such assurances, and immediately dispatches the two men to the United States.[15]

25 October. Jerome Allen is sentenced to death in Florida for the murder of a gas station attendant during a robbery committed when he was 15 years old. The case is unusual because the recent trend in court decisions has been not to execute people for crimes committed before they were 16. In this case, however, the prosecutor insists that Allen is "a juvenile in age only."[16]

The year passes without the Comprehensive Violent Crime Control Act of 1991 becoming law. The bill, which was intended as a part of President George Bush's war on drugs, would have had an enormous effect on the administration of the death penalty in the United States. It called for extending the number of federal crimes punishable by death to more than 50, as well as formally restricting a condemned prisoner to one habeas corpus appeal in the federal courts. (In effect, the Supreme Court seems determined to do this by its own rulings.) The bill passed both houses of Congress in 1991, but President Bush refused to sign it because it did not eliminate the right of habeas corpus altogether.[17]

1992   21 April. Robert Alton Harris is executed in the gas chamber at San Quentin prison. He is the first person to be executed in California in 25 years.

Harris had been sentenced to die for the merciless killings of two 16-year-old boys in 1978. His efforts to escape execution had received the kind of public attention previously granted only to the likes of Caryl Chessman, Roger Keith Coleman, and others who seemed to have serious claims that they might be innocent. Harris had launched a variety of appeals in state and federal courts, including seven to the U.S. Supreme Court.

Harris's last stay was granted by the 9th District Court of Appeals minutes after he was strapped into a chair in the gas chamber around 2 o'clock on this morning. He was then unstrapped and led back to his cell on death row.

However, the U.S. Supreme Court, which had already shown itself intolerant of multiple appeals in *McCleskey v. Zant* (1991), loses all patience. Within hours of the appeals court's stay, the high court overturns it. In an unprecedented move, it sends a fax message to authorities in California. "No further stays of Robert Alton Harris' execution shall be entered by the federal courts except upon order of this court," it declares.[18] In effect, the Court is forbidding lower federal courts to interfere, and ordering the execution to proceed.

Harris is led back into the gas chamber and strapped into the chair again. At roughly 6:05 in the morning, the cyanide pellets are dropped. Within seven minutes, witnesses report, Harris seems to be unconscious. At 6:21, a doctor pronounces him dead.

May. Roger Keith Coleman is executed in Virginia for the murder of his sister-in-law, despite protests and appeals for mercy from around the world. Coleman has claimed that he is innocent of the brutal murder, and many people believe him.

June. The U.S. Supreme Court rules *(Sawyer v. Whittley)* that condemned prisoners may raise certain constitutional claims in federal appeals, even when they have failed to raise them in state proceedings. In effect, the Court is modifying its 1989 ruling in *Dugger v. Adams*, which forbid claims in federal court that had not already been raised in appropriate state court proceedings. It is a limited

1992
(cont.)

modification, however, that can only be used to establish violations that prevented defendants from proving their actual innocence of the crime, not by defendants who merely hope to escape death by mitigating their guilt.

3 November. Voters in Washington, D.C., overwhelmingly reject a referendum calling for the introduction of the death penalty in the District of Columbia.

1993

5 January. Three-time child killer Westley Allan Dodd is hung in Washington State Prison at Walla Walla, Washington. His execution is the first hanging in the United States since 1965. It comes after an unsuccessful attempt by opponents of capital punishment to block the execution on the grounds that hanging is cruel and unusual punishment.

Dodd had refused to cooperate with the effort to block his execution. In fact, he virtually demanded to die, declaring that if he was not killed, he would do everything he could to escape and return to his murderous ways. What's more, he had chosen hanging (over lethal injection) as the method of execution because he had strangled the youngest of his victims, a four-year-old child, and considered it fitting that he should die by a similar method.

The execution was set for just after midnight. Both pro- and anti-death-penalty demonstrators gathered outside the prison as the time approached. Despite the cold, the supporters of capital punishment were in a festive mood. One carried a sign reading, "Hang 'em high." Chanting together, they counted down the final seconds to the appointed time, then cheered and set off fireworks as it arrived. The opponents stood silently, holding candles in the dark.

Inside, witnesses later reported, the execution was carried out with remarkable speed. Dodd was ushered briskly into the execution chamber. Two men slipped a kind of bag over him, then placed the noose around his neck and tightened it. A trap door opened beneath his feet and he dropped seven feet through the air to the end of the rope, apparently dying instantly.

25 January. The United States Supreme Court refuses *(Herrera v. Collins)* to allow a federal court to review new evidence in the case of Leonel Herrera, convicted of murdering a Texas policeman in 1981. Herrera's attorney has argued that new evidence proves that Leonel's brother

committed the crime. Nonetheless, by a 6 to 3 majority the Court rules that the deadline has long since passed for Herrera to appeal on the basis of actual innocence. His only hope is to appeal to the governor of Texas for executive clemency. Justices Blackmun, Stevens, and Souter angrily dissent from the ruling, charging that "[e]xecution of a person who can show that he is innocent comes perilously close to simple murder."[19]

2 March. All charges are dropped against Walter McMillen, who has spent the past six years on death row in Alabama. McMillen, who is black, was convicted in 1988 of killing a white teenager in a trial badly tainted by racism. Even so, the jury that convicted him recommended a life sentence, only to be overruled by the judge who sentenced him to die. Evidence that has surfaced since the trial shows that key witnesses against McMillen—one of whom had apparently been told that he would be spared all risk of the death penalty himself if he incriminated McMillen—lied during the trial, perhaps with the prosecution's knowledge.

Notes

1. Cesare Beccaria, *On Crimes and Punishment,* translated by Henry Paolucci (Indianapolis: Bobbs-Merrill, 1963).

2. Edward Livingston, "Report on the Plan of a Penal Code," in *The Complete Works of Edward Livingston on Criminal Jurisprudence,* vol. 1. (New York: National Prison Association, 1873).

3. *Congressional Digest* (August–September 1927): 242.

4. Kurt Anderson, et al. "An Eye for an Eye," *Time* (24 January 1983): 32.

5. Quoted in James Avery Joyce, *Capital Punishment: A World View* (New York: Thomas Nelson & Sons, 1961), 189.

6. Ibid., 161–162.

7. United Nations, *Capital Punishment* (New York: United Nations Department of Economic and Social Affairs, 1962), 54.

8. Ellen Alderman and Caroline Kennedy, *In Our Defense* (New York: Morrow, 1991), 406.

9. *Chronicle of the 20th Century* (Mount Kisco, N.Y.: Chronicle, 1987), 1120.

10. Amnesty International, *USA Death Penalty: Briefing* (New York: Amnesty International, 1987), 13.

11. Amnesty International, *When the State Kills. . . .* (New York: Amnesty International, 1989), 244.

12. Ibid., 229.

13. Amnesty International, *United States of America: Death Penalty Developments in 1992* (New York: Amnesty International, 1992), 32.

14. "Death Penalty Protocol Adopted. . . ." *UN Chronicle* (March 1990): 85.

15. D'Arcy Jenish and John Howse, "A Momentous Ruling," *Maclean's* (7 October 1991): 62.

16. Amnesty International, *United States of America: Death Penalty Developments in 1991* (New York: Amnesty International, 1992): 21.

17. Ibid., 13.

18. "Execution Witnesses Say Harris Died with Dignity," *Wausau Daily Herald,* 22 April 1992.

19. Dennis Cauchon, "Court: Late Evidence May Not Halt Execution," *USA Today,* 26 January 1993.

4

Biographical Sketches

IN THE END, MOST PUBLIC ISSUES BOIL DOWN to people: people whose lives are affected by the issue; people who frame the arguments and take part in the public debate; people whose actions, good or bad, galvanize support for one side or another.

What is true of most issues is true of the death penalty. For many centuries, capital punishment was not an issue at all, in the sense that there was no real public controversy about it. It was a fact of life—as accepted by most members of society as the changing of the seasons and the divine right of kings. It took individual people, like Cesare Beccaria in Europe and Dr. Benjamin Rush in America, to challenge the inevitability of capital punishment—to transform it from an accepted fact of life into a social and moral issue that had to be examined and debated. We have been wrestling with that issue ever since, and we are still wrestling with it today.

Some of us regard capital punishment primarily as an intellectual question, as framed by philosophers like Jeremy Bentham or social scientists like Walter Berns. Others, however, react to the death penalty in more human terms. Our beliefs on the subject are formed not so much by rational arguments as by personal and often emotional responses to particular people and events. Someone commits a horrible murder, and we instinctively want to see that person punished—eradicated, wiped away, removed from society in the most immediate and final way possible. On the other hand, if someone is convicted and executed on what seems to be flimsy evidence, we begin to doubt whether even society itself has the right to impose such an irrevocable punishment.

The following individuals are representative of the many kinds of people—philosophers and activists, judges and criminals, politicians and executioners—who have helped form modern attitudes toward the death penalty. Of those who have taken a strong stand on the death penalty, there are more abolitionists than retentionists. This may seem odd, considering that the majority of Americans favor the death penalty. The fact is, however, that more abolitionists are prominent for their stand on the death penalty than retentionists.

Why does this imbalance exist? At least part of the reason abolitionists have been the most active side in the battle is because they have had to be on the offensive. For most of our history, retentionism has been the entrenched position. The majority of states have had death penalty statutes on their books, and the majority of the people have supported the practice. Capital punishment, therefore, has not needed a particularly large or powerful force to defend it.

Abolitionists, on the other hand, have been forced to launch assault after assault on a position that has often seemed invulnerable. It is an old military axiom that it takes a larger and more determined force to overrun a well-entrenched position than it does to defend it. So it has been the abolitionists who have made the most noise, firing off the artillery and lobbing the grenades. All retentionists have had to do is hunker down in their legal fortress and weather the occasional fire storm. It is not surprising that they have been relatively content to let the law and public opinion speak for them.

Anthony Guy Amsterdam (1935–)

Prominent attorney who played a leading role in the legal battle to abolish the death penalty in the 1960s and 1970s.

Amsterdam received his law degree from the University of Pennsylvania Law School in 1960, at the threshold of a decade of intense struggle over civil rights of all kinds. A brilliant student, Amsterdam edited the *Pennsylvania Law Review,* for which he wrote at least one article that later influenced the U.S. Supreme Court. Upon graduation, he was picked to serve as a law clerk to the legendary Supreme Court Justice Felix Frankfurter. After his clerkship, he served briefly as assistant U.S. attorney in

Washington, D.C., before taking a teaching job at his old law school.

In 1963 Amsterdam agreed to help out in the case of a black man sentenced to death for intended rape, although he had not physically injured his victim in any way. This led the young lawyer into the struggle to overturn the death penalty, a pursuit that would engage much of his attention for decades. Working with such anti-capital-punishment groups as the NAACP Legal Defense Fund, the National Coalition to Abolish the Death Penalty, and the Southern Poverty Law Center, Amsterdam quickly established himself as one of the most able legal minds working on the issue.

Before long, he was managing the NAACP Legal Defense Fund's growing schedule of capital punishment cases. He played a major role in preparing the brief attacking the constitutionality of the death penalty in the historic *Furman* case. When it came time for oral arguments before the Supreme Court, it was Amsterdam who led the way.

Among his legal honors, Amsterdam was the recipient of the first Distinguished Service Award of the Pennsylvania Law School in 1968, and he was named lawyer of the year by the California Trial Lawyer's Association in 1973. In 1969 he took a position as a law professor at Stanford University in California. He stayed there until moving to New York University in 1981, where he presently remains.

Cesare Beccaria (1738–1794)

The first prominent eighteenth-century European to call for an end to the death penalty. As such, he is considered the founder of the modern abolition movement.

Born a member of the minor Italian aristocracy, Beccaria was trained in the law. In 1764 he published his *Essay on Crimes and Punishments*. It was the first major study of the criminal justice system as it operated in eighteenth-century Europe, as well as the first call for the complete abolition of capital punishment. It remains perhaps the most influential attack on the death penalty ever published.

Beccaria argued that criminal punishments should be just harsh enough to protect society, and no harsher. He attacked several common practices of the time, including the holding of criminal proceedings in secret and the torture of suspects and criminals.

Although he was only 26 years old when his *Essay* was published, it immediately established him as a significant figure in the European Enlightenment. Ironically, for someone who had attacked the penal policies of virtually every government of the time, Beccaria was showered with honors by many of those same governments. Austria even founded a prestigious chair in economics to lure him to that country.

More important than the personal honors was the effect his ideas had on penal reform—not just then, but long after his death. Translations of the *Essay* were quickly published in several languages. The first English translation came out in 1767, and the first American edition was published ten years later. The abolition of capital punishment in Tuscany and Austria in the 1780s has been credited largely to his arguments. Catherine the Great of Russia, where the death penalty had already been abolished for most crimes in the 1750s, summoned Beccaria to help her establish a new criminal code.

Beccaria was not the only Enlightenment figure who favored penal reform. Voltaire, for example, published a detailed commentary on the *Essay*. It was Beccaria, though, who focussed the attention of philosophers and political leaders on the issue. In addition to its effect in Europe, his *Essay* also had a major effect on the thinking of abolitionists in America, including Dr. Benjamin Rush.

Hugo Adam Bedau (1926–)

University professor and author, the most prominent current academic opponent of the death penalty.

Hugo Adam Bedau holds the Austin Fletcher Chair in Philosophy at Tufts University, where he was previously chairman of the Philosophy Department. Professor Bedau was born in Portland, Oregon. He received his undergraduate education at the University of Redlands and went on to obtain a master's degree from Boston University, and another, as well as a Ph.D., from Harvard.

Bedau has served as the president of the American League to Abolish Capital Punishment. His extensive writings on the question include several books, including *The Death Penalty in America* (1964), which has been called "[t]he first completely comprehensive overview on the death penalty attempted by a scholar in this century;"[1] *The Courts, the Constitution and Capital Punishment* (1977); and *Death is Different: Studies in the Morality, Law and Politics of*

Capital Punishment (1987); as well as innumerable studies, essays, and articles.

Although the bulk of his published writings have dealt with the death penalty, he has many other interests as well. They are demonstrated by his editorship of such books as *Civil Disobedience* (1969) and *Justice and Equality* (1971).

Jeremy Bentham (1748–1832)

British social philosopher, legal reformer, and economist.

Bentham was a child prodigy, with a genius for academic studies and a talent for the violin. As a young man, he attended Oxford University and was admitted to the bar. Instead of entering legal practice, however, he devoted himself to the study of ethics and the law. His book, *Introduction to the Principles of Morals and Legislation* (1789), is considered one of the most important philosophical works of the eighteenth century.

Bentham is best known as the cofounder and leading exponent of the philosophical doctrine known as utilitarianism. He believed that social and economic measures should be judged by the happiness or pleasure they produced. The best measures were the ones that produced the greatest happiness for the greatest number of people. Like Beccaria in France, he believed that a kind of moral arithmetic could be used to determine the utility—or usefulness—not only of social policies and institutions, but of the actions of individuals as well.

Also like Beccaria, he believed that the legal systems of his age needed to be reformed. Among the reforms he suggested was the restriction, if not abolition, of capital punishment. Together with Sir Samuel Romilly, who pressed for similar reforms in the British parliament, Bentham helped lay the foundation for the massive reduction in the number of capital crimes in Britain that would occur in the decades following his death.

Walter Berns (1919–)

A political scientist and educator, Berns is a leading spokesman for the retentionist cause.

Born in Chicago, Illinois, Walter Berns received his undergraduate education at the University of Iowa and his postgraduate education at Reed College, the London School of Economics and Political Science, and the University of Chicago. He has served on the faculties of Yale and Cornell universities, among others. From

1979 to 1986 he was a resident scholar at the American Enterprise Institute, where he is currently the John M. Olin Distinguished Scholar, as well as a professor at Georgetown University.

Berns is the author of what has been described as "the landmark book on the death penalty,"[2] *For Capital Punishment: Crime and the Morality of the Death Penalty* (1979). One of the nation's best-known constitutional scholars, Berns challenges the idea that the death penalty should be considered cruel and unusual punishment under the Eighth Amendment. What's more, he argues that the death penalty is justified as an expression of society's moral outrage at certain heinous crimes.

Marvin H. Bovee (1827–1888)

Nineteenth-century champion of the abolitionist cause.

Born and raised in a political family in the state of New York, Bovee moved to the Wisconsin Territory while still a teenager. The territory became a state in 1848, and four years later, Bovee won election as a Democrat to the state legislature.

It was Bovee who led the fight to end the death penalty in Wisconsin. His efforts, helped by a gruesomely botched hanging in the Wisconsin city of Kenosha, were successful in 1853. Not willing to stop there, Bovee determined to carry the abolitionist fight throughout the country. From Nebraska to New Jersey, and from Missouri to Massachussetts, Bovee spent the rest of his life in largely unsuccessful efforts to throw hangmen out of their jobs. Although he did help to impose some restrictions on the use of the death penalty in several places, he was never again as successful as he'd been in Wisconsin.

Bovee published *Christ and the Gallows* (1869), a major collection of anti-capital-punishment letters and essays by prominent Americans.

William Joseph Brennan, Jr. (1906–)

Associate Justice (1956–1990) of the U.S. Supreme Court.

William Brennan was born and raised in Newark, New Jersey. The son of an Irish-immigrant brewery worker and union leader, he grew up with a strong sense of social injustice and the desire to make a difference in the world.

An excellent student, Brennan graduated from the Wharton School and attended the prestigious Harvard Law School on scholarships. He practiced law in New Jersey until World War II broke out. He joined the army, where his background as the son of a union activist was put to wartime use when he was assigned to be a troubleshooter with defense industry unions for the under-secretary for war. After demobilization, he returned to his legal practice in New Jersey, where he was soon appointed to the state supreme court.

When Senator Joseph McCarthy began making wild and ap-parently unfounded charges that hundreds of American scholars, government employees, and ordinary citizens were communists, Brennan spoke out against him. This was considered a brave thing to do at a time when McCarthy seemed to have the power to de-stroy almost any young man's career. This courageous stand didn't damage Brennan, however. McCarthy's vote was the only one cast against him when President Dwight Eisenhower ap-pointed him to the U.S. Supreme Court in 1956.

Eisenhower, who was a Republican, would consider Brennan's appointment a big mistake when the new justice turned out to be much more of a "broad constructionist" than Eisenhower ex-pected him to be. In other words, Brennan tended to view broadly the rights and protections the Constitution grants to individuals. Brennan was, in fact, very much at home in the liberal Court under Chief Justice Earl Warren. He played a leading role in the Warren Court's expansion of the Constitution's protections into areas where they had not been enforced before. These included rulings that encouraged racial desegregation, affirmative action, and civil rights in general. Brennan was particularly strong in upholding the rights of criminal defendants against the power of police and prosecutors.

Over the years, Brennan earned a reputation as a negotiator within the Court, finding ways for justices with differing views to reach consensus on important decisions. Almost a moderate by Warren Court standards, Brennan was considered increasingly liberal as the Burger and Rehnquist Courts of the late 1970s and 1980s became more and more conservative around him.

Brennan was never moderate, however, when it came to the death penalty. He concurred in the *Furman* decision, although he wished it had gone further and unequivocally banned capital pun-ishment forever. He was a bitter dissenter from *Gregg* in 1976 and from all the other decisions that followed upholding various state capital punishment statutes. Together with Justice Thurgood Marshall, he continued to vote against the death penalty in every case. Time and again, they dissented from Court decisions upholding death penalty statutes by repeating what retentionists regarded as a kind of abolitionist mantra: "[T]he death penalty is in all circumstances cruel and unusual punishment prohibited by the Eighth and Fourteenth Amendments."

Brennan retired from the Court in 1990.

Rev. George Cheever (1807–1890)

Clergyman and reformer.

The son of a publisher in Hallowell, Maine, George Cheever attended Bowdoin College and Andover Seminary. He was ordained into the Congregational ministry in 1833, taking up a post in Salem, Massachussetts. He later became pastor of a Presbyterian church in New York, and eventually of the Church of the Puritans in the same city.

A great believer in the power of the pen, Cheever once attacked a rival religion for its failure to produce great literature. Beginning with his stint in Salem, Cheever depended on his writings as much as his preaching to persuade the public to the rightness of his uncompromising beliefs. Combative by temperament and a reformer by conviction, Cheever was ardent in his published calls for an end to slavery and equally ardent in his defense of capital punishment. Early in his career, his printing press was destroyed by a mob angry at something he had written. As though that weren't bad enough, he was sued for libel, forced to pay a fine of $1,000, and thrown into jail for a month.

Undeterred, Cheever continued to pour out his convictions in print, eventually producing 23 books and some 50 pamphlets, speeches, and other literary works. He defended the death penalty on biblical grounds, and his *Defense of Capital Punishment* (1846) is considered the classic presentation of the American Protestant case for the death penalty.

At his death, Cheever left his excellent library to Howard University, the nation's leading black college of the time.

Caryl Chessman (1920–1960)

A convicted thief and kidnapper whose long efforts to avoid execution aroused public sympathy for him and opposition to the death penalty in the 1950s.

Born on 27 May 1920 in St. Joseph, Michigan, Chessman was always a sickly and disturbed child. Quick to cry and equally quick to fly into a rage, he showed an early streak of cruelty, which he later said caused him to strike out even at things he loved.

While he was still very young, the family moved to California. His early life there was wracked with disaster. His mother was partially paralyzed in an accident, and the resulting medical bills impoverished the family. Chessman's criminal career began with childhood thefts to help feed and support them. Before long, however, he had progressed to stealing automobiles for thrill rides and other more serious crimes.

In his mid-teens, he was caught and sentenced to a forestry camp for juvenile delinquents. Escaping twice, he was twice recaptured and transferred to a more secure reform school. There, he became even more hardened than he had been before. Almost as soon as he was released, he began a new career holding up houses of prostitution. He was arrested in the process of committing a burglary on his seventeenth birthday and returned to prison.

Released in 1939, Chessman had ambitions to become a writer, but in the meantime he continued his criminal career. Falling in with a group of other young criminals, he embarked on a string of armed robberies, burglaries, and other crimes. When they were captured in a violent encounter with police, the press referred to them as the Boy Bandit Gang. Except for a brief period during which he escaped, he spent the next several years in various California prisons until he was paroled in December 1947.

Less than two months later, on 23 January 1947, he was arrested in Hollywood, California. Police suspected him of being the notorious "red light bandit" who had been terrorizing couples parked in Los Angeles area lovers' lanes. The bandit had a red light in his car, like the ones the police used. He would approach the couples as though he were a policeman, then pull out a gun and rob them. In some cases, he would force the woman to go off with him and sexually attack her. After questioning by police, Chessman confessed to the crimes, although he later claimed the confession had been beaten out of him.

Chessman was charged with robbery and kidnapping. Under California law at the time, taking a woman anywhere for the purpose of rape was considered kidnapping, and so Chessman was liable to the death penalty, even though no actual rape had taken place. At the trial, Chessman chose to defend himself. He was found guilty, and on 25 June 1948 he was sentenced to death. He was sent back to San Quentin prison, this time to a cell on death row.

For the next 11 years and 11 months, Chessman waged a fierce battle to save his life. Teaching himself the ins and outs of the legal system, he used every device he could think of to delay his execution and reverse his sentence. Fulfilling his earlier ambition to be a writer, he published two best-selling books about his case, *Cell 2455 Death Row* and *Trial by Ordeal.* He also wrote another less popular book, *The Face of Justice,* which dealt with broader issues of life and death.

Altogether, Chessman would file almost 50 appeals against his conviction and sentence, and 15 of them would reach the Supreme Court of the United States. There were many legitimate questions about his conviction. He clearly had not been able to mount a professional defense. The trial judge had shown prejudice against him, and much of the transcript of his trial had been lost. The noted criminologist, Dr. Harry Elmer Barnes, remarked that it would require restraint to describe the trial merely "as one of the most fantastic travesties of justice in the history of civilized criminal jurisprudence."[3]

Thanks to his remarkable talent for publicizing his cause, people around the world were inspired to join in support of Chessman's long battle to escape the executioner. Among the thousands of foreign voices raised in protest were those of the British author J. B. Priestly, humanitarian Dr. Albert Schweitzer, and even the official newspaper of the Vatican. Despite the widespread and emotional sympathy for him, Chessman's appeals eventually ran out. He was put to death in the gas chamber at San Quentin on 2 May 1960. It was the eighth official date that had been set for his execution.

A wave of anti-death-penalty sentiment swept much of the western world in the late 1950s and 1960s. More than any other single cause, it was revulsion at Chessman's death that accelerated that sentiment, which eventually resulted in the abolition of capital punishment in several countries and its temporary abandonment in the United States.

Newton M. Curtis (1835–1910)

Abolitionist congressman.

A native of upstate New York, Curtis distinguished himself as a soldier in the Union Army during the Civil War. He not only achieved the rank of brigadier general, but won the Congressional

Medal of Honor, the highest military award the United States can bestow.

Curtis served with the Reconstruction forces in Virginia for a time after the war before returning to his home state. Back in New York, he took up a series of different jobs before entering the state assembly as a Republican in 1884. As a legislator, he championed the causes of prison reform, humane treatment for the mentally ill, and the abolition of the death penalty. He persuaded his colleagues in the assembly to pass a bill calling for an end to capital punishment, but the state senate refused to go along and the measure never became law.

In 1890 Curtis won election to the U.S. Congress, where he took up the cause of abolition on the national level, introducing a bill to end the death penalty in 1892. Although he never succeeded in persuading his colleagues to ban capital punishment outright, in 1897 he did convince them to lower the number of federal crimes punishable by death from 60 to only three.

George Mifflin Dallas (1792–1864)

A politician and statesman, Dallas was one of the most prominent American political figures of the early nineteenth century to take an active stand against the death penalty.

Dallas was born in Philadelphia, the son of Alexander James Dallas, one of the most important secretaries of the treasury in U.S. history. George attended the College of New Jersey (now Princeton) before entering the bar in 1813. He began his distinguished career in public service as secretary to Albert Gallatin (the financier who had been secretary of the treasury under Thomas Jefferson) on an important peace mission to Moscow.

After his stint abroad, Dallas returned to Pennsylvania, where he became active in Republican politics and served in a series of legal and political offices. Shifting political allegiances, he became a supporter of Andrew Jackson. After Jackson's election as president, Dallas was first named district attorney in Philadelphia, and then, in 1831, appointed to fill out a term in the U.S. Senate. Retiring from the Senate when that term was over, Dallas served briefly as attorney general of Pennsylvania, only to lose that job when his party was turned out in 1835. Two years later, Dallas returned to Russia, this time as U.S. minister, appointed by President Martin van Buren.

A political enemy of James Buchanan, Dallas was nominated to run for vice president of the United States with James Polk. He and Polk were elected in 1844. Not long after, Dallas agreed to address the founding convention of the American Society for the Abolition of Capital Punishment, which picked him to be its first president. He served in both offices at the same time.

In his later years, Dallas was appointed U.S. minister to Great Britain by President Pierce, holding that office until the Republican Abraham Lincoln was elected president and the Civil War began. It was said of Dallas that he "hated abolition [of slavery] and secession both, as he hated all extremes."[4] It might have been added that he hated the extreme punishment of death, as well. To this day, Dallas remains the highest ranking official in U.S. history to take an active and absolute stand against the death penalty.

Clarence Darrow (1857–1938)

Defense attorney and prominent opponent of capital punishment.

Darrow was a product of rural America. Born in Kinsman, Ohio, he passed his law examination in 1878 without ever earning a university degree. He began practicing law in Ashtabula, Ohio, but moved to the big city of Chicago, Illinois, in 1888.

Darrow worked as an attorney for the city of Chicago and later for big business corporations, including the Chicago and Northwestern Railroad. He always felt a natural sympathy with ordinary workers, however, and never felt entirely comfortable with the way most big companies treated their employees. When Eugene V. Debs, the head of a striking railroad workers union, was thrown into jail in 1894, Darrow resigned his job with Chicago and Northwestern and went to work defending Debs. He quickly established himself as the nation's best-known legal champion of underdogs, from political radicals to ordinary citizens charged with capital crimes.

Darrow hated the death penalty and took on many cases just in order to save defendants from the gallows. He prided himself on the fact that he defended more than 100 people who faced potential death sentences, but not one was ever executed. Among them were Big Bill Haywood, the union leader accused of conspiring in the murder of Governor Steuenberg of Idaho in 1905; James and John McNamara, brothers charged with planting a bomb in the offices of the *Los Angeles Times* in 1911; and—most infamous of all—Richard Loeb and Nathan Leopold.

A year after his success in saving Leopold and Loeb from the gallows, Darrow joined with Lewis E. Lawes and others to found the American League to Abolish Capital Punishment. For the next several decades, the League provided the main base for the agitation against the death penalty in the United States.

Darrow's last famous client was John Scopes, a schoolteacher accused of violating a Tennessee law against teaching the theory of evolution. Scopes was prosecuted by the frequent presidential candidate, William Jennings Bryan. Because of the presence of these renowned antagonists, the case generated enormous national interest. Parts of it were actually broadcast live on radio. Scopes was found guilty, but the verdict was later overturned on a technicality.

Darrow retired from the law in 1927, although he spent much of his later years writing. Among his published writings are an early novel, *Farmington* (1904), *Crime: Its Cause and Treatment* (1922), and his autobiography, *The Story of My Life* (1932). A collection of several of Darrow's summations, edited by Arthur Weinberg, was published under the title *Attorney for the Damned* in 1957.

Robert Elliott (?–1939)

One of the most prolific executioners in American history.

Robert Elliott was an electrician and small businessman from Queens who put his talents to use operating the electric chairs of several eastern states during the 1920s and 1930s. Over the roughly 13 years he served as an executioner, he put more than 400 people to death. Among them were some of the most notorious and controversial criminals of the time. They included anarchists Nicola Sacco and Bartolomeo Vanzetti in Massachussetts and Bruno Richard Hauptmann, who was convicted of the kidnapping and murder of the baby of aviation hero Charles Lindburgh, in New Jersey.

Elliott's own death came of natural causes, in his bed, at home in Queens.

Gary Mark Gilmore (1940–1977)

A murderer whose execution in 1977 was the first after the Supreme Court's ruling reinstating capital punishment in the United States in 1976.

Gilmore grew up in Portland, Oregon. His father was a criminal, and Gary, who was a troubled child, seemed determined to follow in his father's footsteps. He began stealing while still in elementary school. By the time he was in his early twenties, he had progressed from simple thievery to armed robbery, and from a relatively short stint in a boys' reformatory to a long sentence in state prison.

Gilmore hated life in prison, and attempted to kill himself several times during his incarceration. All the attempts failed, however. By the time he was released on parole in 1976, he had served half his life in prison.

Gilmore moved to Provost, Utah, where he became obsessed with a young woman named Nicole Baker. When she ran away from him, frightened by his violence and the threats he made toward her, he became desperate. On 19 July 1976, only three months after he'd been paroled, he held up a gas station. Although the station attendant offered no resistance, Gilmore made him lie down on the floor of the station and shot him twice in the back of the head. The next day, Gilmore held up a motel, and killed the clerk. He was soon caught, and three months later, he was found guilty of murder and sentenced to death.

The American Civil Liberties Union and other anti-death-penalty groups attempted to overturn Gilmore's sentence. There had been no executions in a decade, and anti-capital-punishment organizations did not want to see them started up again. Gilmore, however, would have nothing to do with the efforts to save him, and, in fact, he did everything he could to put a stop to them. Even when his mother, Bessie Gilmore, appealed to the U.S. Supreme Court for a stay of execution on his behalf, he instructed his lawyers to protest that she had no right to do so. He then filed papers voluntarily waiving any right to appeal that he might have had himself.

Gilmore was apparently terrified that his sentence would be commuted to life in prison. He was so impatient for the execution order to be carried out that he attempted to kill himself with an overdose of barbiturates his old girlfriend Nicole Baker had smuggled into prison for him.

Finally, on 17 January 1977, Gilmore got his wish. Taken to a largely unused prison warehouse, he was strapped into a chair that faced a canvas wall that had holes cut into it for the guns of his executioners. Despite his request to face his executioners, a black bag was pulled down over his head. Four riflemen, all police volunteers, opened fire at once. Three bullets (the fourth was blank) struck Gilmore, killing him instantly and assuring him a place in the history of capital punishment.

The Gilmore case was the subject of a popular book by Norman Mailer entitled *The Executioner's Song* (1979), as well as a television movie based on the book.

Joseph-Ignace Guillotin (1738–1814)

The French doctor who gave his name to the guillotine.

Guillotin was professor of the medical sciences at the Paris Faculty of Medicine at the time of the French Revolution. He was also an influential member of the revolutionary Assembly. Guillotin was deeply interested in penal reform in general and in the death penalty in particular. A democratic idealist, he believed that legal punishments should be identical for all criminals, regardless of their wealth, power, or social standing.

In December 1789 he proposed to the National Assembly that a beheading machine should be used for all executions in France. The use of such a machine would not only be more democratic than using different methods of execution for criminals who came from different classes, Guillotin argued, it would be quicker and more humane than any of them. The Assembly was not immediately convinced, but eventually did authorize a decapitating machine to be the sole method of executing people in France in 1792.

By that time, Dr. Guillotin had given up his campaign for *la machine,* and the device was originally dubbed the *louisette* or *louison,* after another prominent physician, Dr. Antoine Louis. In later years, however, it became known as the guillotine, after its first sponsor in France. Despite his support for the machine, the idealistic Dr. Guillotin was always uncomfortable with the fact that a death device was known by his name.[5]

Dr. Guillotin died in Paris, of natural causes, on 26 March 1814.

Victor Hugo (1802–1885)

French author of several books that promoted abolition of the death penalty.

Victor Hugo was the leading French literary figure of his time and remains one of the most respected individuals in French history. His talents bloomed early, and he published his first book of poetry at the age of 20. A republican, his novels and other writings frequently attacked what he saw as social injustices of French society in general, and of the French penal system in particular. Several of his works directly or indirectly attacked the death penalty. Among them were *Last Days of a Condemned Man* (1829) and *The Death Penalty* (1854), as well as the monumental novel that many consider his greatest work, *Les Miserables* (1862).

Rev. Joe Ingle (1948–)

Minister, abolitionist, and prison reformer.

Joe Ingle is a minister of the United Church of Christ and one of the nation's most vocal opponents of the death penalty. He lives in Nashville, Tennessee, but works throughout the South—the heartland of the American death penalty. He is the first, and so far the only, director of the Southern Coalition on Jails and Prisons, which was founded in the mid-1970s to promote prison reform and the abolition of capital punishment. As such, he does what he can to minister to the spiritual needs of the hundreds of prisoners on death row in the southern states, while working to remove the threat of execution that hangs over them.

Ingles is fiercely and uncompromisingly opposed to capital punishment, which he believes has made the United States a "society of murderers."[6] He stresses the need for all Americans to take responsibility for the executions that are done in their names. He believes that America's use of the death penalty—directed primarily against the poor, black people, and those of all races who kill white people—parallels the situation in the early days of Nazi rule in Germany. "It is not just a matter of a few DAs or a few wardens who are angry and want to see people killed," he says. "[I]t is a whole system in this country. That's why it is so evil."[7]

Ingle's tireless opposition to the death penalty has attracted international attention. He was nominated for the Nobel Peace Prize in both 1988 and 1989.

Jack Ketch (?–1686)

A legendary executioner in seventeenth-century England.

Jack (or John) Ketch is the most famous—or infamous—executioner in history. He reigned over the English scaffold in the days when victims were hanged or beheaded, and the bodies of some were quartered after death. Because of his varied duties, Ketch is sometimes pictured with a rope in one hand and an axe or hatchet in the other.

The most famous of Ketch's victims was James Scott, the Duke of Monmouth and pretender to the throne of England. Monmouth's beheading on 15 July 1685 was not only the most important execution of Ketch's career, but the most trying. For some reason, Ketch found it much harder than usual to sever the head from the body. After a few blows, he tried to give up the effort entirely, and had to be threatened into returning to complete the job.

In Britain the name "Jack Ketch" means "executioner," in much the way "Benedict Arnold" means "traitor" in the United States. However, Ketch may not have been the infamous executioner's actual name. Tyburn Prison, where criminals were held in Ketch's time, had long been leased to a family named Jacquet; it is thought that Jack Ketch might be a mispronunciation of that name. Whatever his real name, the executioner known as Jack Ketch died in 1686.

Lewis E. Lawes (1883–1947)

Warden of Sing Sing Prison who became a leading advocate of prison reform and the abolition of capital punishment.

Born and raised in upstate New York, Lawes went into the army as a young man. Mustered out in 1904, he got a job as a guard in the New York state prison at Dannemora. He worked his way up in the penal system, serving in a variety of posts at a number of state institutions, until he was appointed to the top job at Sing Sing Prison in Ossining, New York, in 1920.

At that time, Sing Sing was regarded as the toughest state prison in New York. It housed many of the state's most hardened prisoners, as well as the electric chair, which had been moved there from its original home at Auburn.

Lawes was a hard-headed penologist who would run Sing Sing effectively for more than 20 years. He was also a man of compassion and sympathy, even for the worst of the criminals he confined. Both sides of his nature led him to institute a variety of reforms aimed at increasing efforts to rehabilitate prisoners and making the prison experience more humane.

His belief in reform and rehabilitation led him to change his mind about the death penalty. Initially a firm supporter of capital punishment, within three years of his appointment to Sing Sing he came to see executions as primitive, futile, and cruel. He quickly became the nation's most prominent example of an advocate of the death penalty who was converted into an opponent by being required to take part in carrying it out.

In 1925 he helped found the American League to Abolish Capital Punishment, and he remained an active spokesperson for the abolitionist cause, even while continuing to supervise executions in his job as warden. He explained his opposition to the death penalty in *Man's Judgment of Death* in 1923 and again in *Life and Death in Sing Sing* in 1928. Other books by Lewis Lawes include *Twenty-Thousand Years in Sing Sing* (1932) and *Meet the Murderer!* (1940).

Nathan Leopold
(see Richard Loeb and Nathan Leopold below)

Edward Livingston (1764–1836)

A distinguished American lawyer and statesman who wrote an influential argument against capital punishment.

Livingston was born in Clermont, New York. In 1804 he moved west to the territory of Orleans, which had just been purchased from France. He served on Andrew Jackson's staff during the War of 1812, and later represented Louisiana in both the U.S. House of Representatives (1823–1829) and the Senate (1829–1831). Under the presidency of his old commander, Andrew Jackson, Livingston served first as secretary of state (1831–1833) and later as minister to France (1833–1835).

In the 1820s the Louisiana legislature asked Livingston to draft a new penal code for the state. His "Introductory Report," which was originally written in 1824 and published in 1833, presented a detailed argument against capital punishment, providing what Supreme Court Justice Thurgood Marshall would later describe as "a tremendous impetus to the abolition movement for the next half century."[8]

Richard Loeb (1906–1936) and
Nathan Leopold (1905–1971)

Principals in an infamous murder case in Chicago in 1924.

As young men, Loeb and Leopold were drawn together by common backgrounds and interests. Intellectually brilliant, they were both scions of wealthy Chicago families.

Their relationship was unhealthy in a variety of ways. They assured each other that they were fundamentally superior to other people, and somehow above the moral and criminal laws that bound other members of society. At least partly to prove their supposed superiority, they planned and carried out what they expected to be a perfect crime. This turned out to be a surprisingly slapdash kidnapping and murder of a 14-year-old boy. Not nearly as clever as they thought they were, they were soon caught and indicted for the crime.

There was enormous prejudice against the defendants in the city of Chicago. They were not only wealthy in a heavily working class city, but Jewish in a city that was rife with anti-Semitism. What's more, their crime seemed not only heartless but pointless, and they expressed no remorse for it whatsoever.

Frightened for their children's lives, the Leopold and Loeb families hired the famous Chicago attorney Clarence Darrow to defend them. Realizing there was no chance to win an acquittal, Darrow pleaded both his clients guilty. Waiving their right to a jury trial, Darrow appealed directly to the judge, John R. Caverly, to spare their lives. Moved by Darrow's plea, Caverly sentenced the young men to life plus 99 years in prison.

While still a young man, Richard Loeb was stabbed to death in a dispute with a fellow prisoner in 1936. Nathan Leopold became a model prisoner and was eventually paroled in 1958. The same year, he published *Life Plus 99 Years,* telling of what he claimed was his rehabilitation in prison.

Soon after being released, Leopold moved to Puerto Rico, where he would spend the rest of his life working with a religious group. The evidence suggests that he was not only reformed, as his book had implied, but converted into a caring human being.

Thurgood Marshall (1908–1993)

Associate justice (1967–1991) of the U.S. Supreme Court.

First as a civil rights attorney and later on the United States Supreme Court, Thurgood Marshall was a champion of the rights of minorities and a bitter enemy of the death penalty.

Born and raised in Baltimore, Maryland, in the days of segregation, Marshall attended the kind of public schools he would later play a major role in desegregating. He received his higher education in the black college system, getting his A.B. from Lincoln University in 1930 and his law degree from Howard in 1933.

He worked in private practice in Maryland for a while, then moved to New York, where he did legal work for the National Association for the Advancement of Colored People (NAACP). By the late 1930s he had joined the NAACP full time, becoming the director of its Legal Defense and Education Fund in 1940. His position with the Fund put him at the center of the legal battle to end segregation, which would come to a head in the 1950s.

It was Marshall who fought and won the historic *Brown v. Board of Education* (1954) case that put an end to legal segregation in public schools. Even more importantly, it signalled an end to the doctrine of "separate but equal" in society at large.

Marshall was appointed to the United States Circuit Court in 1961 and to the position of Solicitor General of the United States—sometimes called the government's lawyer—in 1965. Two years later, President Lyndon Johnson appointed him associate justice of the United States Supreme Court. He was the first black justice ever to sit on the nation's highest court.

Both his personal experience as a black man in the Middle South and his work with the NAACP had made Marshall bitterly aware of the injustices in American society. It also made him more conscious than most of the value of constitutional rights and the need to enforce and expand them. This became his mission on the Court, which he felt was the greatest engine for change in American society.

When it came to the death penalty, Marshall was a committed abolitionist. He opposed capital punishment both as unjust in itself and because he believed that it would inevitably be applied disproportionately to racial minorities, the poor, and the politically unpopular. Marshall's was the leading voice in the *Furman* decision, which struck down all the existing death penalty statutes in 1972. While some of the five concurring justices held out the possibility that new death penalty laws could be drafted that would be constitutional, Marshall disagreed. In his opinion, he insisted that *any* capital punishment law would be cruel and unusual in a modern society.

Marshall was a bitter dissenter when the Court reinstated capital punishment with the *Gregg* decision four years later, and the night the decision was announced, he had a heart attack.[9]

Despite his collapsing health, Marshall remained on the Court for another 15 years. Throughout that time, he and his fellow abolitionist, William Brennan, continued to dissent from every decision that reaffirmed a death sentence, arguing that "the death penalty is in all circumstances cruel and unusual punishment prohibited by the Eighth and Fourteenth Amendments. . . ."

A conservative, retentionist majority dominated the Court during Marshall's last years there. He and Brennan found themselves increasingly isolated as they fought to hold back the Court's drive to facilitate the use of the death penalty. Marshall hoped to remain on the Court until a more liberal president won the White House, who would replace him with someone of similar views. By the summer of 1991, however, he could no longer fulfill his duties, and he retired.

When Bill Clinton, the more liberal president Marshall had hoped for, was finally elected in 1992, he invited Marshall to swear him in at the inauguration ceremony. Unfortunately when the inauguration day came, Marshall was in the hospital and unable to attend. He died the following week. To the end, he considered his inability to persuade a majority of his colleagues to abolish the death penalty the greatest failure of his career on the Court.

President Clinton eulogized Marshall as "a giant in the quest for human rights,"[10] and Law Professor Lawrence Tribe called him "the greatest lawyer of the twentieth century."[11]

Marshall's body was laid in state in the Supreme Court building that had been the site of his greatest triumphs and his most galling failures. It rested on the same bier that had held the body of Abraham Lincoln more than a century before.

William Marwood (1820–1883)

Marwood was the first hangman to popularize the so-called long drop. Before Marwood, people executed by hanging usually died slowly and painfully of strangulation. Marwood, however, always made sure that the trap on the scaffold was high enough, and the rope long enough, that the victim died instantaneously of a broken neck. The long drop required careful calculation and the right knot, or the head would be ripped from the body. Done properly, however, it produced little visible damage to the corpse at all.

Marwood was born in 1820 in Horncastle, Lincolnshire, England, and he died there in 1883, after plying his trade all over England and Scotland. He became a "public executioner" (his own words) relatively late in life, in 1874. He seems to have been a vain man who liked to talk and even joke about his profession. He laid claim to the long drop as though he had invented it himself, although it had originally been recommended by a group of physicians in Ireland.[12]

Marwood was a religious man. He had been a preacher before he became an executioner, and apparently he saw no conflict between his two callings. "I am doing God's work," he once said of his role as public executioner, "according to the Divine command and the law of the British Crown. I do it as a matter of duty and as a Christian."[13]

Albert Pierrepoint (1905–1992)

The most prolific British executioner of the twentieth century.

The son and nephew of hangmen, Albert determined to follow in his relatives' footsteps while he was still a boy. He achieved his ambition while in his twenties, eventually attaining the position of Britain's chief executioner in 1946.

Pierrepoint's first victim in his new post would prove to be the most notorious: William Joyce, better known as Lord Haw Haw, the Brooklyn-born British and American citizen condemned as a traitor for broadcasting Nazi propaganda into England during World War II.

Before he retired in 1956, Pierrepoint claimed credit for executing 450 people, including 17 women. Although he never admitted any guilt for what he had done, he did become an opponent of capital punishment in his retirement. His change of heart was based, at least partly, on his long experience in the trade.

An autobiography, *Executioner: Pierrepoint,* was published in 1974.

William Hubbs Rehnquist (1924–)

Associate justice (1972–1986) and chief justice of the U.S. Supreme Court (1986–).

Born in Milwaukee, Wisconsin, William Rehnquist graduated from Stanford Law School in 1951. He served as law clerk for Supreme Court Justice Robert H. Jackson for two years before moving to Phoenix, Arizona, to practice law. While there, he was extremely active in conservative political affairs, opposing efforts to encourage racial integration in the city.

Rehnquist returned to Washington, D.C., in 1969 to serve as an assistant attorney general for the Supreme Court's Office of Legal Counsel. President Richard Nixon appointed him associate justice of the Court in 1972, and President Ronald Reagan appointed Rehnquist chief justice in 1986.

In both positions, Rehnquist has been a law and order justice, reliably supporting the rights of law enforcement officials over the rights of the accused in most criminal cases. In particular, Rehnquist argues that, although states are required to treat citizens fairly, the restrictions on governmental power laid down in the Bill of Rights do not necessarily apply to them.

Rehnquist has been a staunch and consistent defender of the death penalty. He was a dissenter in the *Furman* decision, and firmly in the majority in *Gregg*. As the more liberal justices aged and left the Court in the 1980s and more conservative justices came onto it, Rehnquist became the head of a solid pro-capital-punishment majority. While he has been enthusiastically joined by such fellow justices as Antonin Scalia, Byron White, and Sandra Day O'Connor, Rehnquist has been the guiding spirit in the recent drive to see that obstacles to the enforcement of the death penalty are removed.

In recent years, the Rehnquist Court has ruled, among other things, that it is permissible to execute teenagers and the mentally retarded. Convinced that condemned criminals and their attorneys have been abusing the system by taking advantage of technical delays, Rehnquist has led a frequently successful effort to streamline appeal procedures in capital cases.

Under his leadership, the Court has shown increasing reluctance to listen to death sentence appeals. Even when the Court has extended constitutional protections to cover new situations, it has refused to make those protections retroactive and apply them to prisoners already under sentence of death. Writing for the majority, for example, Rehnquist has ordered that defendants may not appeal "good faith interpretations of existing precedents made by state courts even though they are shown to be contrary to later decisions."[14] In addition, the Rehnquist Court has refused to allow inmates to appeal to the federal courts on the basis of issues they neglected to raise earlier in state courts, however much merit those issues may have.

It was the Rehnquist Court that fired off an impatient fax to judges in California, ordering them to stop granting stays of the execution of Robert Alton Harris in 1992. It was also Rehnquist who led the 7 to 2 majority denying the right to a new trial to Leonel Herrara in 1993, despite evidence that the condemned man might have been innocent after all.

Rehnquist's determination to remove procedural obstacles to swift and certain execution are applauded by supporters of capital punishment, who feel that criminals have been allowed to escape justice for far too long. The same efforts, however, are criticized by opponents of the death penalty who see them as a potentially fatal attack on the constitutional right of habeas corpus.

Sir Samuel Romilly (1757–1818)

The most important legal reformer in the British Parliament in the early nineteenth century.

Romilly was admitted to the English bar in 1783. He was deeply influenced by the Enlightenment that was taking place on the continent and was particularly intrigued by the ideas of French thinkers like Rousseau. His *Letters Containing an Account of the Late Revolution in France* (1792) welcomed the French Revolution, while his *Thoughts on Executive Justice* (1786) was heavily influenced by Cesare Beccaria's calls for penal reform. Appointed solicitor general in 1806 and later becoming a member of Parliament, he attempted to put Beccaria-inspired reforms into practice.

Romilly was particularly appalled by the excessive use of the death penalty. When he first took office, more than 200 crimes were punishable by death in England, most of them relatively minor offenses. As Jeremy Bentham's chief ally in Parliament, he set out to reduce that number. Although only somewhat successful during his lifetime, his efforts began a legislative process that would lead to the abolition of the death penalty for the vast majority of criminal offenses by the middle of the nineteenth century.

Dr. Benjamin Rush (1745–1813)

"The father of the movement to abolish capital punishment in the United States."[15]

Born in Pennsylvania, Rush was a highly educated man for his time. He received his colonial education at what is now known as Princeton University, then went abroad to complete his studies at the University of Edinburgh in Scotland. Returning to America, he became a professor of chemistry at the College of Philadelphia.

Considered the leading American medical man of his time, he had an enormous influence on the development of medicine in the United States. Among other medical distinctions, he is regarded as the founder of American psychiatry, and he authored the first book on the subject to be published in the United States.

A physician by profession, Rush was a crusading reformer by temperament. Active in the movement for American independence, he was both a signer of the Declaration of Independence and a member of the Continental Congress. During the Revolution itself, he was made surgeon general of the Continental Army.

Even compared to many of his fellow revolutionaries, Rush was a fiercely independent thinker. He took pride in attacking popular ideas that he believed were wrong or misguided. Among them was the traditional practice of executing criminals.

In 1787 Rush presented a talk on the reform of the American criminal justice system at the home of his friend, Benjamin Franklin. He proposed that the new nation being formed should deal with its criminals in an entirely new way. He urged the establishment of a new kind of jail, one that would not just imprison criminals but reform them as well. This was a novel idea in the eighteenth-century United States, but Rush believed that such prisons would not only protect law-abiding citizens from criminals, but they would redeem the criminals themselves and transform them into decent and useful members of society. Rush urged abandonment of the death penalty as a central element of his reforms.

Rush's address was published in the form of an essay entitled *An Enquiry into the Effects of Public Punishments upon Criminals and upon Society*. In 1788 he published a second essay, which dealt in more detail with the specific issue of capital punishment. Entitled *Considerations on the Injustice and Impolicy of Punishing Murder by Death*, it was, in his own words, "the boldest attack" he ever made on any public policy. It aroused a storm of controversy, causing him to publish two revised versions. The final version, entitled *An Enquiry into the Consistency of the Punishment of Murder by Death, With Reason and Revelation*, was published in 1798.[16]

Although the main thrust of Rush's quarrel with capital punishment was religious, he also put forth many secular arguments that have a surprisingly modern ring. Several are still being put forward today by people who base their opposition to capital punishment not on Rush, but on recent psychological and sociological research. According to Philip Mackey, in his book *Voices against Death*, "Rush apparently invented his argument[s] that capital punishment makes convictions harder to obtain, that murderers are usually not hardened criminals likely to murder again, and that the death penalty invites murders by those who want the state to help them commit suicide."[17]

Nicola Sacco (1891–1927) and Bartolomeo Vanzetti (1888–1927)

Anarchists whose execution for participation in a murderous armed robbery raised questions about whether the death penalty was being used as a means of eliminating political enemies of the state.

Nicola Sacco and Bartolomeo Vanzetti were Italian immigrants to the United States. Sacco was a shoe worker and Vanzetti a fish peddler. Both were proud and active anarchists who had been under investigation by the police because of their anti-government political activities even before their 1920 arrest following a bank robbery in South Braintree, Massachussetts. Two people had been killed in the robbery, so the men were charged with murder as well as armed robbery. Both insisted they were innocent of the crime and that they were being railroaded because of their political beliefs.

The trial received an enormous amount of attention, not only in the United States, but in Europe as well. In many people's minds, here and abroad, it was a test of whether the U.S. government could deal fairly with political radicals accused of crime.

People everywhere took sides either for or against Sacco and Vanzetti. Much of the American public was hostile to the defendants, either because they were immigrants or because they were anarchists, or both. The Russian revolution had taken place only a few years before, and many Americans feared that "foreign" communists and anarchists were plotting to stage a similar violent uprising here.

Others firmly believed that the men were innocent. They were suspicious of the state's motives, and regarded the case less as a criminal prosecution than as political persecution. To these observers, the trial seemed obviously unfair and the judge hopelessly prejudiced against the defendants. The jury took practically no time at all to return a verdict of guilty, and the judge seemed delighted to impose a sentence of death.

Tens of thousand of people around the world vehemently protested against the scheduled executions. Among them were a number of famous and influential figures, including the American poet Edna St. Vincent Millay, who carried a sign in one demonstration that read: "Free them and save Massachussetts! American honor dies with Sacco and Vanzetti!" Among those who worked to overturn the death sentences was a man who would later become one of the century's most respected Supreme Court justices, Felix Frankfurter.

The men bore their fate with dignity while they waited in prison for their sentences to be carried out. From his cell, Sacco wrote a letter to his 13-year-old son, Dante. "But remember always, Dante," he wrote, "in the play of happiness, don't you use all for yourself only, but . . . help the weak ones that cry for help. . . ."[18] Vanzetti wrote to the boy as well. "One day you will understand," he told him, "that your father has sacrificed everything dear and sacred to the human heart and soul for his fate in liberty and justice for all."[19] When these touching letters were made public, they only served to deepen the conviction of Sacco and Vanzetti's supporters that the pair were innocent. Men capable of such noble sentiments could not be cold-blooded killers, they insisted.

Despite appeals from around the world, the two men were executed by electric chair in 1927. They continued to protest their innocence and proclaim their beliefs to the end. Sacco called out "Long live anarchy!" in Italian from the electric chair.

Sacco and Vanzetti were only two of a great many condemned prisoners executed despite widespread doubts about their guilt. Still, their deaths haunt the American judicial system more stubbornly than any of the others—more than Chessman's, or the Rosenbergs', or, recently, even Roger Keith Coleman's.

Part of the reason the memory of Sacco and Vanzetti has such power lies in the interest aroused in their case by influential writers and artists who took up their cause at the time. Another part of the reason lies in the strength and character of the two men themselves. Most other executed criminals, whether guilty of the crimes that bring them to death or not, are shady and unpleasant characters at best. Sacco and Vanzetti, on the other hand, were seen as honorable and even noble—men who were ready to live and to die for a cause they believed in with all their hearts, however misguided their belief may have been.

The thought that men like these may have been killed unjustly is especially troubling, even to many who are relatively unconcerned about the fates of most ordinary death row residents.

Henry Schwarzschild (1926–)

One of the leading U.S. campaigners against the death penalty.

Born in Germany, Henry Schwarzschild fled his native country as a young man at the start of World War II. Like many of his fellow refugees from Naziism, he came to the United States. Here, he attended Columbia University, receiving his degree in time to serve with U.S. Counterintelligence during the war. He later served in important research posts with the U.S. State Department and the Rand School of Social Science, and in various positions with organizations such as the International Rescue Committee and the Anti-Defamation League of B'Nai B'rith.

Vitally concerned with social justice, he joined the civil rights movement early, putting his body on the line as well as his professional abilities. He participated in sit-ins in the early 1960s and later served as executive director of the Lawyers Constitutional Defense Committee in the deep South. In the 1970s he was director of the ACLU's Project on Amnesty for Vietnam War Resisters, which helped make it possible for thousands of young Americans to return to their homes. It is the battle against the death penalty, however, that has been his major work.

For years now, Schwarzschild has been one of the nation's most active abolitionists and one of the movement's most prominent voices. He was the founder and first director of the National Coalition to Abolish the Death Penalty (NCADP), which has proven vital to the abolitionist movement in its role as a bridge and clearinghouse for anti-death-penalty groups all over the country. Even while staying active with the NCADP, Schwarzschild served as director of the American Civil Liberties Union Capital Punishment Project until 1992, when his place was taken by Diann Rust-Tierney.

Potter Stewart (1915–1985)

Associate justice (1958–1981) of the U.S. Supreme Court.

Potter Stewart was born and bred in Ohio. People said that it was this Midwestern background that nurtured the common-sense attitude and gift for negotiation he brought with him to the U.S. Supreme Court.

The son of an Ohio Supreme Court judge and one-time mayor of Cincinnati, Stewart was all but predestined for the bench. After graduating from college, he won a fellowship at Cambridge University in England. Returning to the United States, he attended the prestigious Yale Law School, entering the bar in 1941. An extremely promising career as a Wall Street lawyer was interrupted by a stint in the navy during World War II. After returning briefly to Wall Street, he moved back to Cincinnati to follow in his father's footsteps, becoming prominent in both politics and the law.

President Dwight Eisenhower appointed Stewart to the Sixth Circuit Federal Appeals Court in 1954 and to the U.S. Supreme Court in 1958. Stewart was not an ideological judge. He liked to base his rulings on narrow questions of the law rather than on grand constitutional issues. At the same time, he could couch his judicial decisions in no-nonsense language that everyone could understand. Although he might not be able to define pornography, he admitted in one ruling, "I know it when I see it."[20]

Stewart's lack of ideology earned him a reputation as an important and influential swing vote on the Supreme Court. He sometimes voted with the liberals like Marshall, and sometimes with the conservatives like Rehnquist, and often he helped find ways for majorities to solidify in the middle ground between the two. His tendency to be a swing vote was particularly apparent on votes involving the death penalty.

Stewart voted with the majority in *Furman,* helping to strike down the capital punishment laws in 1972. He wrote a separate opinion, though, arguing that it was primarily the capriciousness and arbitrariness of the laws that made them unconstitutional, not the death penalty itself.

When the majority of the Court was ready to reinstate the death penalty in the *Gregg* case in 1976, it was Stewart's negotiating ability and instinct to find compromise that helped them find the way to do it. More than anyone else, Stewart was the architect of the plurality decision that he announced for the Court.[21] For better or worse, that decision laid the foundation for the approach the Court has taken toward the death penalty ever since.

Bartolomeo Vanzetti
(see Nicola Sacco and Bartolomeo Vanzetti)

NOTES

1. Ian Gray and Moira Stanley, *A Punishment in Search of a Crime* (New York: Avon, 1989), 225.

2. David L. Bender and Bruno Leone, et al., eds. *The Death Penalty, Opposing Viewpoints* (St. Paul: Greenhaven, 1986), 68.

3. James Avery Joyce. *Capital Punishment: A World View* (New York: AMS Press, 1961), 27.

4. *Dictionary of American Biography, Vol. III* (New York: Charles Scribner's Sons, 1958), 39.

5. Simon Schama, *Citizens* (New York: Knopf, 1989), 622.

6. Gray and Stanley, 145.

7. Ibid., 143.

8. *Furman v. Georgia,* 408 U.S. 238 (1972).

9. Bob Woodward and Scott Armstrong, *The Brethren: Inside the Supreme Court* (New York: Simon and Schuster, 1979), 441.

10. Judy Keen, "A Giant in the Quest for Human Rights," *USA Today*, 25 January 1993.

11. News reports, CNN Television, 24 January 1993.

12. John Laurence. *A History of Capital Punishment* (New York: Citadel Press, 1960), 47–48.

13. Ibid., 115.

14. *Butler v. McKellar,* 494 U.S. 407 (1990).

15. Hugo Adam Bedau, ed. *The Death Penalty in America* (Chicago: Aldine, 1968), 8.

16. Philip Mackey, *Voices against Death* (New York: Burt Franklin & Company, 1976), 1–2.

17. Ibid., 2.

18. Quoted in Francis Russell's *Tragedy in Dedham* (New York: McGraw-Hill, 1971), 438.

19. Ibid., 439.

20. *Jacobellis v. Ohio,* 378 U.S. 184 (1964).

21. Woodward and Armstrong, 430–441.

5

Facts and Documents

AS WE HAVE SEEN, CAPITAL PUNISHMENT is not merely a social question, but a philosophical and moral issue as well. In this chapter we will look at a variety of materials that, between them, provide a range of perspectives on the capital punishment debate.

The chapter begins with excerpts from some fundamental political documents, both national and international. It moves on to present some historic arguments both for and against capital punishment, the major biblical texts most often referenced in debates over the death penalty, and key U.S. Supreme Court decisions, as well as a variety of other facts and data relating to capital sentencing and executions.

The United States Constitution

The Constitution of the United States is the supreme law of the land. No law, policy, or practice of the federal government or any state is legally valid if it conflicts with the Constitution.

The Constitution is made up of a preamble, seven articles, and 26 amendments. Three of those amendments relate to the death penalty:

Amendment V

No person shall be held to answer for a capital, or otherwise infamous crime, unless on a presentment or indictment of a Grand Jury, except in cases arising in the land or naval forces, or in the militia, when in actual service in time of War or public danger; nor shall any person be subject for the same offence to be twice put in jeopardy of life or limb; nor shall be compelled in any criminal case to be a witness against himself, nor be deprived of life, liberty, or property, without due process of law; nor shall private property be taken for public use, without just compensation.

Amendment VIII

Excessive bail shall not be required, nor excessive fines imposed, nor cruel and unusual punishments inflicted.

Amendment XIV

Section 1. All persons born or naturalized in the United States and subject to the jurisdiction thereof, are citizens of the United States and of the State wherein they reside. No State shall abridge the privileges or immunities of citizens of the United States; nor shall any State deprive any person of life, liberty, or property, without due process of law; nor deny to any person within its jurisdiction the equal protection of the laws. . . .

International Standards

Various international groups and bodies have issued standards regarding the death penalty. They have been included in a number of treaties and other international agreements and resolutions, some of which have been signed by the United States.

Declarations and Resolutions of the United Nations and Other International Bodies

No institution speaks for all the nations of the world, but the United Nations comes as close as any international body can. The UN has never attempted to ban the death penalty outright—far too many of its members are committed to the practice for that. It has made clear, though, in a number of resolutions, that the nations of the world, speaking through the voice of the world's most inclusive international organization, see the abolition of capital punishment as a desirable goal. Excerpts from several U.N. documents follow.

The Universal Declaration of Human Rights
(adopted 10 December 1948)

ARTICLE 3

Everyone has the right to life, liberty, and the security of the person.

Resolution 1984/50 of the UN Economic and Social Council (adopted 25 May 1984 and endorsed by the UN General Assembly in resolution 39/118, adopted without vote, 14 December 1984)

SAFEGUARDS GUARANTEEING PROTECTION OF THE RIGHTS OF THOSE FACING THE DEATH PENALTY

1. In countries which have not abolished the death penalty, capital punishment may be imposed only for the most serious crimes, it being understood that their scope should not go beyond intentional crimes, with lethal or other extremely grave consequences.

2. Capital punishment may be imposed only for a crime for which the death penalty is prescribed by law at the time of its commission, it being understood that if, subsequent to the commission of the crime, provision is made by law for the imposition of a lighter penalty, the offender shall benefit thereby.

3. Persons below 18 years of age at the time of the commission of the crime shall not be sentenced to death, nor shall the death penalty be carried out on pregnant women, or on new mothers or persons who have become insane.

4. Capital punishment may be imposed only when the guilt of the person charged is based upon clear and convincing evidence leaving no room for an alternative explanation of the facts.

5. Capital punishment may only be carried out pursuant to a final judgement rendered by a competent court after legal process which gives all possible safeguards to ensure a fair trial, at least equal to those contained in Article 14 of the International Covenant on Civil and Political Rights,

including the right of anyone suspected of or charged with a crime for which capital punishment may be imposed to adequate legal assistance at all stages of the proceedings.

6. Anyone sentenced to death shall have the right to appeal to a court of higher jurisdiction, and steps should be taken to ensure that such appeals shall become mandatory.

7. Anyone sentenced to death shall have the right to seek pardon, or commutation of sentence; pardon or commutation of sentence may be granted in all cases of capital punishment.

8. Capital punishment shall not be carried out pending any appeal or other recourse procedure or other proceeding relating to pardon or commutation of the sentence.

9. Where capital punishment occurs, it shall be carried out so as to inflict the minimum possible suffering.

United Nations Resolution 32/61, as adopted by the UN General Assembly 8 December 1977

CAPITAL PUNISHMENT

The General Assembly,
Having regard to Article 3 of the Universal Declaration of Human Rights, which affirms everyone's right to life, and Article 6 of the International Covenant on Civil and Political Rights, which also affirms the right to life as inherent to every human being. . . .

1. Reaffirms that, as established by the General Assembly in resolution 2857 (XXVI) and by the Economic and Social Council in resolutions 1574 (L), 1745 (LIV) and 1930 (LVIII), the main objective to be pursued in the field of capital punishment is that of progressively restricting the number of offences for which the death penalty may be imposed with a view to the desirability of abolishing this punishment. . . .

American Convention on Human Rights

ARTICLE FOUR: RIGHT TO LIFE

1. Every person has the right to have his life respected. This right shall be protected by law and, in general, from the moment of conception. No one shall be arbitrarily deprived of his life.

2. In countries that have not abolished the death penalty, it may be imposed only for the most serious crimes and pursuant to a final judgement rendered by a competent court and in accordance with a law establishing such punishment, enacted prior to the commission of the crime.

The application of such punishment shall not be extended to crimes to which it does not presently apply.

3. The death penalty shall not be reestablished in the states that have abolished it.

4. In no case shall capital punishment be inflicted for political offences or related common crimes.

5. Capital punishment shall not be imposed upon persons who, at the time the crime was committed, were under 18 years of age or over 70 years of age; nor shall it be applied to pregnant women.

6. Every person condemned to death shall have the right to apply for amnesty, pardon, or commutation of sentence, which may be granted in all cases. Capital punishment shall not be imposed while such a petition is pending decision by the competent authority.

The following historic protocol was the first binding agreement between nations to require the abolition of the death penalty for ordinary crimes. It needed ratification by at least five member states of the Council of Europe to go into effect. The first state to ratify it was Denmark, on 1 December 1983, followed over the next two years by Austria, Sweden, Spain, and Luxembourg, bringing the protocol into effect in 1985. It has since been formally ratified by several other members of the Council as well.

Protocol Number Six of the Convention for the Protection of Human Rights and Fundamental Freedoms, as opened for signature on 28 April 1983

The member States of the Council of Europe, signatory to this Protocol to the Convention for the Protection of Human Rights and Fundamental Freedoms, signed at Rome on 4 November 1950. . . .
    Considering that the evolution that has occurred in several member States of the Council of Europe expresses a general tendency in favour of abolition of the death penalty;
    Have agreed as follows:

ARTICLE 1 The death penalty shall be abolished. No one shall be condemned to such penalty or executed.

ARTICLE 2 A State may make provision in its law for the death penalty in respect of acts committed in time of war or of imminent threat of war; such penalty shall be applied only in the instances laid down in the law and in accordance with its provisions. The States shall communicate to the Secretary General of the Council of Europe the relevant provisions of that law.

Two Historic Views on Capital Punishment

No one has had a greater influence on the capital punishment issue than the eighteenth-century Italian jurist, Cesare Beccaria. It was Beccaria, more than anyone else, who launched the modern debate on the subject with the publication of his famous essay.

Excerpts from Cesare Beccaria's
An Essay on Crimes and Punishments,
as published in England in 1775

The useless profusion of punishments, which has never made men better, induces me to enquire, whether the punishment of death be really just or useful in a well governed state? What right, I ask, have men to cut the throats of their fellow-creatures? Certainly not that on which the sovereignty and laws are founded. The laws, as I have said before, are only the sum of the smallest portions of the private liberty of each individual, and represent the general will, which is the aggregate of that of each individual. Did any one ever give to others the right of taking away his life? Is it possible, that in the smallest portions of the liberty of each, sacrificed to the good of the public, can be contained the greatest of all good, life? If it were so, how shall it be reconciled to the maxim which tells us, that a man has no right to kill himself? Which he certainly must have, if he could give it away to another.

But the punishment of death is not authorized by any right; for I have demonstrated that no such right exists. It is therefore a war of a whole nation against a citizen, whose destruction they consider as necessary, or useful to the general good. But if I can further demonstrate, that it is neither necessary nor useful, I shall have gained the cause of humanity.

ONLY ONE REASON FOR THE DEATH PENALTY

The death of a citizen cannot be necessary, but in one case. When, though deprived of his liberty, he has such power and connections as may endanger the security of the nation; when his existence may produce a dangerous revolution in the established form of government. But even in this case, it can only be necessary when a nation is on the verge of recovering or losing its liberty; or in times of absolute anarchy, when the disorders themselves hold the place of laws. But in a reign of tranquillity; in a form of government approved by the united wishes of the nation; in a state well fortified from enemies without, and supported by strength within, and opinion, perhaps more efficacious; where all power is lodged in the hands of a true sovereign; where riches can purchase pleasures and not authority, there can be no necessity for taking away the life of a subject.

If the experience of all ages be not sufficient to prove, that the punishment of death has never prevented determined men from injuring society; if the example of the Romans; if twenty years reign of Elizabeth, empress of Russia, in which she gave the fathers of their country an example more illustrious than many conquests bought with blood; if, I say, all this be not sufficient to persuade mankind, who always suspect the voice of reason, and who choose rather to be led by authority, let us consult human nature in proof of my assertion.

It is not the intenseness of the pain that has the greatest effect on the mind, but its continuance; for our sensibility is more easily and more powerfully affected by weak but repeated impressions, than by a violent, but momentary, impulse. The power of habits is universal over every sensible being. As it is by that we learn to speak, to walk, and to satisfy our necessities, so the ideas of morality are stamped on our minds by repeated impressions. The death of a criminal is a terrible but momentary spectacle, and therefore a less efficacious method of deterring others, than the continued example of a man deprived of his liberty, condemned, as a beast of burthen, to repair, by his labour, the injury he has done to society. *If I commit such a crime,* says the spectator to himself, *I shall be reduced to that miserable condition for the rest of my life.* A much more powerful preventative than the fear of death, which men always behold in distant obscurity.

THE EFFECT OF VIOLENCE IS MOMENTARY

The terrors of death make so slight an impression, that it has not force enough to withstand the forgetfulness natural to mankind, even in the most essential things; especially when assisted by the passions. Violent impressions surprise us, but their effect is momentary; they are fit to produce those revolutions which instantly transform a common man into a Lacedaemonian or a Persian; but in a free and quiet government they ought to be rather frequent than strong.

The execution of a criminal is, to the multitude, a spectacle, which in some excites compassion mixed with indignation. These sentiments occupy the mind much more than that salutary terror which the laws endeavour to inspire; but in the contemplation of continued suffering, terror is the only, or a least predominant sensation. The severity of a punishment should be just sufficient to excite compassion in the spectators, as it is intended more for them than for the criminal.

A punishment, to be just, should have only that degree of severity which is sufficient to deter others. Now there is no man, who upon the least reflection, would put in competition the total and perpetual loss of his liberty, with the greatest advantages he could possibly obtain in consequence of a crime. Perpetual slavery, then, has in it all that is necessary to deter the most hardened and determined, as much as the punishment of death. I say it has more. There are many who can look at death with intrepidity and firmness; some through fanaticism, and others through vanity, which attends us even to the grave; others from a desperate resolution, either to get rid of their misery, or cease to live: but fanaticism and vanity forsake the criminal in slavery, in chains and fetters, in an iron cage; and despair seems rather the beginning than the end of their misery. The mind, by collecting itself and uniting all its force, can, for a moment, repel assailing grief; but its most vigorous efforts are insufficient to resist perpetual wretchedness.

In all nations, where death is used as a punishment, every example supposes a new crime committed. Whereas in perpetual slavery, every criminal affords a frequent and lasting example; and if it be necessary that men should often be witnesses of the power of the laws, criminals should often be put to death; but this supposes a frequency of crimes; and from hence this punishment will cease to have its effect, so that it must be useful and useless at the same time.

SLAVERY AND THE DEATH PENALTY

I shall be told, that perpetual slavery is as painful a punishment as death, and therefore as cruel. I answer, that if all the miserable moments in the life of a slave were collected into one point, it would be a more cruel punishment than any other; but these are scattered through his whole life, whilst the pain of death exerts all its force in a moment. There is also another advantage in the punishment of slavery, which is, that it is more terrible to the spectator than to the sufferer himself; for the spectator considers the sum of all his wretched moments, whilst the sufferer, by the misery of the present, is prevented from thinking of the future. All evils are increased by the imagination, and the sufferer finds resources and consolations, of which the spectators are ignorant; who judge by their own sensibility of what passes in a mind, by habit grown callous to misfortune.

. . . The punishment of death is pernicious to society, from the example of barbarity it affords. If the passions, or the necessity of war, have taught men to shed the blood of our fellow creatures, the laws, which intended to moderate the ferocity of mankind, should not increase it by examples of barbarity, the more horrible, as this punishment is usually attended with formal pageantry. Is it not absurd, that the laws, which detest and punish homicide, should, in order to prevent murder, publicly commit murder themselves? What are the true and most useful laws? Those compacts and conditions which all would propose and observe, in those moments when private interest is silent, or combined with that of the public.

. . . .

What are the natural sentiments of every person concerning the punishment of death? We may read them in the contempt and indignation with which everyone looks on the executioner, who is nevertheless an innocent executor of the public will; a good citizen, who contributes to the advantage of society, the instrument of the general security within, as good as soldiers are without. What then is the origin of this contradiction? Why is this sentiment of mankind indelible, to the scandal of reason? It is, that in a secret corner of the mind, in which the original impressions of nature are still preserved, men discover a sentiment which tells them, that their lives are not lawfully in the power of any one, but of that necessity only, which with its iron scepter rules the universe.

. . . .

If it be objected, that almost all the nations in all ages have punished certain crimes with death, I answer, that the force of these examples vanishes, when opposed to truth, against which prescription is urged in vain. The history of mankind is an immense sea of errors, in which few obscure truths may here and there be found.

But human sacrifices have also been common in almost all nations. That some societies only, either few in number, or for a very short time, abstained from the punishment of death, is rather favourable to my argument, for such is the fate of great truths, that their duration is only as a flash of lightning in the long and dark night of error. The happy time is not yet arrived, when truth, as falsehood has been hitherto, shall be the portion of the greatest number.

In the nineteenth century, the anti-capital-punishment and antislavery causes were often championed by the same people. A similar religious fervor prompted many of their leaders to attack what they saw as twin evils—two practices that were not only unjust but un-Christian.

One exception to this rule was the Reverend George Cheever, a popular preacher who may have been the most influential defender of the death penalty in the nineteenth century. Cheever was himself a zealous Christian reformer—and an abolitionist when it came to slavery—and so was able to challenge the opponents of capital punishment on their own terms. What may be his best summary of the pro-death-penalty position appeared in the December 1881 issue of the *North American Review*.

Rev. George Cheever: The Death Penalty

The basis of argument for the death penalty against murder is found, along with the reason given for it, in Gen. v. 6: "Whoso sheddeth man's blood, by man shall his blood be shed; for in the image of God made he man." Nothing is plainer, by consent of the most accurate critics and scholars, than the translation and interpretation of this sentence. 1. The Creator is its author. 2. It is his benevolent statute for man's protection against the violence of man, because man is made in the image of God. 3. It being an acknowledged legal axiom that a law is in force while the reason for it remains, its universal and perpetual obligations are demonstrated. 4. The origin, institution, sanction, and right of human governments with penal inflictions are here determined by authority of the Creator, and not by any imagined compacts of mankind. 5. The nature and requisitions of justice, righteousness, equity, duty, expediency are in the terms of this legislation. The social obligations of mankind, and all governmental responsibilities, being referred exclusively to the will and word of the Creator, and the dictate of a conscience toward him, there is no other possible safeguard from man's evil passions. 6. The grasp of this law—thou shalt love thy fellow creature, in God's image, as thyself— is upon human interests, temporal and eternal, as revealed by God. Obedience to it would insure the highest and most perfect protection of all races in virtue and happiness. It is the very beginning of God's humane legislation for the new world, after a thousand years' demonstration of incurable hereditary depravity in the old, and the consequent perversion and abuse of God's lenity toward Cain, filling the earth with violence. 7. Every state, being a trustee for God and the people, is bound to see to it that the people for whom God's whole law is promulgated are taught these truths, with the consequent sacredness of law and conscience toward God, were it only for the security of men's households and their own lives. If God's covenant with mankind had been kept conscientiously by mankind, there never would have been another murderer on earth from the time of the deluge to this day, nor even a religious persecutor. For God that made the world hath made of one blood all nations of men, and hath determined the times and bounds of their habitation, with this intent, that they should seek after God, and worship him in freedom, as being his offspring, who giveth to all life, and breath, and all things. And the powers that be are ordained of God, whose minister in an earthly government, prophetic of the divine, beareth not the sword in vain. 8. The death penalty was to be restricted to the crime of murder, and thence all penalties were to be graduated according to the offense, with the same unmistakable regard to the divinely constituted rights of family, character, property, and person, and the entire freedom and independence of a conscience toward God. With the same extreme of carefulness and exact justice, and for the perfection of its efficacy, the penalty was to be guarded from any possible mistake in its application through reliance on merely circumstantial evidence. Thus the legislation was as perfect as the benevolence and justice of God could make it.

Evidently there was required, in the foundations of a new social state, a penalty against murder to the last degree dreadful and deterring, fatal and final, with all the powers of human government ordained and pledged for its execution. God himself would make Cain's own dread of being murdered, through all men's sense of justice, inextinguishable, by having it established as the first law of humanity that, if any man destroyed another's life, his own life should go for it. And all the fiends of remorse, detection, and a righteous vengeance, with all the energies and vigilance of human selfishness itself, aghast with horror, should combine to arrest and exterminate the miscreant. This uproar of indignation and wrath was what Cain himself expected, when driven forth from the presence and protection of God.

The penalty is restricted to murder, though some crimes against personal rights are equivalent to murder, and produce it, and even worse, as, for example, slavery, and, in consequence, all the infinite horrors of the slave trade. And, therefore, there shines forth, illuminating and illustrating the law against murder, like another sun risen on mid-noon, that other and later unparalleled Hebrew law in behalf of the enslaved: "He that stealeth a man and selleth him, or if he be found in his hands, he shall surely be put to death." This is the polarized light of the first penalty, crystallizing for all generations the meaning and insurance of the primal blood-statute; for no man in his senses will pretend that this grand edict of God's protecting and avenging mercy was never intended as a law, but was merely a prediction of the prevalence of legal murder. And so of the statute, in such absolute, imperative terms: "Ye shall take no satisfaction for the life of a murderer which is guilty of death, but he shall be surely put to death." (Num. xxxv. 31.) There was this assurance of the death penalty laid upon every generation. It grew into one of the ever-present Eumenides in men's minds, as in the Book of Proverbs, "A man that doth violence to the blood of any person shall flee to the pit; let no man stay him." Hence, also the careful and just definitions of what constitutes a murderer, and the requirement of witnesses as to the fact of the crime, evil intention being always essential, and mere circumstantial evidence not to be relied upon.

Malice aforethought once proved, the crime is demonstrated, and nothing shall save the murderer, not even the city of refuge provided by God himself for a just trial, nor the intervention of any pardoning or interceding power, nor the altar of God. "Thou shalt take the murderer from mine altar, that he may die." (Ex. xxi. 14.) If not, if the murderer is let off with his life, then the whole land remains guilty, and the blood of the murdered man crieth unto God from the ground; for the primal curse is on this crime against God's image in mankind, and no atonement or restitution can be made for it by man; none shall be accepted.

This is the secret of some of the most terrific tragedies of retribution by the Divine Vengeance otherwise so unaccountable, but as startling and warning for nations as for individuals. (See II. Sam. xxi. 1-14. See, also, the awful charge laid upon Solomon by David on his death-bed, II. Kings ii. 5,6,31,33.) These are illustrative instances of that profound intuitive sense of the sacredness of retributive justice, manifested by the inhabitants of Melita in the case of Paul. "No doubt this is a murderer, whom, though he hath escaped the sea, yet . . . —divine vengeance—suffereth not to live." This is the wonderful inspiration of similar classic utterances, so abundant, solemn, and familiar in the loftiest heathen tragedians and philosophers, whose beliefs in the providence of a just and righteous God were shared by these uncultured but thoughtful barbarians.

This law is the perfection of heavenly mercy itself, taking all right of revenge away from individuals and reserving the retribution for injuries as belonging to God's own attribute of impartial universal justice. The Sermon on the Mount is not more entirely God's law of love for all mankind than was the statute given through Noah for the whole world's good a covenant of divine wisdom for the education of the world in righteousness. It sets forgiveness in the heart of every human being, and proclaims revenge as murder. So the handwriting of God in the rainbow binding the storm was but the prophecy and prelude of that eternal melody in the song of the angels, "Glory to God in the highest, on earth peace, good-will to men," and of that celestial doxology, belonging to the perfection of all religion, in the worship of faultless prayer, "For thine is the kingdom, the power and the glory, forever. Amen." As everything needful for mankind to ask is in our Lord's Prayer, so in that august, comprehensive transaction of God with Noah there was the perfection of all moral discipline, and just and peace-assuring criminal jurisprudence, by which men needed to be ruled on earth and educated for citizenship in heaven.

Thus, all retributive punishment, and all the securities and arrangements of God for it, are a concentration of all the lessons and energies of true moral discipline. All right training of the mind, the accurate tracing of consequences, an equitable connection of cause and event, and all disposal of awards, all retributions for guilt, must be grounded, first of all, in absolute justice. Otherwise, if utility alone were wisdom, and men the judges, the world's Caiaphases of expediency would become its glorified statesmen and saviours.

Now, the impossibility for any but an Omniscient Being to know and measure the absolute desert of every action, throws the whole power and right of governmental retribution upon the revealed authority and will of God, making government itself a divine, paternal, protecting, educating institution, maintaining its permanence and right by a conscience in the people instructed toward God. The knowledge of God's law is in such education, securing obedience, independence, liberty, prosperity, and whatsoever things are true, honest, just, pure, lovely, and of good report. The God of peace is in and with such a socialism, and not the savageness and selfishness of the survival of the fittest. And this is the mighty educating power of law proceeding from the bosom of God as the Father of his intelligent creatures, and acknowledged and executed by human governments.

The efficacy of the penalty against murder can be demonstrated (1st) by restricting it to murder, and (2d) by making it immutable and certain. The man who murders another kills himself. When the most hardened villain is made sure of that, who will strike the blow? Make the penalty exceptional and inevitable, as it ought to be, and murder would be unknown under a government of infallible justice. The divine edict would be found of such deterring efficacy that the government would never need to execute it. The known certainty of the penalty would put a stop to the crime.

But the certainty that a murderer cannot at any rate be punished with death would inevitably increase the crime, presenting such a powerful temptation to murder in self-defense, during the commission of any other crime whatever. This would make murderers out of common villains. It would tempt the midnight burglar even to begin his work of robbery even with assassination for security in the process, and then to complete it, double-locked from discovery by the death of all the witnesses.

The law of God says to the criminal, Become a murderer and you are lost. The abolition of the penalty says, Murder, and you are saved. The removal of the dreaded penalty holds out an inducement so diabolical to the highest crime, that it seems incredible that any humane form of socialism should entertain it for a moment. You may save your own life, it says, by killing the witnesses against you. You can only be imprisoned, even if you kill; but if anyone tries to kill you, you have the right to kill him. You may even escape condemnation, if tried, by the plea of sudden insanity, into which the threat of death and the desire to escape are affirmed to have driven you.

Kill, and you may be defended, even by charge of the judge, and verdict of the jury, on the ground of sudden, irresistible frenzy, or delirium from intoxication, and therefore not punishable. But the stealing of a million dollars is never thus protected; a well-planned burglary, never. Therefore the assassin has the advantage. The killing

of the owner of the money may be a sudden madness; it may even be
argued that it was accidental, or in self-defense, without intention to
kill, and therefore not punishable: see the trial of Webster, for the
murder of Parkman; also the case of Colt. If the owner had chosen,
he might have saved his life by the sacrifice of his property, and so
prevented the murder. By attempting to defend his property, he has
compelled the burglar to become a murderer, because that crime was
the safest—an insurance against punishment, all things considered,
having made it profitable.

Thus, but too surely the abolition of the death penalty would
offer a recompense to the highest criminal sagacity and boldness. And
the more hardened the criminal may have become, through the laxity
of law and the absence of any appeal to conscience and to God, the
more the law defends him, in case of any midnight conflict; and he
knows this beforehand, and reasons accordingly. If he breaks into a
house, and stabs its sleeping owner, that he may not testify against
him, his victim is abandoned by the law to the death-blow of the
murderer, who secures his own life by taking that of the sleeper, while
the assassin is as effectively protected as if a reward of his ferocity had
been guaranteed.

Then, again, the moment the murderer is being tried for his life,
the sympathies of the public and the press are moved in his behalf, so
that even the sternest jury feels the impulse; and, if they convict,
extenuating circumstances are pleaded; and even if the murderer is
sentenced, petitions for reprieve, for a new trial, for pardon, for
commutation of the punishment, are gotten up, and powerful reasons
of humanity are urged, which, if resisted by the Governor, bring
upon him and upon the law itself the accusation of being the actual
murderers.

And the more effectively God's law and a future final retribution
are denied, or obscured in the murderer's consciousness, by his never
having heard of these truths in the common schools through which he
graduated, and by the legal and social habit of denying the authority
of the Scriptures of God over both government and people (a habit
which the exclusion of positive religion from the state, its constitutions,
and its schools, fosters from childhood), the more rational and
righteous it appears, in his own view, to take care of only himself, no
matter what becomes of others. He has never been taught that God
requires murder to be punished by death, much less that there is an
endless retribution, in another world, for crime unrepented of in this.

Had the state done its duty in his education, he would never have
been a murderer. It is moral assassination by the state to have let him
grow up in such brutality. A law so benevolent and illuminating as
that of God against murder, with its very reason grounded in the
immortality of man and his accountability to God, and his obligations

to love his fellow-man in God's image, binds the government to teach its whole meaning, and to proclaim it with all the light thrown upon it from God's successive revelations, from the precedents broadening down through ages, and from the final teachings of Christ. Government, in assuming the authority to punish, is bound to flash the whole lightning of the statute to the uttermost depths of society, till its divine meaning penetrates the entire mass.

To withhold such instruction, and thus educate the masses in ignorance both of God's claims and care, and then and thus to apply the penalty of death for crime, is at once such contempt of God, and such a process of cruelty and despotism against man, as would make government an agency of perdition. The acknowledgment of responsibility to God for the protection of human life, and for the enlightenment and freedom of the conscience, is incontrovertibly, therefore, the duty of all governments. Law is thus enthroned in God, and God in law; and the state, for insurance of its own permanence and usefulness, must wear its appointed seal and robes of majesty, as "a power ordained of God," proclaiming that it maintains an authority received from God, by enlightened conscience of its citizens toward God. This is the only perfect security for human freedom. The law, without such education of the people, and without the appeal to God, becomes a defiance and violation of his will. Its efficacy depends on its divine sanction being taught, and necessitates that teaching by the state. How otherwise can any government be honest, or any of its penalties be just, humane, and reformatory?

Immediately after the dreadful murder of our revered and beloved Lincoln, President Garfield, then a member of the United States Congress, delivered in New York an address on the duty of the Government and the people, closing with these memorable words: "Love is at the front of the throne of God; but justice and judgment, with inexorable dread, follow behind. This nation is too great to look for mere revenge; but for the good of the future I would do everything."

In the United States, amidst increasing perils from the socialism of ignorant masses, annually multiplying by millions; with all conflicting infidel speculations and political theories, from Nihilism to Mormonism, let loose, and sensual and intoxicating habits unrestrained; with the suffrage universal, and violent factions, and strifes for office, gain, and power universal also; with scientific dynamites of revenge inviting every disappointed villain's handling—the proposed abolition of the divine law against murder would be more inhuman, reckless, and unjust than it would be to make a breach in one of the dikes in Holland, letting in the sea. God proposes to abolish the crime; man to abolish the penalty. God seeks our deliverance from sin; man our evasion of its consequences. Self-government under God is heaven. Self-government without God is anarchy and hell. Which will we choose?

Biblical References Used in the Debate over the Death Penalty

Rev. Cheever is not the only person to base his or her position on the death penalty on Scripture. In the United States, the moral debate over capital punishment has always had a distinctly religious flavor. Those on both sides have traditionally used both the Hebrew Bible and the Christian New Testament as authority for their beliefs. The following are the passages most often quoted in the death penalty debate.

The Hebrew Bible

And Cain talked with Abel his brother: and it came to pass, when they were in the field, that Cain rose up against Abel his brother, and slew him.

And the LORD said unto Cain, Where is Abel thy brother? And he said, I know not; Am I my brother's keeper?

And he said, What hast thou done? The voice of thy brother's blood crieth unto me from the ground.

And now art thou cursed from the earth, which hath opened her mouth to receive thy brother's blood from thy hand:

When thou tillest the ground, it shall not henceforth yield unto thee, her strength; a fugitive and a vagabond shalt thou be in the earth.

And Cain said unto the LORD, My punishment is greater than I can bear.

Behold, thou hast driven me out this day from the face of the earth; and from thy face shall I be hid; and I shall be a fugitive and a vagabond in the earth; and it shall come to pass, that everyone that findeth me shall slay me.

And the LORD said unto him, Therefore whosoever slayeth Cain, vengeance shall be taken on him sevenfold. And the LORD set a mark upon Cain, lest any finding him should kill him.

And Cain went out from the presence of the LORD, and dwelt in the land of Nod, on the east of Eden.

(Genesis 4:8–16)

Whoso sheddeth man's blood, by man shall his blood be shed, for in the image of God made he man.

(Genesis 9:6)

Thou shalt not kill.

(Exodus 20:13)

He that smiteth a man, so that he die, shall be surely put to death.

(Exodus 21:12)

But, if a man come presumptuously upon his neighbor, to slay him with guile; thou shalt take him from mine altar, that he may die.

And he that smiteth his father, or his mother, shall be surely put to death.

And he that stealeth a man, and selleth him, or if he be found in his hand, he shall surely be put to death. And he that curseth his father, or his mother, shall be surely put to death.

(Exodus 21:14–17)

If men strive, and hurt a woman with child, so that her fruit depart from her, and yet no mischief follow; he shall be surely punished, according as the woman's husband shall lay upon him; and he shall pay as the judges determine.

And if any mischief follow, then thou shalt give life for life,
Eye for eye, tooth for tooth, hand for hand, foot for foot,
Burning for burning, and wound for wound, stripe for stripe.

(Exodus 21:22–25)

If an ox gore a man or woman that they die; then the ox shall be surely stoned, and his flesh shall not be eaten; but the owner of the ox shall be quit;

But if the ox were wont to push with his horn in time past, and it hath been testified to its owner, and he hath not kept him in, but that he hath killed a man or a woman; the ox shall be stoned, and his own also shall be put to death.

If there be laid on him a sum of money, then he shall give, for the ransom of his life, whatsoever is laid upon him.

(Exodus 21: 28–30)

Thou shalt not suffer a witch to live.

(Exodus 22:18)

Whosoever lieth with a beast shall surely be put to death.

(Exodus 22:19)

He that sacrificeth unto any god, save unto the LORD only, he shall be utterly destroyed.

(Exodus 22:20)

Ye shall keep the sabbath therefore, for it is holy unto you: everyone that defileth it shall surely be put to death: for whosoever doeth any work therein, that soul shall be cut off from among his people.

Six days may work be done; but in the seventh is the sabbath of rest, holy to the LORD: whosoever doeth any work in the sabbath day, he shall surely be put to death.

(Exodus 31:14–15)

And he that blasphemeth the name of the LORD, he shall surely be put to death, and all the congregation shall certainly stone him: as well the stranger as he that is born in the land, when blasphemeth the name of the LORD, shall be put to death.

And he that killeth any man shall surely be put to death.

(Leviticus 24:16–17)

Whoso killeth any person, the murderer shall be put to death by the mouth of witnesses: but one witness shall not testify against any person to cause him to die.

Moreover, ye shall take no satisfaction for the life of a murderer, which is guilty of death; but he shall be surely put to death.

(Numbers 35:31–32)

So ye shall not pollute the land wherein ye are; for blood it defileth the land: and the land cannot be cleansed of the blood that is shed therein, but by the blood of him that shed it.

(Numbers 35:33)

If thy brother, the son of thy mother, or thy son, or thy daughter, or the wife of thy bosom, or thy friend, which is as thine own soul, entice thee secretly, saying, Let us go and serve other gods, which thou hast not known, thou, nor thy fathers:

Namely, of the gods of the people which are round about you, nigh unto thee, or far off from thee, from the one end of the earth even unto the other end of the earth;

Thou shalt not consent unto him, nor hearken unto him; neither shall thine eye pity him, neither shalt thou spare, neither shalt thou conceal him;

But thou shalt surely kill him; thine hand shall be first upon him to put him to death, and afterwards the hand of all the people.

And thou shalt stone him with stones, that he die; because he hath sought to thrust thee away from the LORD thy God, which brought thee out of the land of Egypt, from the house of bondage.

(Deuteronomy 13:6–10)

That innocent blood be not shed in the land, which the LORD thy God giveth thee for an inheritance, and so blood be upon thee.

But if any man hate his neighbor, and lie in wait for him, and rise up against him, and smite him mortally that he die, and fleeth into one of these cities:

Then the elders of his city shall send and fetch him thence, and deliver him into the hand of the avenger of blood, that he may die.

Thine eye shall not pity him, but thou shalt put away the guilt of innocent blood from Israel, that it may go well with thee.

(Deuteronomy 19:10–13)

And thine eye shall not pity; but life shall go for life, eye for eye, tooth for tooth, hand for hand, foot for foot.

(Deuteronomy 19:21)

But if this thing be true, and the tokens of virginity be not found for the damsel:

Then they shall bring out the damsel to the door of her father's house, and the men of her city shall stone her with stones that she die; because she hath wrought folly in Israel, to play the whore in her father's house: so shall thou put evil away from among you.

If a man be found lying with a woman married to an husband, then they shall both of them die, both the man that lay with the woman, and the women: so shalt thou put evil away from Israel.

If a damsel that is a virgin be betrothed unto an husband, and a man find her in the city, and lie with her;

Then ye shall bring them both out unto the gate of that city, and ye shall stone them with stones that they die; the damsel, because she cried not, being in the city; and the man, because he hath humbled his neighbor's wife: so thou shalt put evil from among you.

But if a man find a betrothed damsel in the field, and the man force her, and lie with her; then the man only that lay with her shall die:

But unto the damsel thou shalt do nothing; there is in the damsel no sin worthy of death. . . .

(Deuteronomy 22:20–26)

The New Testament

Ye have heard that it was said by them of old time, Thou shalt not kill: and whosoever shall kill shall be in danger of the judgment:

But I say unto you, That whosoever is angry with his brother without a cause, shall be in danger of the judgment: and whosoever shall say to his brother, Raca, shall be in danger of the council: but whosoever shall say, Thou fool, shall be in danger of hell fire.

(Matthew 5:21, 22)

Ye have heard that it hath been said, An eye for an eye, and a tooth for a tooth:

But I say unto you, That ye resist not evil; but whosoever shall smite thee on thy right cheek, turn to him the other also.

(Matthew 5:38, 39)

And behold, one of them, which were with Jesus, stretched out his hand and drew his sword, and struck a servant of the high priest's, and smote off his ear.

Then said Jesus unto him, Put up again thy sword into his place: for all they that take the sword, shall perish with the sword.

(Matthew 26:51, 52)

And the scribes and Pharisees brought unto him a woman taken in adultery: and when they had set her in the midst, they say unto him, Master, this woman was taken in adultery, in the very act.

Now Moses in the law commanded us that such should be stoned: but what sayest thou?

This they said, tempting him, that they might have to accuse him. But Jesus stooped down, and with his finger wrote on the ground, as though he heard them not.

So when they continued asking him, he lifted up himself, and said unto them, He that is without sin among you, let him first cast a stone at her.

And again he stooped down, and wrote on the ground.

And they which heard it, being convicted by their own conscience, went out one by one, beginning at the eldest, even unto the last, and Jesus was left alone, and the woman standing in the midst.

When Jesus had lifted up himself, and saw none but the woman, he said unto her, Woman, where are those thine accusers? Hath no man condemned thee?

She said, No man, Lord. And Jesus said unto her, Neither do I condemn thee; go, and sin no more.

Then spake Jesus again unto them, saying, I am the light of the world: he that followeth me shall not walk in darkness, but shall have the light of life.

(John 8:3–12)

Dearly beloved, avenge not yourselves; but rather, give place unto wrath: for it is written, Vengeance is mine; I will repay, saith the Lord.

(Romans 12:19)

For rulers are not a terror to good works, but to the evil. Wilt thou then not be afraid of the power? Do that which is good, and thou shalt have praise of the same:

For he is the minister of God to thee for good. But if thou do that which is evil, be afraid; for he beareth not the sword in vain: for he is the minister of God, a revenger to execute wrath upon him that doeth evil.

Wherefore, ye must needs be subject, not only for wrath, but also for conscience sake.

(Romans 13:3–5)

A Lawyer's Plea

When the famous defense attorney Clarence Darrow undertook to save the lives of Nathan Leopold and Richard Loeb, there was no doubt that they were guilty of the murder of a 14-year-old boy named Bobby Franks. Seeing no hope for an acquittal, Darrow had them plead guilty. What was more, he decided to waive their right to a trial by jury and place their fates solely in the hands of the sitting judge, John R. Caverly. The plea he directed to Judge Caverly was not a legal argument, but a passionate appeal against the death penalty itself. By all accounts, it was one of the most effective speeches ever given in a courtroom. It was reported that it brought tears even to the judge's eyes, who proceeded to sentence the two young men to life plus 99 years in prison.

Clarence Darrow: Plea to the Judge for the Lives of Nathan Leopold and Richard Loeb (excerpts)

Your honor, it has been almost three months since the great responsibility of this case was assumed by my associates and myself. I

am willing to confess that it has been three months of great anxiety—
a burden which I gladly would have been spared excepting for my
feelings of affection toward some of the members of one of these
unfortunate families. This responsibility is almost too great for anyone
to assume, but we lawyers can no more choose than the court can
choose.

Our anxiety over this case has not been due to the facts that are
connected with this most unfortunate affair, but to the almost unheard-
of publicity it has received; to the fact that newspapers all over this
country have been giving it space such as they have almost never
before given to any case. The fact that day after day the people of
Chicago have been regaled with stories of all sorts about it, until
almost every person has formed an opinion.

And when the public is interested and demands a punishment
no matter what the offense, great or small, it thinks of only one
punishment, and that is death.

It may not be a question that involves the taking of human life; it
may be a question of pure prejudice alone; but when the public speaks
as one man it thinks only of killing.

. . . .

We have said to the public and to this court that neither the
parents, nor the friends, nor the attorneys would want these boys
released. That they are as they are. Unfortunate though it be, it is
true, and those closest to them know perfectly well that they should
not be released, and that they should be permanently isolated from
society. We have said that, and we mean it. We are asking this court to
save their lives, which is the least and most a judge can do.

We did plead guilty before Your Honor because we were afraid to
submit our case to a jury. I would not for a moment deny to this court
or to this community a realization of the serious danger we were in
and how perplexed we were before we took this more unusual step.

I can tell Your Honor why.

I have found that years and experience with life tempers one's
emotions and make him more understanding of his fellow-man. . . .
I am aware that as one grows older he is less critical. He is not so
sure. He is inclined to make some allowance for his fellow-man. I am
aware that a court has more experience, more judgement and more
kindliness than a jury.

Your Honor, it may be hardly fair to the court; I am aware that I
have helped to place a serious burden upon your shoulders. And at
that, I have always meant to be your friend. But this was not an act of
friendship.

I know perfectly well that where responsibility is divided by
twelve, it is easy to say: "Away with him." But, Your Honor, if these

boys hang, you must do it. There can be no division of responsibility here. You can never explain that the rest overpowered you. It must be by your deliberate, cool, premeditated act, without a chance to shift responsibility.

It was not a kindness to you. We placed this responsibility on your shoulders because we were mindful of the rights of our clients, and we were mindful of the unhappy families who have done no wrong.

Now, let us see, Your Honor, what we had to sustain us. Of course, I have known Your Honor for a good many years. Not intimately. I could not say that I could even guess from my experience what Your Honor might do, but I did know something. I knew, Your Honor, that ninety unfortunate human beings had been hanged by the neck until dead in the city of Chicago in our history. We would not have civilization except for those ninety who were hanged, and if we cannot make it ninety-two we will have to shut up shop. Some ninety human beings have been hanged in the history of Chicago, and of those only four have been hanged on the plea of guilty—one out of twenty-two.

I know that in the last ten years four hundred and fifty people have been indicted for murder in the city of Chicago and have pleaded guilty. Four hundred and fifty have pleaded guilty in the city of Chicago, and only one has been hanged! And my friend who is prosecuting this case deserves the honor of that hanging while he was on the bench. But his victim was forty years old.

Your Honor will never thank me for unloading this responsibility upon you, but you know that I would have been untrue to my clients if I had not concluded to take this chance before a court, instead of submitting it to a poisoned jury in the city of Chicago. I did it knowing that it would be an unheard-of thing for any court, no matter who, to sentence these boys to death.

. . . .

Let me tell you something that I think is cowardly. . . . Here is Dickie Loeb, and Nathan Leopold, and the State objects to anybody calling one "Dickie" and the other "Babe" although everybody does, but they think they can hang them easier if their names are Richard and Nathan, so we will call them Richard and Nathan. Eighteen and nineteen years old at the time of the homicide.

Here are three officers watching them. They are led out and in this jail and across the bridge waiting to be hanged. Not a chance to get away. Handcuffed when they get out of this room. Not a chance. Penned in like rats in a trap. And for a lawyer with psychological eloquence to wave his fist in front of their faces and shout "Cowardly!" does not appeal to me as a brave act. It does not commend itself to me as a proper thing for a state's attorney or his assistant; for even defendants not yet hanged have some rights with an official.

Cold-blooded? Why? Because they planned, and schemed, and arranged and fixed? Yes. But here are the officers of justice, so-called, with all the power of the state, with all the influence of the press, to fan this community into a frenzy hate; with all of that, who for months have been planning and scheming, and contriving and working to take these two boys' lives.

You may stand them on the trap door of the scaffold, and choke them to death, but that act will be infinitely more cold-blooded, whether justified or not, than any act that these boys have committed or can commit.

Cold-blooded! Let the state, who is so anxious to take these boys' lives, set an example in consideration, kindheartedness and tenderness before they call my clients cold-blooded.

I have heard this crime described—this most distressing and unfortunate homicide, as I would call it; this cold-blooded murder as the State would call it. I call it a homicide particularly distressing because I am defending. They call it a cold-blooded murder because they want to take human lives. Call it what you will.

I have heard this case talked of, and I have heard these lawyers say that this is the coldest-blooded murder that the civilized world has ever known. I don't know what they include in the civilized world. I suppose Illinois. Although they talk as if they did not. But we will assume Illinois. This is the most cold-blooded murder, says the State, that ever occurred.

Now, Your Honor, I have been practicing law a good deal longer than I should have, anyhow for forty-five or forty-six years, and during a part of that time I have tried a good many criminal cases, always defending. It does not mean that I am better. It probably means that I am more squeamish than the other fellows. It means neither that I am better nor worse. It means the way I am made. I cannot help it.

I have never yet tried a case where the state's attorney did not say that it was the most cold-blooded, inexcusable, premeditated case that ever occurred. If it was murder, there never was such a murder. If it was robbery, there never was such a robbery. If it was conspiracy, it was the most terrible conspiracy since the Star Chamber passed into oblivion. If it was larceny, there never was such a larceny.

Now, I am speaking moderately. All of them are the worst. Why? Well it adds to the credit of the state's attorney to be connected to a big case. That is one thing. They can say: "Well I tried the most cold-blooded murder case that ever was tried, and I convicted them, and they are dead," or: "I tried the worst forgery case that ever was tried, and I won that. I never did anything that was not big."

Lawyers are apt to say that.

And then there is another thing, Your Honor: Of course, I generally try cases to juries, and these adjectives always go well with juries; bloody, cold-blooded, despicable, cowardly, dastardly, cruel, heartless—the litany of the state's attorney's office generally goes well with a jury. The twelve jurors, being good themselves, think it is a tribute to their virtue if they follow the litany of the state's attorney.

I suppose it may have some effect with the court; I do not know. Anyway, those are the chances we take when we do our best to save life and reputation.

"Here, your clients have pleaded guilty to the most cold-blooded murder that ever took place in the history of the world. And how does a judge dare to refuse to hang by the neck until dead two cowardly ruffians who committed the coldest-blooded murder in the history of the world?"

That is a good talking point.

. . . .

Of course, Your Honor, I admit that I hate killing, and I hate it no matter how it is done—whether you shoot a man through the heart, or cut his head off with an ax, or kill him with a chisel, or tie a rope around his neck. I hate it. I always did. I always shall.

But there are degrees, and if I might be permitted to make my own rules I would say that if I were estimating what was the most cruel murder, I might first consider the sufferings of the victim.

Now, probably the State would not take that rule. They would say the one that had the most attention in the newspapers. In that way they have got me beaten at the start. But I would say the first thing to consider is the degree of pain to the victim.

Poor little Bobby Franks suffered very little. There is no excuse for his killing. If to hang these two boys would bring him back to life, I would say let them hang, and I believe their parents would say so, too. But:

> The moving finger writes, and having writ,
> Moves on; nor all your piety nor wit
> Shall lure it back to cancel half a line,
> Nor all your tears wash out a word of it.

Robert Franks is dead, and we cannot call him back to life. It was all over in fifteen minutes after he got into the car, and he probably never knew or thought of it. That does not justify it. It is the last thing I would do. I am sorry for the poor boy. I am sorry for his parents. But it is done.

Of course I cannot say with the certainty of Mr. Savage that he would have been a great man if he had grown up. At fourteen years of age I don't know whether he would or not. Savage, I suppose, is a mind reader, and he says that he would. He has a fantasy, which is hanging. So far as the cruelty to the victim is concerned, you can scarce imagine one less cruel.

.   .   .   .

I have heard the state's attorney talk of mothers.

Mr. Savage is talking for the mothers, and Mr. Crowe is thinking of the mothers, and I am thinking of the mothers. Mr. Savage, with the immaturity of youth and inexperience, says that if we hang them then there will be no more killing. This world has been one long slaughterhouse from the beginning until today, and killing goes on and on and on, and will forever. Why not read something, why not study something, why not think instead of blindly shouting for death?

Kill them. Will that prevent other senseless boys or other vicious men or vicious women from killing? No!

It will simply call on every weak-minded person to do as they have done. I know how easy it is to talk of mothers when you want to do something cruel. But I am thinking of the mothers too. I know that any mother could be the mother of a little Bobby Franks, who left his home and went to his school, and who never came back. I know that any mother might be the mother of Richard Loeb and Nathan Leopold, just the same. The trouble of this, that if she is the mother of a Nathan Leopold or of a Richard Loeb, she has to ask herself the question:

"How came my children to be what they are? From what ancestry did they get this strain? How far removed was the poison that destroyed their lives? Was I the bearer of the seal that brings them to death?"

Any mother might be the mother of any of them. But these two are the victims. I remember a little poem that gives the soliloquy of a boy about to be hanged, a soliloquy such as these boys might make:

> *The night my father got me*
> *His mind was not on me;*
> *He did not plague his fancy*
> *To muse if I should be*
> *The son you see.*
>
> *The day my mother bore me*
> *She was a fool and glad,*
> *For all the pain I cost her,*
> *That she had borne The lad*
> *That borne she had.*

My father and my mother
Out of the light they lie;
The warrant would not find them,
And here, 'tis only I
Shall hang so high

O let not man remember
The soul that God forgot,
But fetch the county sheriff
And noose me in a knot
And I will rot

And so the game is ended,
That should have not begun.
My father and my mother
They had a likely son,
And I have none.

No one knows what will be the fate of the child he gets or the child she bears; the fate of the child is the last thing they consider. This weary old world goes on, begetting, with birth and with living and with death; and all of it is blind from the beginning to the end. I do not know what it was that made these boys do this mad act, but I do know there is a reason for it. I know they did not beget themselves. I know that any one of an infinite number of causes reaching back to the beginning might be working out in these boys' minds, whom you are asked to hang in malice and in hatred and injustice, because someone in the past has sinned against them.

I am sorry for the fathers as well as the mothers, for the fathers who give their strength and their lives for educating and protecting and creating a fortune for the boys that they love; for the mothers who go down into the shadow of death for their children, who nourish them and care for them, and risk their lives, that they may live, who watch them with tenderness and fondness and longing, and who go down into dishonor and disgrace for the children that they love.

All of these are helpless. We are all helpless. But when you are pitying the mother and father of poor Bobby Franks, what about the fathers and mothers of these two unfortunate boys, and what about the unfortunate boys themselves, and what about all the fathers and all the mothers and all the boys and all the girls who tread a dangerous maze in darkness from birth to death?

Do you think you can cure it by hanging these two? Do you think you can cure the hatreds and the maladjustments of the world by hanging them? You simply show your ignorance and your hate when you say it. You may here and there cure hatred with love and understanding, but you can only add fuel to the flames by cruelty and hate.

What is my friend's idea of justice? He says to this court, whom he says he respects—and I believe he does—Your Honor, who sits here patiently, holding the lives of these two boys in your hands: "Give them the same mercy that they gave to Bobby Franks."

Is that the law? Is that justice? Is this what a court should do? Is this what a state's attorney should do? If the state in which I live is not kinder, more humane, more considerate, more intelligent than the mad act of these two boys, I am sorry that I have lived so long.

I am sorry for all fathers and all mothers. The mother who looks into the blue eyes of her little babe cannot help musing over the end of the child, whether it will be crowned by the greatest promises which her mind can image or whether he may meet death upon the scaffold. All she can do is to rear him with love and care, to watch over him tenderly, to meet life with hope and trust and confidence, and to leave the rest with fate.

.   .   .   .

I could say something about the death penalty that, for some mysterious reason, the State wants in this case. Why do they want it? To vindicate the law? Oh, no. The law can be vindicated without killing anyone else. It might shock the fine sensibilities of the state's counsel that this boy was put into a culvert and left after he was dead, but, Your Honor, I can think of a scene that makes this pale into insignificance. I can think, and only think, Your Honor, of taking two boys, one eighteen the other nineteen, irresponsible, weak, diseased, penning them in a cell, checking off the days and the hours and the minutes until they will be taken out and hanged. Wouldn't it be a glorious day for Chicago? Wouldn't it be a glorious triumph for the state's attorney? Wouldn't it be a glorious triumph of justice in this land? Wouldn't it be a glorious illustration of Christianity and kindness and charity? I can picture them, wakened in the gray light of morning, furnished a suit of clothes by the State, led to the scaffold, their feet tied, black caps drawn over their heads, stood on a trap door, the hangman pressing a spring so that it gives way under them; I can see them fall through space—and—stopped by the rope around their necks.

This would surely expiate placing Bobby Franks in the culvert after he was dead. This would doubtless bring immense satisfaction to some people. It would bring a greater satisfaction because it would be done in the name of justice. I am always suspicious of righteous indignation. To hear young men talk glibly of justice. Well, it would make me smile if it did not make me sad. Who knows what it is? Does Mr. Savage know? Does Mr. Crowe know? Do I know? Does Your Honor know? Is there any human machinery for finding it out? Is there any man who can weigh me and say what I deserve? Can Your Honor? Let us be honest. Can Your Honor appraise yourself, and say what you deserve? Can Your Honor appraise these two young men and say what they deserve? Justice must take account of infinite circumstances which a human being cannot understand.

If there is such a thing as justice it could only be administered by one who knew the inmost thoughts of the man to whom he was meting it out. Aye, who knew the father and mother and the grandparents and the infinite number of people back of him. Who knew origin of every cell that went onto the body, who could understand the structure and how it acted. Who could tell how the emotions that sway the human being affected that particular frail piece of clay. It means more than that. It means that you must appraise every influence that moves men, the civilization where they live, and all society which enters into the making of the child or the man! If Your Honor can do it—if you can do it you are wise, and with wisdom goes mercy.

No one with wisdom and with understanding, no one who is honest with himself and his own life, whoever he may be, no one who has seen himself the prey and the sport and the plaything of the infinite forces that move man, no one who has tried and has failed—and we have all tried and we have all failed—no one can tell what justice is for someone else or for himself; and the more he tries and the more responsibility he takes, the more he clings to mercy as being the one thing which he is sure should control his judgement of men.

It is not so much mercy either, Your Honor. I can hardly understand myself pleading to a court to visit mercy on two boys by shutting them into a prison for life. For life! Where is the human heart that would not be satisfied by that?

Where is the man or woman who understands his own life and who has a particle of feeling that could ask for more? Any cry for more roots back to the hyena; it roots back to the hissing of the serpent; it roots back to the beast and the jungle. It is not a part of man. It is not a part of that feeling which, let us hope, is growing, though scenes like this make me sometimes doubt that it is growing. It is not a part of that feeling of mercy and pity and understanding of each other which we believe has been slowly raising man from his low estate. It is not a part of the finer instincts which are slow to develop; of the wider knowledge which is slow to come, and slow to move us when it comes. It is not a part of all that makes the best in man. It is not a part of all that promises any hope for the future and any justice for the present. And must I ask that these boys get mercy by spending the rest of their lives in prison, year following year, month following month, and day following day, with nothing to look forward to but hostile guards and stone walls? It ought not to be hard to get that much mercy in any court in the year 1924.

. . . .

Can you administer law without consideration? Can you administer what approaches justice without it? Can this court or any court administer justice by consciously turning his heart to stone and being deaf to all the finer instincts which move men? Without those instincts I wonder what would happen to the human race?

If a man could judge his fellow in coldness without taking account of his own life, without taking account of what he knows of human life, without some understanding—how long would we be a race of real human beings? It has taken the world a long time for man to get even where he is today. If the law was administered without any feeling of sympathy or humanity or kindliness, we would begin our long, slow journey back to the jungle that was formerly our home.

How many times has assault with intent to rob or kill been changed in these courts to assault and battery? How many times has felony been waived in assault with a deadly weapon and a man or boy given a chance? And we are asking the chance to be shut up in stone walls for life. For life. It is hard for me to think of it, but that is the mercy we are asking from this court, which we ought not be required to ask, and which we should have as a matter of right in this court and which I have faith to believe we will have as a matter of right.

Is this new? Why, I undertake to say that even the state's attorney's office—and if he denies it I would like to see him bring in the records—I will undertake to say that in three cases out of four in all kinds and all degrees, clemency has been shown.

Three hundred and forty murder cases in ten years with a plea of Guilty in this county. All the young who pleaded guilty, every one of them—three hundred in ten years with one hanging on a plea of Guilty, and that a man of forty years of age. And yet they say we come here with a preposterous plea for mercy. When did any plea for mercy become preposterous in any tribunal in all the universe?

We are satisfied with justice, if the court knows what justice is, or if any human being can tell what justice is. If anybody can look into the minds and hearts and lives and the origin of these two youths and tell what justice is, we would be content. But nobody can do it without imagination, without sympathy, without kindliness, without understanding, and I have faith that this Court will take this case, and his conscience, and his judgement and his courage and save these boys' lives.

Many may say now that they want to hang these boys; but I know that giving the people blood is something like giving them their dinner. When they get it they will go to sleep. They may for the time being have an emotion, but they will bitterly regret it. And I undertake to say that if these two boys are sentenced to death and are hanged, on that day a pall will settle over the people of this land that will be dark and deep, and at least cover every humane and intelligent person with its gloom. I wonder if it will do good. I wonder if it will help the children—and there is an infinite number like these. I marveled when I heard Mr. Savage talk. I do not criticize him. He is young and enthusiastic. But has he ever read anything? Has he ever thought? Was there ever any man who had studied science, who has read anything of criminology or philosophy—was there ever any man who knew himself who could speak with the assurance with which he speaks?

What about this matter of crime and punishment, anyhow? I may know less than the rest, but I have at least tried to find out, and I am fairly familiar with the best literature that has been written on that subject in the last hundred years. The more men study, the more they doubt the effect of severe punishment on crime. And yet Mr. Savage tells this court that if these boys are hanged, there will be no more murder.

Mr. Savage is an optimist. He says that if the defendants are hanged there will be no more boys like these.

I could give him a sketch of punishment—punishment beginning with the brute which killed something because something hurt it; the punishment of the savage. If a person is injured in the tribe, they must injure somebody in the other tribe; it makes no difference who it is, but somebody. If one is killed his friends or family must kill in return.

You can trace it all down through the history of man. You can trace the burnings, the boilings, the drawings and quarterings, the hanging of people in England at the crossroads, carving them up and hanging them as examples for all to see.

We can come down to the last century when nearly two hundred crimes were punishable by death, and by death in every form; not only hanging—that was too humane—but burning, boiling, cutting into pieces, torturing in all conceivable forms.

You can read the stories of the hangings on a high hill, and the populace for miles around coming out to the scene, that everybody might be awed into goodness. Hanging for picking pockets—and more pockets were picked in the crowd that went to the hanging than had been known before. Hangings for murder—and men were murdered on the way there and on the way home. Hangings for poaching, hangings for everything, and hangings in public, not shut up cruelly and brutally in a jail, out of the light of day, wakened in the nighttime and led forth and killed, but taken to the shire town on a high hill, in the presence of a multitude, so that all might see that the wages of sin were death.

. . . .

I know that every step in the progress of humanity has been met and opposed by prosecutors, and many times by the courts. I know that when poaching and petty larceny were punishable by death in England, juries refused to convict. They were too humane to obey the law; and judges refused to sentence. I know that when the delusion of witchcraft was spreading over Europe, claiming its victims by millions, many a judge so shaped his cases that no crime of witchcraft could be punished in his court. I know that these trials were stopped in America because juries would no longer convict. I know that every step in the progress of the world in reference to crime has come from the human feelings of man. It has come from that deep well of sympathy which, in spite of all our training and all our conventions and all our teaching, still lives in the human breast. Without it there could be no human life on this weary old world.

Gradually the laws have been changed and modified, and men look back with horror at the hangings and the killings of the past. What did they find in England? That as they got rid of these barbarous statutes, crimes decreased instead of increased; as the criminal law was modified and humanized, there was less crime instead of more. I will undertake to say, Your Honor, that you can scarcely find a single book written by a student—and I will include all the works on criminology of the past—that has not made the statement over and over again that as the penal code was made less terrible, crimes grew less frequent.

.   .   .   .

If these two boys die on the scaffold—which I can never bring myself to imagine—if they do die on the scaffold, the details of this will be spread over the world. Every newspaper in the United States will carry a full account. Every newspaper of Chicago will be filled with the gruesome details. It will enter every home and every family.

Will it make men better or make men worse? I would like to put that to the intelligence of man, at least such intelligence as they have. I would like to appeal to the feelings of human beings so far as they have feelings—would it make the human heart softer or would it make hearts harder? How many men would be colder and crueler for it? How many men would enjoy the details? And you cannot enjoy human suffering without being affected for better or for worse; those who enjoyed it would be affected for the worse.

What influence would it have upon the millions of men who will read it? What influence would it have upon the millions of women who will read it, more sensitive, more impressionable, more imaginative than men? Would it help them if Your Honor should do what the state begs you to do? What influence would it have upon the infinite number of children who will devour its details as Dickie Loeb has enjoyed reading detective stories? Would it make them better or would it make them worse? The question needs no answer. You can answer it from the human heart. What influence, let me ask you, will it have for the unborn babes still sleeping in the mother's womb? And what

influence will it have on the psychology of the fathers and mothers yet
to come? Do I need to argue to Your Honor that cruelty only breeds
cruelty?—that hatred only causes hatred?—that if there is any way to
soften this human heart, which is hard enough at best, if there is any
way to kill evil and hatred and all that goes with it, it is not through
evil and hatred and cruelty; it is through charity, and love and
understanding?

How often do people need to be told this? Look back at the world.
There is not a man who is pointed to as an example to the world who
has not taught it. There is not a philosopher, there is not a religious
leader, there is not a creed that has not taught it. This is a Christian
community, so-called, at least it boasts of it, and yet they would hang
these boys in a Christian community. Let me ask this court, is there
any doubt about whether these boys would be safe in the hands of the
founder of the Christian religion? It would be blasphemy to say they
would not. Nobody could imagine, nobody could even think of it. And
yet there are men who want to hang them for a childish, purposeless
act, conceived without the slightest malice in the world.

Your Honor, I feel like apologizing for urging it so long. It is not
because I doubt this court. It is not because I do not know something
of the human emotions and the human heart. It is not that I do not
know that every result of logic, every page of history, every line of
philosophy and religion, every precedent in this court, urges this court
to save life. It is not that. I have become obsessed with this deep
feeling of hate and anger that has swept across this city and this land.
I have been fighting it, battling with it, until it has fairly driven me
mad, until I sometimes wonder whether every religious human
emotion has not gone down in the raging storm.

I am not pleading so much for these boys as I am for the infinite
number of others to follow, those who perhaps cannot be as well
defended as these have been, those who may go down in the storm
and the tempest without aid. It is of them that I am thinking, and for
them I am begging of this court not to turn backward toward the
barbarous and cruel past.

. . . The easy thing and the popular thing to do is to hang my
clients. I know it. Men and women who do not think will applaud.
The cruel and thoughtless will approve. It will be easy today; but in
Chicago, and reaching out over the length and breadth of the land,
more and more fathers and mothers, the humane, the kind and the
hopeful, who are gaining an understanding and asking questions not
only about these poor boys, but about their own—these will join in no
acclaim at the death of my clients. They would ask that the shedding
of blood be stopped, and that the normal feelings of man resume their
sway. And as the days and the months and the years go on, they will
ask it more and more. But, Your Honor, what they shall ask might not

count. I know the easy way. I know Your Honor stands between the future and the past. I know the future is with me, and what I stand for here; not merely the lives of these two unfortunate lads, but for all boys and girls; for all of the young, and, as far as possible, for all of the old. I am pleading for life, understanding, charity, kindness, and the infinite mercy that considers all. I am pleading that we overcome cruelty with kindness, and hatred with love. I know the future is on my side.

Your Honor stands between the past and the future. You may hang these boys; you may hang them by the neck until they are dead. But in doing it you will turn your face toward the past. In doing it you are making it harder for every other boy who, in ignorance and darkness, must grope his way through the mazes which only childhood knows. In doing it you will make it harder for unborn children. You may save them and make it easier for every child that sometime may stand where these boys stand. You will make it easier for every human being with an aspiration and a vision and a hope and a fate.

I am pleading for the future; I am pleading for a time when hatred and cruelty will not control the hearts of men, when we can learn by reason and judgment and understanding and faith that all life is worth saving, and that mercy is the highest attribute of man.

. . . If I should succeed in saving these boys' lives and do nothing for the progress of the law, I should feel sad, indeed. If I can succeed, my greatest reward and my greatest hope will be that I have done something for the tens of thousands of other boys, for the countless unfortunates who must tread the same road in blind childhood that these poor boys have trod; that I have done something to help human understanding, to temper justice with mercy, to overcome hate with love.

The Supreme Court Speaks

The Supreme Court has dealt often with the death penalty, but two rulings stand out: *Furman v. Georgia,* which temporarily ended capital punishment in 1972, and *Gregg v. Georgia,* which reinstated it in 1976. The key question in each case was whether the death penalty was cruel and unusual punishment under the Eighth and Fourteenth Amendments.

The Court's decisions reflected the controversy and mixed feelings among society at large. In each case the decision was split: 5 to 4 in *Furman* and 7 to 2 in *Gregg.* What's more, each case produced several concurring opinions, in which even those justices who agreed on the ultimate decision insisted on explaining their different, and sometimes conflicting, reasons for arriving at the same result.

Most of the justices on the majority in *Furman v. Georgia* argued that the death penalty was unconstitutional because of the discriminatory way in which it was then administered. Justices Thurgood Marshall and William Brennan, however, argued that the death penalty would be unconstitutional no matter how it was administered. The Appendix at the back of this book includes extracts from a concurring decision in each case.

Other notable Court decisions on the death penalty follow. Chapter 3 includes information about many of them.

Beck v. Alabama, 447, U.S. 625, 100 S.Ct. 2382 (1980)
Booth v. Maryland, 482 U.S. 496, 96 L Ed 2d 440, 107 S.Ct. 2529 (1987)
Bullington v. Missouri, 451 U.S. 430, 101 S.Ct. 1852 (1981)
Butler v. McKellar, 494 U.S. 407 (1990).
Coker v. Georgia, 433 U.S. 584, 97 S.Ct. 2861 (1977)
Coleman v. Thompson, iii S.Ct. 2546 (1991)
Endmund v. Florida, 458 U.S. 782 (1982)
Ford v. Wainwright, 477 U.S. 399 (1986)
Gilmore v. Utah, 429 U.S. 1012, 97 S.Ct. 436. (1976)
Herrera v. Collins, 112 S.Ct. 1074 (1993)
In re Kemmler, 136 U.S. 436, 10 S.Ct. 930 (1890)
Jurek v. Texas, 428 U.S. 262, 96 S.Ct. 2950 (1976)
Lockett v. Ohio, 438 U.S. 586, 98 S.Ct. 2954 (1978))
Lockhart v. McCree, 476 U.S. 162 (1986)
Maxwell v. Bishop, 398 U.S. 262 (1970)
McCleskey v. Kemp, 481 U.S. 279 (1987)
McCleskey v. Zant, iii S.Ct. 1454 (1991)
McGautha v. California, 402 U.S. 183, 91 S.Ct. 1454 (1971)
Murray v. Giarratano, 492 U.S. 1 (1989)
Penry v. Lynaugh, 492 U.S. 302 (1989)
Proffitt v. Florida, 428 U.S. 242, 96 S.Ct. 2960 (1976)
Roberts v. Louisiana, 431 U.S. 633, 97 S.Ct. 1993 (1977)
Rudolph v. Alabama, 375 U.S. 889 (1963)
Sawyer v. Whitley, 112 S.Ct. 2514 (1992)
South Carolina v. Gathers, 490 U.S. 805, 109 S.Ct. 2207 (1989)
Stanford v. Kentucky, 492 U.S. 106 L Ed 2d #06, 109 S.Ct. 2969 (1989)
State ex rel. Francis v. Resweber, 329 U.S. 459 (1947)

Tison v. Arizona, 481 U.S. 137 (1987)
Thompson v. Oklahoma, 487 U.S. 815 (1988)
Trop v. Dulles, 356 U.S. 86, 100 (1958)
United States v. Jackson, 390 U.S. 570 (1968)
Weems v. United States, 217 U.S. 349, 373 (1910)
Wilkerson v. Utah, 99 U.S. 130 (1879)
Wilkins v. Missouri, 492 U.S. 361 S.Ct. 2969 (1989)
Woodson v. North Carolina, 428 U.S. 280, 96 S.Ct. 2978 (1976)

Model Penal Code of the American Law Institute, Proposed Official Draft 1962

The U.S. Supreme Court has ruled that in order for a death sentence to be constitutional, the jury must consider the circumstances of the crime. Circumstances that would mitigate, or lessen, the defendant's guilt must be weighed against those that would aggravate it, or make it worse.

But what kinds of circumstances mitigate or aggravate a criminal offense? What, in the eyes of the law, makes a particular murder worse than another murder? What makes one guilty defendant less guilty than another?

In the late 1950s and early 1960s, the American Law Institute set about writing a "model penal code" to serve as an example to lawmakers of a rational system of criminal punishment. The proposal contained the following examples of aggravating and mitigating circumstances for juries to take into account when deciding whether to impose the death penalty on a particular defendant:

AGGRAVATING CIRCUMSTANCES

(a) The murder was committed by a convict under sentence of imprisonment.

(b) The defendant was previously convicted of another murder or of a felony involving the use or threat of violence to the person.

(c) At the time the murder was committed the defendant also committed another murder.

(d) The defendant knowingly created a great risk of death to many persons.

(e) The murder was committed while the defendant was engaged or was an accomplice in the commission of, or an attempt to commit, or flight after committing or attempting to commit robbery, rape or deviate sexual intercourse by force or threat of force, arson, burglary or kidnapping.

(f) The murder was committed for the purpose of avoiding or preventing a lawful arrest or effecting an escape from lawful custody.

(g) The murder was committed for pecuniary gain.

(h) The murder was especially heinous, atrocious or cruel, manifesting exceptional depravity.

MITIGATING CIRCUMSTANCES

(a) The defendant has no significant history of prior criminal activity.

(b) The murder was committed while the defendant was under the influence of extreme mental or emotional disturbance.

(c) The victim was a participant in the defendant's homicidal conduct or consented to the homicidal act.

(d) The murder was committed under circumstances which the defendant believed to provide a moral justification or extenuation for his conduct.

(e) The defendant was an accomplice in a murder committed by another person and his participation in the homicidal act was relatively minor.

(f) The defendant acted under duress or under the domination of another person.

(g) At the time of the murder, the capacity of the defendant to appreciate the criminality [wrongfulness] of his conduct or to conform his conduct to the requirements of law was impaired as a result of a mental disease or defect or intoxication.

(h) The youth of the defendant at the time of the crime.

Methods of Execution Past and Present

Over the course of history, governments have been extremely inventive in devising ways to execute people. At one time or another, in one place or another, victims were:

Flayed, their skin cut from their bodies, strip by strip

Sawed into pieces

Beaten to death

Shot with arrows

Thrown from a high place onto rocks or stakes

Boiled alive in water or in oil

Eaten by insects

Bitten by poisonous snakes

Buried alive, or walled up in cement

Drowned

Suffocated in a bog, quicksand, or soft pit of ashes

Whipped to death

Left in a cell to die of starvation or thirst

Left outdoors to die of exposure

Common Historical Methods of Execution

Stoning

One of the most primitive possible methods of execution, stoning dates back at least as far as the law of Moses. Traditionally, a crowd of ordinary citizens would gather around the condemned to act as executioners. The one who had made the accusation against the victim threw the first stone, after which everyone picked up stones and pelted the victim with them until he or she either died from brain damage or was smothered or crushed beneath the weight of the stones. Stoning is still prescribed by law in a few countries, all of which have Islamic traditions. It is typically reserved for crimes involving illicit sexual activities. The only place known to have used it with any frequency recently is Iran.

Crucifixion

A slow and torturous method of execution, crucifixion was used in the Middle East and classical Greece, as well as the outlying areas of the Roman Empire. Forms of this punishment later appeared in some portions of Europe during the early Middle Ages and in Japan as recently as the nineteenth century. The victim was hung on a tree or some kind of constructed cross, and left to die of exposure or starvation, whichever came first. At times, however, the victim was impaled or pierced with a spear before that happened, which brought a quicker death, if not a less painful one.

Burning

Burning at the stake was a common method of punishment in Europe during the Middle Ages and for some centuries after that; it was also used by certain North American Indian tribes. In Europe the typical victim was female. In several countries burning was the prescribed penalty for witches. In England, where witches were usually hanged, it was often used for those guilty of treason—not only "high treason" against the government, but "petty treason," which meant the murder of a husband by his wife. Burning carried a special horror for medieval Christians because it destroyed the body. It was a religious age in which even many of the worst criminals hoped to be forgiven their sins and to spend eternity in paradise. This would not happen, they believed, without a Christian burial. When a body was burnt, and the ashes scattered, a proper burial was impossible.

Breaking on the Wheel

In medieval France and Germany, as well as in some other countries, breaking on the wheel was as much a form of torture as of execution. Condemned criminals were stretched out and splayed on a large wooden wheel. The bones in their arms and legs were smashed with a large iron bar, after which their chests were caved in with the same instrument. A skilled executioner could perform these operations without breaking the skin, or rendering the victim unconscious, much less immediately killing him or her. Victims were left to hang there, gasping for breath with their shattered bones pressing on their lungs, until they died of thirst, hunger, or exposure. A much messier variation began with the process explained above, but with no effort made to keep the skin intact. Then the wheel was spun, sending the victim's insides flying.

Drawing and Quartering

A gruesome method of execution in which the victim's body was literally torn limb from limb. Each arm and leg of the victim was tied to a different horse, and the horses spurred to pull in four directions. In order to make the horses' task easier and to assure that the body was ripped into several pieces, the tendons and large muscles were sometimes cut through in advance. Sometimes the victim was hanged before being drawn and quartered; sometimes not.

Peine forte et dure

Also known as pressing, this was a method of slowly crushing—or pressing—a prisoner to death. It was primarily used in England from the fifteenth to the eighteenth centuries as a way of forcing accused criminals to plead either guilty or not guilty to a crime. If they refused to plead long enough, they would die. Typically the prisoner was stripped and made to lie down on his or her back. A board or other flat object was laid on the prisoner's chest. Iron weights were piled on top of the board, one after another, steadily increasing the weight bearing down on him or her. This process often went on for several days, during which food and drink was kept to a minimum. Typically three scraps of bread might be given on one day, three drinks of water on the next. Pressing was used in colonial America during the 1692 witch trials in Salem, Massachusetts, when an 80-year-old Salem man named Giles Cory was crushed to death.

Garotting

A garotte is a strangling device. The simplest version consisted of a board with a hole in it. A loop of rope or cord was stuck through the hole and placed around the victim's neck. Two executioners stood behind the board and pulled with all their strength on the ends of the rope, slowly choking the victim to death. Later versions of the garotte used lever and screw mechanisms to make the executioner's job easier. One version of the garotte used an iron band that could be tightened, in place of a cord. Another used two collars, one set above the other. Each was placed to surround a different adjoining vertebra in the victim's neck. The collars were operated by a screw that, when turned quickly, would pull one collar forward and the other one back, abruptly snapping the victim's neck. Still another version of the garotte, employed in some Spanish-American countries until well into the twentieth century, used a steel spike attached to a collar. When the collar was tightened, the spike was driven into the back of the victim's neck, slicing the spinal cord.

Beheading or Decapitation

This is the means of execution from which "capital punishment" gets its name. (The Latin word *capitalis* means "the head," and it is the root of both the English words *capital* and *decapitation*.) Nations differed in the preferred weapon of decapitation—some preferred the sword and others the axe. Whatever the weapon, the condemned person was made to kneel before the executioner, leaning forward with neck extended to receive the blade. In some cases the victim was required to rest his or her head on a chopping block, which made the executioner's job easier. Even with a block, however, it took a strong and steady arm to lop off a head with a single blow. Expert headsmen were highly prized—by the victim most of all—since a botched blow could result in enormous pain. In time, decapitating machines were invented to replace the unreliable hands and arms of unsteady human executioners. Although not foolproof themselves, these machines helped remove human uncertainty from the beheading process. Beheading was practiced in ancient Greece and Rome, as well as in Japan, China and throughout Europe, from the late Middle Ages until fairly recent times. Even today, decapitation is an official method of punishment in Belgium, the Congo, Mauritania, Saudi Arabia, Qatar, the United Arab Emirates, and the Arab Republic of Yemen.

Shooting

With the invention of the firearm, it became possible to execute criminals more easily than ever before. It even became possible to do it from a distance. There are two main methods of execution by firearm. One involves a single executioner, the other a group, or firing squad. The single executioner typically stands within arm's length of the victim and fires a handgun directly into the victim's brain. This method offers the advantage of simplicity, and (if the executioner has a steady hand) the virtual certainty of an immediate "clean" kill. A firing squad usually involves at least four executioners using rifles and standing some distance away. A firing squad is more impersonal than an individual executioner, and also less accurate. In the state of Utah, executioners shoot through a hole in a canvas barrier that conceals them from the victim's view. To make a good target, the victim is usually seated, stood against a wall, or tied in a standing position to a pole or board. In some places, one of the executioners' rifles contains a blank round, so no individual is ever sure whether they actually fired a fatal shot or not.

Hanging

It is probable that more criminals have died by hanging than by any other method of execution. Hanging was practiced in the

Middle East in biblical times, and it has survived in many countries—including the United States—until today. The first hangings in Europe, however, were not executions, but exhibitions. Corpses of criminals killed by other means were dangled from tree branches or the cross beams of makeshift gibbets. It was probably the Germanic tribes of Europe who first used hanging as a way of actually executing people. For centuries most hanging victims where hung from a short rope and died by agonizingly slow strangulation. In the past century techniques were developed to drop the victim at the end of a rope long enough to break the neck, thus killing more quickly.

Some Modern Methods of Execution

Shooting and hanging remain the most frequently used methods of execution in the world today. Shooting is used in 86 nations, hanging in 78. Both methods are prescribed by the laws of at least one state of the United States, although they are rarely used here.

The other three methods of execution in the United States are peculiar to this country—that is, this is the only country that uses any of them. They are:

Gas

The gas chamber was the first new means of execution actually developed in the twentieth century. The condemned prisoner is strapped into a chair in a small, airtight chamber, with windows in its walls through which official witnesses can view the death. Below the death chamber chair is a container of sulfuric acid. At the appointed moment, a white cloth bag containing cyanide pellets is dropped into the acid. A chemical reaction takes place, releasing the cyanide gas, which rises up around the chair, filling the room and the lungs of the victim. The cyanide interferes with enzymes in the victim's respiratory system that transfer oxygen from the blood to the cells of the body. Starved of oxygen, the brain loses consciousness, and soon the other vital organs give out.

Electrocution

First used in the United States in 1890, electrocution is currently the second most commonly used method of execution in this country. The victim is strapped into a wooden chair, and copper electrodes are attached to his or her head and legs. At the appropriate time, a massive electrical charge is passed through them, burning the body's internal organs and causing respiratory paralysis and cardiac arrest.

Lethal Injection

First adopted by Kansas in 1977, and by Texas later in the same year, lethal injection has become the most common method of execution in the United States today, prescribed by more states than any other two methods combined. It involves the transmission of deadly chemicals—typically a combination of sodium thiopental, pancuronium bromide, and potassium chloride—directly into the veins of the condemned criminal. An execution by lethal injection mimics a medical procedure, with the condemned man or woman strapped down on a hospital gurney. The execution device itself is similar to the apparatus used to intravenously feed or medicate patients in a hospital. A flexible tube is attached to a container of chemicals on one end and a needle on the other. The end with the needle extends through a hole in the wall of the execution chamber to the gurney, where the needle is inserted into a vein of the condemned person. At the appropriate time, the tube is opened and the chemicals are allowed to flow into the victim's bloodstream.

Tables and Figures

The information contained in the following set of figures and tables throws light on death penalty practice, both in the United States and in the world at large.

TABLE 1

Number of People Executed by Jurisdiction, 1930–1991

State	Number Executed	
	Since 1930	Since 1977
Georgia	381	15
Texas	339	42
New York	329	
California	292	
North Carolina	267	4
Florida	197	7
Ohio	172	
South Carolina	166	4
Mississippi	158	4
Pennsylvania	152	
Louisiana	151	20
Alabama	143	8
Arkansas	120	2
Virginia	105	
Kentucky	103	13
Tennessee	93	
Illinois	91	1
New Jersey	74	
Maryland	68	
Missouri	68	6
Oklahoma	61	1
Washington	47	
Colorado	47	
Indiana	43	2
West Virginia	40	
District of Columbia	40	
Arizona	38	
Nevada	34	5
Federal System	33	
Massachusetts	27	
Connecticut	21	
Oregon	19	
Iowa	18	
Utah	16	3
Kansas	15	
Delaware	12	
New Mexico	8	
Wyoming	7	
Montana	6	
Vermont	4	
Nebraska	4	
Idaho	3	
South Dakota	1	
New Hampshire	1	
Wisconsin	0	
Rhode Island	0	
North Dakota	0	
Minnesota	0	
Michigan	0	
Maine	0	
Hawaii	0	
Alaska	0	
U.S. Total	4916	157

Sources: Bureau of Justice Statistics Bulletin, "Capital Punishment 1990," U.S. Department of Justice; "United States of America Death Penalty Developments," Amnesty International, February 1992.

TABLE 2

Disposition of Death Row Residents 1973–1990

Year of Sentence	Prisoners on Death Row				Prisoners Leaving Death Row				Still on Death Row at Start of 1991
	Number Sentenced	Executed	Died From Other Causes	Statute Overturned	Conviction Overturned	Sentence Overturned	Sentence Commuted	Other/ Unknown	
1973	42	2	0	14	9	8	9	0	0
1974	151	8	4	65	15	28	22	1	8
1975	299	5	3	171	23	62	21	2	12
1976	234	9	5	137	16	37	15	0	15
1977	139	13	2	40	26	31	7	0	20
1978	187	23	3	21	34	55	8	0	43
1979	157	11	8	2	27	48	6	0	55
1980	184	13	11	3	29	41	4	1	83
1981	238	15	8	0	35	61	3	0	115
1982	274	13	10	0	21	50	4	1	176
1983	257	11	8	1	16	39	2	0	179
1984	291	13	7	1	29	45	4	1	185
1985	286	1	2	1	23	44	2	7	209
1986	314	1	6	0	28	37	3	4	234
1987	303	3	3	1	25	27	0	5	242
1988	310	1	3	0	8	19	0	4	277
1989	267	1	1	0	2	3	0	0	260
1990	244	0	1	0	0	0	0	0	243
Total 1973–1990	4,177	143	85	457	366	635	110	25	2,356

Source: Bureau of Justice Statistics Bulletin, "Capital Punishment, 1990," U.S. Department of Justice.

TABLE 3
Prisoners under Sentence of Death 1990

	Number				Percent		
All Races	White	Black	Hispanic	All Races	White	Black	Hispanic
Total							
2356	1215	933	172	100%	100%	100%	100%
Prior Felony Convictions							
Yes							
1522	757	642	105	69.2%	66.5%	74.3%	64.4%
No							
678	382	222	58	30.8%	33.5%	25.7%	35.6%
Not Reported							
156	76	69	9	—	—	—	—
Prior Homicide Convictions							
Yes							
179	83	76	15	8.7%	7.8%	9.4%	9.9%
No							
1880	981	736	136	91.3%	92.2%	90.6%	90.1%
Not Reported							
297	151	121	21	—	—	—	—
Legal Status at Time of Capital Offense Charges Pending							
139	78	50	7	6.8%	7.3%	6.2%	4.8%
Probation							
161	92	57	10	7.8%	8.6%	7.1%	6.8%
Parole							
417	171	205	37	20.3%	16.0%	25.5%	25.3%
Prison Escapee							
36	21	12	2	1.8%	2.0%	1.5%	1.4%
Prison Inmate							
64	33	24	7	3.1%	3.1%	3.0%	4.8%
Other Status*							
28	16	10	1	1.4%	1.5%	1.2%	0.7%
None							
1206	658	445	82	58.8%	61.6%	55.4%	56.2%
Not Reported							
305	146	130	26	—	—	—	—

Notes: Percents do not include those for whom data was not reported.
* Includes furlough or work releases, mandatory conditional releases, bail, halfway houses, prerelease centers, local jails, house arrests, road gangs, and accelerated release programs, etc.
Source: Bureau of Justice Statistics Bulletin, "Capital Punishment 1990," U.S. Department of Justice.

TABLE 4
Women Sentenced to Death, by Race: December 31, 1990

State Total	Total 32	White 20	Black 12
Alabama	5	3	2
North Carolina	5	5	0
Ohio	4	0	4
Oklahoma	4	3	1
Texas	3	2	1
Florida	2	2	0
Mississippi	2	0	2
California	1	1	0
Kentucky	1	1	0
Missouri	1	1	0
Nevada	1	0	1
Pennsylvania	1	0	1
South Carolina	1	1	0
Tennessee	1	1	0

Source: Bureau of Justice Statistics Bulletin, "Capital Punishment 1990," U.S. Department of Justice.

TABLE 5
Minimum Age for Infliction of Capital Punishment

Age less than 18	Age 18	None Specified
Arkansas (14)	California	Alabama
Georgia (17)	Colorado	Arizona
Indiana (16)	Connecticut	Delaware
Kentucky (16)	Illinois	Florida
Louisiana (16)	Maryland	Idaho
Mississippi (16)*	New Jersey	Nebraska
Missouri (14)	New Mexico	Pennsylvania
Montana**	Ohio	South Carolina
Nevada (16)	Oregon	Washington
New Hampshire (17)	Tennessee	
North Carolina	Federal System***	
Oklahoma (16)		
South Dakota		
Texas (17)		
Utah (16)		
Virginia (15)		
Wyoming (16)		

Notes: *Statutory age in Mississippi is 13, but effective age is 18, based on interpretation of Supreme Court decisions.
**Age in Montana depends on age defendant is transferred to adult court, which theoretically may be as young as 10.
***Age normally 18, but can be younger if defendant is waived from a juvenile court.
Source: Bureau of Justice Statistics Bulletin, "Capital Punishment 1990," U.S. Department of Justice.

TABLE 6
Methods of Execution

Lethal Injection	Electrocution	Lethal Gas	Hanging	Firing Squad
Arkansas	Alabama	Arizona	Montana	Idaho
Colorado	Arkansas	California	New Hampshire	Utah
Delaware	Connecticut	Maryland	Washington	
Idaho	Florida	Mississippi		
Illinois	Georgia	Missouri		
Mississippi	Indiana	North Carolina		
Missouri	Kentucky			
Montana	Louisiana			
Nevada	Nebraska			
New Hampshire	Ohio			
New Jersey	South Carolina			
New Mexico	Tennessee			
North Carolina	Virginia			
Oklahoma				
Oregon				
Pennsylvania				
South Dakota				
Texas				
Utah				
Washington				
Wyoming				

Notes: Some states employ more than one method. Federal executions are carried out by the method employed by the state in which the execution takes place.
Source: Bureau of Justice Statistics Bulletin, "Capital Punishment 1990," U.S. Department of Justice.

TABLE 7
Abolitionist Countries

Country	Date of Abolition	Abolished by Constitution
Austria	1968 (for ordinary crimes, 1950)	yes
Bolivia	1961	yes
Cape Verde	(date cannot be established)	yes
Colombia	1910	yes
Costa Rica	1882	yes
Denmark	1978 (for ordinary crimes, 1930)	no
Dominican Republic	1966	yes
Ecuador	1897 (for "political crimes," 1852)	yes
Finland	1972 (for ordinary crimes, 1949)	no
France	1981	no
Germany, W.	1949	yes
Haiti	1987 (with reinstatement of 1987 constitution	yes
Honduras	1965	yes
Iceland	1928	no
Kiribati	1965	no
Luxemburg	1979	no
Monaco	1964	yes
Netherlands	1983 (for ordinary crimes, 1870)	yes
Nicaragua	Before 1900	yes
Norway	1979 (for ordinary crimes, 1905)	no
Panama	1902	yes
Portugal	1976 (for ordinary crimes, 1867)	yes
Solomon Islands	1966	no
Sweden	1973 (for ordinary crimes in peacetime,1921)	no
Tuvalu	1975	yes
Uruguay	End 19th century	yes

Source: "Capital Punishment," Law Library of Congress, September 1989 (Rev. April 1990).

TABLE 8
Countries with Death Penalty for Ordinary as Well as Exceptional Crimes

Afghanistan	Grenada	Qatar
Albania	Guatemala	Romania
Algeria	Guinea	Rwanda
Andorra	Guyana	St. Kitts-Nevis
Angola	Hong Kong	St. Lucia
Antigua & Barbuda	Hungary	St. Vincent and the Grenadines
Bahamas	India	Sao Tome and Principe
Bahrain	Indonesia	Saudi Arabia
Bangladesh	Iran	Senegal
Barbados	Iraq	Sierra Leone
Belgium	Ivory Coast	Singapore
Belize	Jamaica	Somalia
Benin	Japan	South Africa
Bermuda	Jordan	Sri Lanka
Bhutan	Kenya	Sudan
Botswana	Korea(DPR)	Suriname
Brunei	Korea(Rep)	Swaziland
Bulgaria	Kuwait	Syria
Burkina Faso	Laos	Tanzania
Burma	Lebanon	Thailand
Burundi	Lesotho	Togo
Cambodia	Liberia	Tonga
Cameroon	Libya	Trinidad & Tobago
Central African Republic	Liechtenstein	Tunisia
Chad	Madagascar	Turkey
Chile	Malawi	Uganda
China(PRC)	Malaysia	United Arab Emirates
China(Taiwan)	Mali	USSR
Comoros	Maldives	Vietnam
Congo	Mauritania	Western Samoa
Cuba	Mauritius	Yemen(YAR)
Czechoslovakia	Mongolia	Yemen(PDR)
Djibouti	Morocco	Yugoslavia
Dominica	Mozambique	Zaire
Egypt	Nauru	Zambia
Equatorial Guinea	Niger	Zimbabwe
Ethiopia	Nigeria	
Fiji	Oman	
Gabon	Pakistan	
Gambia	Paraguay	
Germany, E.	Peru	
Ghana	Philippines	
Greece	Poland	

Source: "Capital Punishment," Law Library of Congress, September 1989 (Rev. April 1990).

Figure 1
Death Sentences by Year
1973–1990

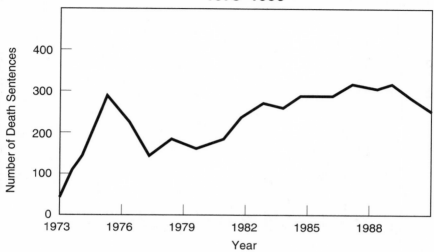

Source: "Capital Punishment 1990," Bureau of Justice Statistics
Bulletin, U.S. Department of Justice.

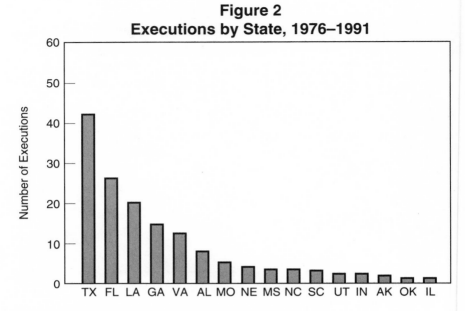

Figure 2
Executions by State, 1976–1991

Source: "1991 Death Penalty Developments in the U.S.A.,"
Amnesty International, 1992.

Figure 3
Executions in the United States, 1976–1992

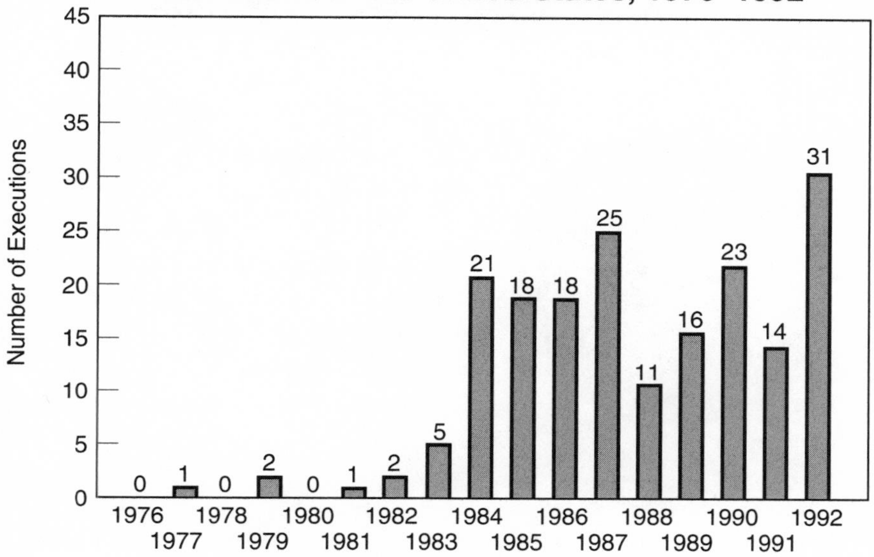

Number of Executions

Year	Value
1976	0
1977	1
1978	0
1979	2
1980	0
1981	1
1982	2
1983	5
1984	21
1985	18
1986	18
1987	25
1988	11
1989	16
1990	23
1991	14
1992	31

Source: NAACP Legal Defense and Education Fund Inc.

Figure 4
Ethnic Group or Color of Victims and Defendants in Death Penalty Cases 1976 to April 1991

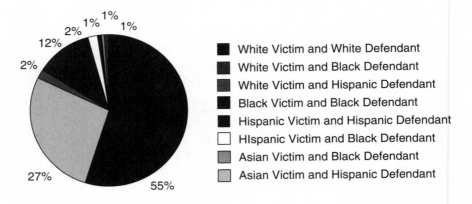

White Victim and White Defendant
White Victim and Black Defendant
White Victim and Hispanic Defendant
Black Victim and Black Defendant
Hispanic Victim and Hispanic Defendant
HIspanic Victim and Black Defendant
Asian Victim and Black Defendant
Asian Victim and Hispanic Defendant

Note: Two defendants were sentenced for the deaths of one white and one black victim.

Source: NAACP Legal Defense and Educational Fund Inc.

Figure 5
Ethnic Group or Color of Defendants Executed
1976 to April 1991

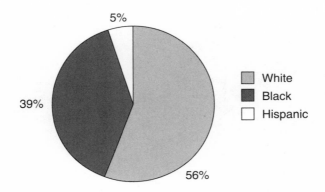

Source: NAACP Legal Defense and Educational Fund Inc.

Figure 6
Number of Victims Whose Murderer Received the Death Penalty 1976 to April 1991, by Ethnic Group or Color

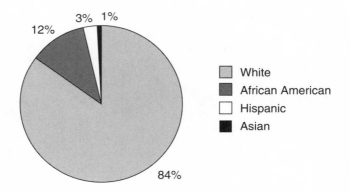

Source: NAACP Legal Defense and Educational Fund Inc.

6

Organizations

THIS CHAPTER CONTAINS A DIRECTORY of organizations, private and governmental, that are either active in matters involving the death penalty or serve as sources of information about it. The overwhelming majority of these organizations would like to see the death penalty abolished. This discrepancy requires some explanation.

Supporters of the death penalty may suspect that this imbalance indicates deliberate bias. Abolitionists, on the other hand, may assume that it reflects the relative strength of their arguments. While the author does confess a personal bias against the death penalty, the disparity on this list does not reflect that bias. Instead, it reflects the disparity that actually exists among the organizations that concern themselves with the death penalty. On a national or regional scale at least, there are many more groups actively opposing the death penalty than promoting it.

What's more, most of the pro-death-penalty organizations that do spring up tend to be ad hoc and temporary—a specific reaction to a particularly heinous crime or the trial of a notorious criminal. They are frequently made up of victims' families and friends, who unite with others to call for the criminal's death or to gather outside the prison to celebrate on the night of his (or potentially her) execution. Their members are drawn together by an immediate sense of outrage, rather than the kind of on-going, determined commitment demonstrated by death penalty opponents.

Alabama Prison Project
410 S. Perry Street
Montgomery, AL 36104
(205) 264-7416

Abolitionist group active in public education in Alabama. In specific cases, the Project participates in investigations to supply evidence of mitigation to the defense in capital trials, and in campaigns appealing for clemency on behalf of condemned inmates.

American Civil Liberties Union—Death Penalty Project
122 Maryland Avenue NE
Washington, DC 20002
(202) 675-2321

This division of the ACLU concentrates on efforts to end the death penalty through public education and legislative action. It has been particularly active in attempting to influence federal legislation on the subject.

ACLU publications, and information about the organization's activities in general, are available from the national headquarters:

Capital Punishment Project
132 West 43rd Street
New York, NY 10036
(212) 944-9800

In addition, there are the following regional offices:

Mountain States Regional Office
6825 E. Tennessee Avenue
Building 2, Suite 262
Denver, CO 80224
(303) 321-4828

Southern Regional Office
44 Forsythe Street NW
Suite 202
Atlanta, GA 30303
(404) 523-2721

National Prison Project
1875 Connecticut Avenue NW
Suite 410
Washington, DC 20009
(202) 234-4830

For those wishing to become active in local efforts of the ACLU, there are affiliate offices in every state and the District of Columbia. Some states have more than one. Addresses and telephone numbers can be found in the appropriate local telephone directories or by calling or writing the national office in New York. Other cities with offices include the following, listed by state:

Alabama
Montgomery

Alaska

Anchorage

Arizona
Phoenix

Arkansas
Little Rock

California
Los Angeles, San Diego,
San Francisco

Colorado
Denver

Connecticut
Hartford

Delaware
Wilmington

District of Columbia
Washington

Florida
Miami

Georgia
Atlanta

Hawaii
Honolulu

Idaho
Boise

Illinois
Chicago

Indiana
Indianapolis

Iowa
Des Moines

Kansas
Kansas City (Mo.)

Kentucky
Louisville

Louisiana
New Orleans

Maine
Portland

Maryland
Baltimore

Massachussetts
Boston

Michigan
Detroit

Minnesota
Minneapolis

Mississippi
Jackson

Missouri (eastern)
St. Louis

Missouri (western)
Kansas City

Montana
Billings

Nebraska
Lincoln

Nevada
Las Vegas

New Hampshire
Concord

New Jersey
Newark

New Mexico
Albuquerque

New York New York	**Tennessee** Nashville
North Carolina Raleigh	**Texas** Austin, Dallas, Houston
Ohio Cleveland	**Utah** Salt Lake City
Oklahoma Oklahoma City	**Vermont** Montpellier
Oregon Portland	**Virginia** Richmond
Pennsylvania Philadelphia, Pittsburgh	**Washington** Seattle
Rhode Island Providence	**West Virginia** Charleston
South Carolina Columbia	**Wisconsin** Milwaukee
South Dakota Sioux Falls	**Wyoming** Laramie

American Friends Service Committee
1501 Cherry Street
Philadelphia, PA 19102
(215) 241-7123

One of the most active of all the U.S. religious organizations opposed to the death penalty.

Amnesty International
International Secretariat
1 Easton Street
London WC1X 8DJ
United Kingdom
(44) (71) 413-5500

Amnesty International USA Program to Abolish the Death Penalty
322 Eighth Avenue
New York, NY 10001
(212) 807-8400

Amnesty International USA (Regional Headquarters)
322 Eighth Avenue
New York, NY 10001
(212) 807-8400

58 Day Street, Davis Square
Somerville, MA 02144
(617) 623-0202

608 Massachussetts Avenue NE
Washington, DC 20002
(212) 544-0200

730 Peachtree, Room 982
Atlanta, GA 30308
(404) 876-5661

53 W. Jackson, Room 1162
Chicago, IL 60604
(312) 427-2060

9000 W. Washington
Culver City, CA 90232
(310) 815-0450

Winner of the Nobel Peace Prize, Amnesty International collects and disseminates information about human rights abuses around the world, including the United States. "Amnesty International opposes the death penalty in all cases, believing it to be the ultimate cruel, inhuman and degrading treatment and a violation of the right to life as proclaimed in the Universal Declaration of Human Rights and other international human rights instruments." For general information, you can get in touch with any of the regional offices listed above. For information about publications, write or phone the national office in New York.

Capital Punishment Research Project
P.O. Drawer 277
Headland, AL 36345
(205) 693-5225

Directed by Watt Espy, one of the leading historians of the death penalty in the United States, who has documented more than 15,750 executions since colonial times.

Catholics Against Capital Punishment
P.O. Box 3125
Arlington, VA 22203
(703) 522-5014

A Roman Catholic abolitionist group.

Death Penalty Information Center

1606 20th Street NW
Lower Level
Washington, DC 20005
(202) 347-2531
Richard C. Dieter, Executive Director

Established to "serve the media and the larger community as clearinghouse for data and resources on the myriad issues surrounding capital punishment," including "polls, academic studies, and newspaper coverage." Although it clearly opposes the death penalty, it attempts to provide objective information on the subject. It has several publications available, as well as a speakers' bureau of "informed sources on capital punishment, including unexpected voices [opposing the death penalty] from the law enforcement community and families of victims."

Defense for Children International USA

21 South 13th Street
Philadelphia, PA 19107
(215) 569-3996

Advocacy group for the protection of children (has information on juveniles and the death penalty).

Law Enforcement Against Death

11 Leicester Road
Belmont, MA 12178
(617) 489-1708

Anti-capital-punishment organization that argues against the effectiveness of the death penalty as a deterrent.

Loyola Death Penalty Research Center

348 Baronne Street
Suite 421
New Orleans, LA 70112
(504) 522-0578

Collects information related to death penalty issues.

Mennonite Central Commission, U.S. Office of Crime and Justice

P.O. Box 500
Akron, PA 17501
(717) 859-3889

Provides abolitionist literature and other educational materials.

Murder Victims' Families for Reconciliation
2093 Willow Creek Road
Portage, IN 46368
(219) 763-2170

The director is William Pelke, the grandson of an elderly woman murdered by four teenage girls in Gary, Indiana. One of the girls was sentenced to death at the age of 16.

NAACP Legal Defense & Educational Fund—
Capital Punishment Project
Suite 1600
99 Hudson Street
New York, NY 10013
(212) 219-1900

Once headed by Thurgood Marshall, the NAACP Legal Defense & Educational Fund (LDF) was founded by the National Association for the
Advancement of Colored People in the 1940s. While it is still allied with
the NAACP, it is no longer a part of it. Among its other activities, LDF
helps to defend black defendants charged with, or convicted of, capital
crimes. Partly because it believes the death penalty has traditionally been
unfairly applied to minorities, it works against the death penalty in more
general ways as well, particularly against its application to young people
and the mentally retarded.

National Bar Association
1225 11th Street NW
Washington, DC 20001-4217
(202) 842-3900

The national professional association for attorneys can provide information on legal questions surrounding the death penalty.

National Coalition to Abolish the Death Penalty (NCADP)
1419 V Street NW
Washington, DC 20009
(202) 347-2411

The most inclusive of the national groups working to end capital punishment, the NCADP helps consolidate the efforts of a broad range of
national and local organizations and institutions active in the abolitionist
cause.

National Criminal Justice Statistics Clearinghouse
P.O. Box 6000
Rockville, MD 20850
(800) 732-3277

A subdivision of the U.S. Department of Justice that provides information on all aspects of the U.S. criminal justice system, including the death penalty.

National Legal Aid & Defender Association
Death Penalty Litigation Section
1625 K Street NW
Eighth Floor
Washington, DC 20006
(202) 452-0620

Devoted to the needs and interests of those actively engaged in defending people liable to the death penalty. Publishes the "Capital Report" (newsletter).

Northern California Coalition to Abolish the Death Penalty
1212 Broadway
Suite 830
Oakland, CA 94612
(510) 836-3013

An active branch of the National Coalition, which works to educate the public on death penalty issues by various means, including pamphlets and forums in high schools. Along with its other activities, the group participates in demonstrations against the death penalty; it was especially active in organizing the demonstrations outside San Quentin Prison in the weeks leading up to the execution of Robert Alton Harris.

Penny Resistance
8319 Fulham Road
Richmond, VA 23227-1712
(804) 266-7400

Religious Action Center of Reform Judaism
2027 Massachussetts Avenue
Washington, DC 20036
(202) 387-2800

Affiliated with the Union American Hebrew Congregations, which represents the nation's reform congregations, the Religious Action Center actively opposes capital punishment.

Washington Legal Foundation
1705 N Street
Washington, DC 20036
(202) 857-0240

A "nonpartisan public interest law institution organized to engage in litigation and the administrative process in matters affecting the broad public interest," the Foundation supports the retention of the death penalty. In addition to its efforts on behalf of capital punishment, it is active in promoting the "defense of individual rights," aiding crime victims, supporting a strong defense, and "challenging regulations which impede a free market economy." Publishes studies on matters of public policy, including the death penalty.

7

Selected Print Resources

THIS CHAPTER IS DESIGNED TO DIRECT readers to a variety of sources that deal with the subject of capital punishment in a variety of ways. The intention has been to include the major available sources likely to be of use to a student, as well as a selection of other interesting, if less important, works. This is by no means a complete list. For further possibilities consult the bibliography below.

Some of the works listed here defend the death penalty. Some oppose it. Some take no stand either way. There has been no effort to weight this list either in favor of or against any position. There is no question, however, that more of these works oppose the death penalty than support it. That imbalance, in favor of the abolitionist side in the debate over the death penalty, reflects the imbalance in the literature of capital punishment as a whole. There are simply more abolitionist books and other sources available than retentionist ones.

Books

Abbott, Jack Henry. **In the Belly of the Beast.** New York: Random House, 1981. (Out of print.)

Abbott had spent almost his entire teenage and adult life in prison by the time he wrote this book. Growing out of several passionate, angry letters he wrote to author Norman Mailer, it vividly describes a killing in which

Abbott took part, as well as the dehumanizing and embittering effects of long prison terms. Introduction by Norman Mailer.

Amnesty International. **The Death Penalty.** London: Amnesty International Publications, 1979. 222p. $5. ISBN 0-900058-88-9.

An Amnesty International Report. Prepared by the worldwide human rights organization that opposes capital punishment, the book begins with a brief chapter presenting arguments against the death penalty. A second chapter deals with "The Death Penalty in International Law and Organization." The bulk of the book is taken up with a country-by-country survey of the death penalty as practiced in 138 different nations in the mid-1970s. A final chapter discusses cases of "Murder Committed or Acquiesced in by Government." The book concludes with four appendices and an addendum that brings the information up to date as of 1979. See also, *When the State Kills . . .* below. With photographs.

Amnesty International. **When the State Kills . . . The Death Penalty: A Human Rights Issue.** New York: Amnesty International USA, 1989. 268p. $10. ISBN 0-939994-45-3.

Similar to Amnesty International's 1979 volume, *The Death Penalty.* Roughly the first third of the book is taken up with arguments and evidence marshalled against the death penalty. As in *The Death Penalty,* the bulk of the book is taken up with a country-by-country survey of capital punishment. Concludes with 17 appendices, including charts and tables, as well as the texts of several international agreements and declarations relating to the death penalty. Comparing this book with *The Death Penalty,* readers can explore the changes in the use of capital punishment around the world over the past quarter century. With photographs. Also available in Spanish and Arabic.

Bailey, Lloyd R. **Capital Punishment: What the Bible Says.** Nashville, TN: Abingdon Press, 1987. 112p. $6.95. ISBN 0-687-04626-2.

Attempts to place Bible texts relating to the death penalty in the context of the time in which they were written, rather than to use particular texts to make a case either for or against capital punishment.

Baldus, David C., George Woodworth, and Charles A. Pulaski, Jr. **Equal Justice and the Death Penalty: A Legal and Empirical Analysis.** Boston: Northeastern University Press, 1990. 752p. $55. ISBN 1-55553-056-7.

An extensive study of death penalty sentencing between the landmark *Furman* and *McCleskey v. Kemp* decisions of the Supreme Court. It concludes that, while things have gotten somewhat better, death sentencing remains unfair in its impact on disadvantaged minorities. What's more, "given the Supreme Court's decision in *McCleskey v. Kemp*, little improvement in this regard appears likely."

Beccaria, Cesare. **On Crimes and Punishments.** Edited and translated by David Young. Indianapolis: Hackett Publications, 1986. 129p. $22.50. ISBN 915144-99-9.

Originally published in Italian as *Dei delitti e delle pene* in 1764. This is the landmark essay that launched the great drive for abolition in the nineteenth and twentieth centuries. Beccaria attacked such widespread penal practices of the time as secret accusations and punishments, torture, and, of course, the death penalty. In his central argument, Beccaria declares "[t]hat a punishment may not be an act of violence. . . . " What's more, "it should be public, immediate, and necessary, the least possible in the case given, proportioned to the crime, and determined by the laws."

Bedau, Hugo Adam. **The Death Penalty in America.** 3d ed. Chicago: Aldine, 1982. $24.95 ISBN 0-19-502986-0 (hardcover). New York: Oxford University Press, 1982. $11.95. ISBN 0-19-502987-9 (paperback).

An anthology of articles and essays on the death penalty by various writers, including the editor, who is a prominent, long-time opponent of capital punishment. Entries are grouped under various chapter headings, such as "The Argument for the Death Penalty," "The Argument Against the Death Penalty," and "Abolition: Success or Failure?" With bibliography.

————. **Death Is Different: Studies in the Morality, Law and Politics of Capital Punishment.** Boston: Northeastern University Press, 1987. 360p. $37.50. ISBN 1-55553-008-7.

Berger, Raoul. **Death Penalties: The Supreme Court's Obstacle Course.** Cambridge, MA: Harvard University Press, 1982. 256p. $25. ISBN 0-674-19426-8.

A distinguished defender of capital punishment looks at the Supreme Court's attitude toward the death penalty. In essence, the book is an argument against what Berger sees as a too broad reading of the "cruel and unusual" clause, which he believes is "depriving" the people of the right to decide whether or not they want criminals executed.

Berns, Walter. **For Capital Punishment: Crime and the Morality of the Death Penalty.** New York: Basic Books, 1981. $12.95. ISBN 0-465-02474-2.

The case in favor of capital punishment, argued by a distinguished constitutional law expert and adjunct scholar at the American Enterprise Institute.

Black, Charles L., Jr. **Capital Punishment: The Inevitability of Caprice and Mistake.** Rev. ed. New York: W.W. Norton, 1982. $6.95. ISBN 0-393-95289-4.

A classic presentation of the abolitionist argument that the death penalty cannot realistically be applied fairly, and that any effort to apply it "inevitably" leads to tragic and uncorrectable mistakes.

Bovee, Marvin H. **Christ and the Gallows; or, Reasons for the Abolition of Capital Punishment.** New York: AMS Press, 1983 reprint of 1869 edition. $40. ISBN 0-404-62403-0.

The classic collection of letters and essays by prominent opponents of the death penalty, including Henry Longfellow, Elizabeth Cady Stanton, and Bovee himself.

Bowers, William J., Glenn L. Pierce, and John F. McDevitt. **Legal Homicide: Death as Punishment in America, 1864–1982.** Boston: Northeastern University Press, 1984. (Out of print.)

A historical review.

Brown, Edmund G. (Pat), with Dick Adler. **Public Justice, Private Mercy: A Governor's Education on Death Row.** New York: Grove Press, 1989. 320p. $18.95. ISBN 1-55585-253-4.

A governor's-eye view of the commutation process. As governor of California, Brown had to face the decision of whether or not to commute death sentences 59 times. Although an opponent of the death penalty, Brown decided in favor of "public justice" 36 of those times, and in favor of "private mercy" only 26 times. In this book, he explains the circumstances and agonies of those decisions.

Carrington, Frank. **Neither Cruel nor Unusual: The Case for Capital Punishment.** New York: Crown, 1978. (Out of print.)

A forceful presentation of the pro-death-penalty position.

Cheever, George B. **Punishment by Death: Its Authority & Expediency.** New York: AMS Press, reprint of 1842 edition. $37.50. ISBN 0-404-62409-X.

The case for capital punishment, laid out by the clergyman who was, perhaps, its strongest nineteenth-century defender.

Chessman, Caryl. **Cell 2455 Death Row.** Englewood Cliffs, N.J.: Prentice-Hall, 1954. Reissued, Westport, CT: Greenwood Press, 1969. 361p. ISBN 8371-1631-7. (Out of print.)

The autobiography of Caryl Chessman, who was executed in 1960 for kidnapping. In "Author's Note," Chessman describes the book as a plea "for the criminally damned and doomed." The title is taken from the number of the author's cell on San Quentin's death row. Beginning with a description of the gas chamber death of a fellow prisoner, Chessman goes on to describe the life that brought him to the brink of a similar fate. It is a vividly written account of the author's criminal career, in which he maintains his innocence of the crimes for which he was condemned, and declares his determination "to cheat the executioner out of his day off and his hundred dollar fee." The book became a best-seller and helped to focus public attention on the issue of capital punishment in the mid-1950s.

————. **Trial by Ordeal.** Englewood Cliffs, NJ: Prentice-Hall, 1955. 309p. Library of Congress Catalog No. 55-10671. (Out of print.)

An account by Caryl Chessman of his efforts to save himself from execution for robbery and kidnapping. It includes descriptions of his life in prison and his reflections on his own death sentence. (By 1955 he had been on death row for over six years.)

The Churches Speak On—Capital Punishment. Detroit: Gale Research, 1989. 165p. (Out of print.)

Official statements from a variety of religious and ecumenical groups, including the Roman Catholic and Eastern Orthodox churches, as well as various Protestant and Jewish organizations.

Cytron, Barry D., and Earl Schwartz. **Hayim ben ha-shemashot; or When Life Is in the Balance: Life and Death Decisions in the Light of the Jewish Tradition.** New York: United Synagogue of America, 1986. 238p. (Out of print.)

The fifth chapter of this book discusses the relevant biblical and rabbinical texts that are taken as either supporting or opposing capital punishment.

Darrow, Clarence. **Clarence Darrow on Capital Punishment.** Evanston, Ill.: Chicago Historical Bookworks, 1991. 192p. $11.95. ISBN 0-685-49004-1.

The renowned criminal defense attorney's views on the death penalty.

————. **The Story of My Life.** Cutchogoe, NY: Buccaneer Books, 1992. 476p. $28.95. ISBN 0-89966-918-0.

An autobiography of the great criminal lawyer, abolitionist, and co-founder of the American League to Abolish Capital Punishment. Chapter 10 consists of an attack on the death penalty.

Dicks, Shirley, ed. **Death Row: Interviews with Inmates, their Families and Opponents of Capital Punishment.** Jefferson, NC: McFarland, 1990. 146p. ISBN 0-87975-679-9.

The first section of this three-part book deals with opponents of capital punishment, the second with people sentenced to death, and the third with the families of the condemned.

————. **Congregation of the Condemned: Voices against the Death Penalty.** New York: Prometheus, 1991. 250p. $24.95. ISBN 0-87975-679-9.

Similar to above.

Draper, Thomas, ed. **Capital Punishment.** The Reference Shelf Series. New York: H. W. Wilson, 1985. ISBN O-8242-0711-4. (Out of print.)

Like its sister volume, *The Death Penalty,* edited by Irwin Isenberg, this anthology of brief articles provides some interesting information and perspectives. With bibliography.

Duffy, Clinton T. **Eighty-Eight Men and Two Women.** New York: AMS Press, reprint of 1962 edition. $32.50. ISBN 0-404-62412-X.

Thoughts of an ex-warden on the executions he oversaw while in charge of California's San Quentin Prison.

Flanders, Stephen A. **Capital Punishment.** Library in a Book series. New York: Facts on File, 1991. 240p. $22.95. ISBN 0-8160-1912-6.

A history and chronology of the death penalty, as well as a discussion of important Supreme Court cases. With an annotated bibliography.

Gray, Ian, and Moira Stanley. **A Punishment in Search of a Crime.** New York: Avon, 1989. 400p. $8.95. ISBN 0-380-75923-3.

Subtitled "Americans Speak Out Against the Death Penalty," the book consists primarily of more than 40 selections by people opposed to capital punishment. Contributors include such prominent figures as author William Styron, Congressman John Conyers, and Hugo Adam Bedau, along with many lesser-known scholars, lawyers, death row inmates, and prison officials. With bibliography. Foreword by M. Kerry Kennedy.

Gross, Samuel R., and Robert Mauro. **Death and Discrimination: Racial Disparities in Capital Sentencing.** Boston: Northeastern University Press, 1989. 268p. $32.50. ISBN 1-55533-040-0.

An examination of how race influences death penalty sentencing. The book includes a detailed study of the way eight states applied death sentences in a given period, as well as discussions of the causes and effects of the racial disparities it finds. Foreword by Marvin Wolfgang.

Haas, Kenneth C., and James A. Inciardi, eds. **Challenging Capital Punishment: Legal & Social Sciences Approaches.** Criminal Justice System Annual Series: vol. 24. Newbury Park, CA: Sage Publications, 1988. 302p. $42.95. ISBN 0-8039-2909-9.

Presents examples of how social science and law can facilitate our understanding of some of the questions and issues involved in the death penalty.

Hook, Donald D., and Lothor Kahn. **Death in the Balance: The Debate over Capital Punishment.** New York: Free Press, 1990. 131p. $12.95. ISBN 0-669-2090646.

Presenting cases both for and against the death penalty, the authors argue that society should overcome its ambivalence toward the death penalty: either enforce it consistently and wholeheartedly or abolish it altogether. With bibliography.

Huie, William Bradford. **The Execution of Private Slovik.** New York: New American Library, 1954. 152p. (Out of print.)

A short but absorbing account of the case of the only American military person executed for desertion during World War II.

Ingle, Joseph B. **Last Rights: 13 Fatal Encounters with the State's Justice.** Nashville, TN: Abingdon Press, 1990. 300p. $21.95. ISBN 0-687-21124-7.

The author, a minister who has worked with the Southern Coalition on Jails and Prisons, recounts his experiences with inmates of death rows in a variety of prisons. Ingles declares that "capital punishment is a spiritual question," and insists that the God he worships would not condone the killing of anyone, including the most hardened criminal.

Isenberg, Irwin, ed. **The Death Penalty.** The Reference Shelf Series. New York: H. W. Wilson, 1977. 160p. ISBN O-8242-0604-5. (Out of print.)

An anthology of articles from magazines and newspapers relating to the death penalty. With bibliography.

Johnson, Robert. **Death Work: A Study of the Modern Execution Process.** Edited by Roy R. Roberg. Pacific Grove, Cal.: Brooks/Cole: 1990. 200p. $18.25. ISBN 0-534-12828-9.

Following a description of execution procedures from ancient times to the present, this book describes the execution process as it is carried out in the United States today. It details the experiences and impressions of condemned prisoners and executioners alike as they prepare for, and finally face, the grim ordeal.

Joyce, James Avery. **Capital Punishment: A World View.** New York: AMS Press, reprint of 1961 edition. $34.50. ISBN 0-404-62422-7.

Using as a starting point an account of convicted kidnapper Caryl Chessman's efforts to save himself from the gas chamber, Joyce discusses the history of the movement to abolish the death penalty in Europe, Great Britain, the United States, and ultimately in the United Nations. In later chapters, the debate over the death penalty is related to broader questions of war, peace, and nuclear deterrence. With bibliography and two appendices.

Koestler, Arthur. **Reflections on Hanging.** New York: AMS Press, reprint of 1957 edition. $30. ISBN 0-404-62423-5.

Meditations on the death penalty by the renowned Hungarian-born author who was himself imprisoned under sentence of death in Spain for some time during the Spanish Civil War. Contains the famous abolitionist distinction: "The division is not between rich and poor, highbrow and lowbrow, Christians and atheists: it is between those who have charity and those who have not."

Laurence, John. **The History of Capital Punishment.** New York: Citadel, 1960. 230p. $4.95. ISBN 0-80650840-X (paperback). Reprinted in 1983 by Carol Publishing Group. ISBN 0-8065-0840-X.

According to its preface, "This book does not state the pros and cons for Capital Punishment. It is an outline of scaffold history." With a chapter by Clarence Darrow from his book, *Crime and Its Causes,* and an editorial from the *New York Herald Tribune.*

Lawes, Lewis E. **Life and Death in Sing Sing.** Garden City, NY: Garden City Publications, 1928. (Out of print.)

An account of Lawes's thoughts and experiences as warden of the famous prison. It contains what Philip English Mackey has described as "the reformer's best attack on capital punishment."

————. **Man's Judgment of Death.** New York: G.P. Putnam's Sons, 1969 (reprint of 1924 edition). 146p. $10. ISBN 0-87585-062-6.

The first published attack on the death penalty by the Sing Sing warden who would become one of the most active, and most effective, opponents of the death penalty in the twentieth century.

Leopold, Nathan. **Life Plus 99 Years.** New York: Greenwood Press, reprint of 1958 edition. 381p. $55. ISBN 0-8371-7207-1.

An account of his experiences, and reflections on them, by the convicted killer who was spared a death sentence in 1924 and served the next 34 years in prison.

Mackey, Philip English. **Voices against Death: American Opposition to Capital Punishment, 1787–1975.** New York: Burt Franklin & Co., 1976. ISBN 0-89102-062-4. (Out of print.)

An invaluable collection of essays, speeches, etc., by a wide variety of death penalty opponents from Benjamin Rush to Bedau. Included, among many others, are Edward Livingston, Robert Rantoul, Jr., John Greenleaf Whittier, Walt Whitman, Horace Greeley, William Dean Howells, Clarence Darrow, Kathleen Norris, Caryl Chessman, and Thorsten Sellin. With bibliography and an introduction by Hugo Adam Bedau.

Masur, Louis P. **Rites of Execution: Capital Punishment and the Transformation of American Culture, 1776–1865.** New York: Oxford University Press, 1989. 224p. $13.95. ISBN 0-19-506663-4.

A study of capital punishment during the first near century of United States history, with special attention to the changing public attitudes toward hanging, particularly in the northeastern and mid-Atlantic states.

Meltsner, Michael. **Cruel and Unusual: The Supreme Court and Capital Punishment.** New York: Random House, 1973. ISBN 0-394-47231-4. (Out of print.)

An account of the temporarily successful efforts of a group of civil rights attorneys, led by Anthony Amsterdam, to have the death penalty declared cruel and unusual punishment by the U.S. Supreme Court.

Miller, Arthur Selwyn, and Jeffrey H. Bowman. **Death by Installments: The Ordeal of Willie Francis.** New York: Greenwood Press, 1988. 189p. $47.95. ISBN 0-31326-009-5.

An account of the harrowing case of Willie Francis, the teenager whose botched execution led to a major U.S. Supreme Court decision in 1947. The book reports on the way the Court dealt with the issue at the time, and discusses the constitutional issues raised by the case, some of which may not yet be resolved.

NAACP Legal Defense & Educational Fund Staff. **Death Row U.S.A. Reporter, Nineteen Seventy-Five to Nineteen Eighty-Eight.** Buffalo, NY: W. S. Hein, 1990. 1068p. $225. ISBN 0-89941-708-6.

A massive resource provided by what has long been one of the most active organizations opposing the death penalty.

Nathanson, Stephen. **An Eye for an Eye: The Morality of Punishing by Death.** Lanham, MD: Rowman and Littlefield, 1987. 161p. $14.95. ISBN 0-8476-7561-0.

"In writing this book," Nathanson declares, "I have tried to make as good a case as I can against the use of death as a punishment. That has not been my sole aim, however, I have also tried to give serious consideration to the concerns and arguments of those who favor the death penalty." With a foreword by Arthur J. Goldberg.

Otterbein, Keith F. **The Ultimate Coercive Sanction: A Cross-Cultural Study of Capital Punishment.** New Haven, CT: HRAF Press, 1986. 164p. $16. ISBN 0-87536-346-6.

Argues that the death penalty is, or has been, used by every culture at one time or another.

Radelet, Michael L. **Facing the Death Penalty: Essays on a Cruel and Unusual Punishment.** Philadelphia: Temple University Press, 1989. 264p. $34.95. ISBN 0-87722-611-3.

Deals with the experiences of condemned inmates, and those working on their behalf. "Little support for capital punishment will be found in these pages." Includes a foreword by Henry Schwartzschild.

Russell, Francis. **Tragedy in Dedham: The Story of the Sacco-Vanzetti Case.** New York: McGraw-Hill, 1962. 478p. (Out of print.)

A detailed accounting of the infamous Sacco-Vanzetti case, in which two Italian-American anarchists were executed for a double murder, despite international protests from people who believed they were innocent.

Schneir, Walter and Miriam. **Invitation to an Inquest.** Garden City, NY: Doubleday, 1965. 467p. (Out of print.)

Considered one of the best accounts of the espionage case of Julius and Ethel Rosenberg and their convicted fellow conspirator Martin Sobell.

Scott, George R. **The History of Capital Punishment: Including an Examination of the Case for & against Capital Punishment.** New York: AMS Press, reprint of 1950 edition. $38.50. ISBN 0-404-62428-6.

A valuable standard work.

Sheleff, Leon Shaskolski. **Ultimate Penalties: Capital Punishment, Life Imprisonment, Physical Torture.** Columbus, OH: Ohio State University Press, 1987. 492p. $39.50. ISBN 0-8142-0436-8 (hardcover). 1990. $15.95. ISBN 0-8142-0531-3 (paperback).

Is death really the worst penalty society can inflict on an individual? This book sheds light on that question by examining the ramifications of the drastic penalties described in its title.

Sorell, Tom. **Moral Theory and Capital Punishment.** New York: R. Blackwell, in association with the Open University, 1988. 172p. $15.95. ISBN 0-631-15321-7.

A philosophical examination of the possible justifications for the death penalty, concluding that it is a fit punishment for a limited category of murderers.

Stevens, Leonard A. **Death Penalty: the Case of Life and Death in the United States.** Great Constitutional Issues: the Eighth Amendment. New York: Coward, McCann & Geoghegan, 1978. 160p. ISBN 0-698-30701-1. (Out of print.)

A study of capital punishment as an issue in the United States, in the form of a detailed account of the historic *Furman* case. With a foreword by Michael Meltsner.

Szumski, Bonnie and others, eds. **The Death Penalty.** The Opposing Viewpoints series. St. Paul, MN: Greenhaven, 1986. 175p. ISBN 0-089908-381-1. (Out of print.)

An anthology of writings both for and against the death penalty, from 1701 up to the 1980s. Selections are grouped under four chapter headings: "Three Centuries of Debate on the Death Penalty," "Is the Death Penalty Immoral?" "Does the Death Penalty Deter Murder?" and "Should the Death Penalty Be Used for Political Crimes?" Notable authors include John Stuart Mill, Clarence Darrow, Horace Greeley, Walter Berns, and Ernest van den Haag. With bibliography.

van den Haag, Ernest, and John P. Conrad. **The Death Penalty: A Debate.** New York: Plenum, 1983. 305p. $19.95. ISBN 0-306-41416-3.

An unusually extended debate on the issue, with van den Haag supporting the death penalty and Conrad opposing it. Their intent "is to reach the thoughtful citizen who is concerned about the condition of criminal justice—its effectiveness, its humaneness, and its fairness." Foreword by Arthur J. Goldberg.

van den Haag, Ernest. **Punishing Criminals: Concerning a Very Old and Painful Question.** Lanham, MD: University Press of America, 1991. 308p. $32.50. ISBN 0-8191-8172-2.

Most recent thoughts of the noted proponent of capital punishment on the issue of criminal punishment in general.

Wexley, John. **The Judgement of Julius and Ethel Rosenberg.** New York: Cameron & Kahn, 1955. 672p. (Out of print.)

An extensive contemporary account of the Rosenberg case, in which a middle-aged couple was executed for slipping atomic secrets to the Soviet Union.

White, Welsh S. **The Death Penalty in the Eighties: An Examination of the Modern System of Capital Punishment.** Ann Arbor, MI: University of Michigan Press, 1987. 198p. ISBN 0-472-10088-2. (Out of print.)

Discusses a variety of issues involved in the capital punishment debate, including some that are rarely discussed, such as the rights of the defendant in the penalty phase of a trial and the question of defendants who choose to be electrocuted.

————. **The Death Penalty in the Nineties: An Examination of the Modern System of Capital Punishment.** Ann Arbor, MI: University of Michigan Press, $36.50. ISBN 0-472-09461-0 (hardcover). $18.95. ISBN 0-472-06461-4 (paperback).

Expanded and updated version of the above.

Woodward, Bob, and Scott Armstrong. **The Brethren: Inside the Supreme Court.** New York: Avon, 1981. 467p. $5.95. ISBN 0-380-52183-0.

An inside look at the workings of the U.S. Supreme Court from the 1969 through 1975 terms. It includes valuable information on the justices' deliberations concerning the death penalty and the Eighth Amendment's ban on cruel and unusual punishment that resulted in the historic *Furman* and *Gregg* decisions of the 1970s.

Articles and Essays

Baldus, David C., Charles A. Pulaski, Jr., and George Woodworth. **"Arbitrariness and Discrimination in the Administration of the Death Penalty: A Challenge to State Supreme Courts."** *Stetson Law Review* 15 (1986): 133–261.

Barzun, Jacques. **"In Favor of Capital Punishment."** *The American Scholar,* vol. 31, no. 2 (Spring 1962).

The classic essay calling for capital punishment as a way of ridding society of "uncontrollable brutes."

Bedau, Hugo Adam, and Michael L. Radelet. **"Miscarriages of Justice in Potentially Capital Cases."** *Stanford Law Review,* 40 (November 1987): 21–179.

In an important defense of the abolitionist argument that capital punishment is bound to result in tragic and fatal mistakes, the authors present an alphabetical listing of 350 cases in which people convicted of crimes for which they could have been sentenced to death were eventually proved to be innocent. With statistical tables.

Camus, Albert. **"Reflections on the Guillotine,"** in the author's *Resistance, Rebellion, and Death.* (New York: Alfred A. Knopf, 1966), 173–234.

The Nobel Prize winner's classical essay opposing the death penalty.

Cheever, the Rev. George B., D.D., Samuel Hand, and Wendell Phillips. **"The Death Penalty."** *North American Review* (December 1881).

Three essays on the death penalty from the varying perspectives of three nineteenth-century reformers. Cheever and Hand come down in favor of the practice, Phillips against.

Erlich, Isaac. **"The Deterrent Effect of Capital Punishment: A Question of Life and Death."** *American Economic Review* (June 1975): 398–414.

The best known of the very few statistical studies to conclude that the death penalty does, in fact, deter crime. Using a controversial method called regression analysis, Erlich argues that capital punishment has a "pure deterrent effect" and that the number of executions for murder in a particular jurisdiction can have a direct effect on the number of murders that take place there.

Filler, Louis. **"Movements To Abolish the Death Penalty in the United States."** *Annals of the American Academy of Political & Social Science* (November 1954): 124–136.

A historical review.

Frady, Marshall. **"Death in Arkansas."** *The New Yorker* (22 February 1993): 105–133.

A detailed and revealing look at the case of Rickey Ray Rector, a brain-damaged black man executed in Arkansas in 1992 for the murder of a small town policeman. The Rector case is of special interest for several reasons, among them the fact that Bill Clinton, who was then the governor of Arkansas, interrupted his presidential campaign to return to the state in order to deny any last minute requests for a stay of execution.

Geimer, William S., and Jonathan Amsterdam. **"Why Jurors Vote Life or Death: Operative Factors in Ten Florida Death Penalty Cases."** *American Journal of Criminal Law* 15 (1987–1988): 1–54.

A rare exploration of the reasoning of jurors when deciding the question of life or death.

Goldberg, Steven. **"On Capital Punishment."** *Ethics* 85 (1974).

A retentionist takes a critical look at the question of deterrence and the death penalty.

Various authors. **"Should the Death Penalty Be Retained?"** *Congressional Digest* (August–September 1927): 227–250.

Brief selections from several authors, judges, penologists, politicians, and others with opinions on the death penalty. Among the pro-capital-punishment views represented are those of Judge Alfred J. Talley, Ambrose Bierce, and Albert Einstein. Among those opposed are Henry Ford, Clarence Darrow, and Thomas Mott Osborne.

Studies and Reports

Great Britain, **Royal Commission on Capital Punishment, 1949–1953.** *1953 Report.* London, H.M. Stationary Office, 1953.

A landmark study by a royal commission of the British government, examining the question of whether or not Great Britain should retain the death penalty. It would eventually be abandoned, at first on an experimental basis, in 1965.

New York State Defenders Association. **Capital Losses: The Price of the Death Penalty for New York State.** Albany, N.Y.: New York State Defenders Association, 1982.

A study of the financial costs of maintaining the death penalty, concluding that reinstituting the death penalty in New York would cost the state upwards of $1.8 million dollars per execution.

Sellin, Thorsten. **The Death Penalty: A Report for the Model Penal Code Project of the American Law Institute.** Philadelphia: American Law Institute, 1959. 84p.

Sellin's classic study.

Shinn, Rinn-Sup. **Crime and Crime Control: National Public Opinion Polls, 10 December 1990.** Washington, D.C.: Congressional Research Service, 1990. 54p.

A report on public opinion polls relating to crime and the criminal justice system, prepared for the Congressional Research Service. The fifth chapter of the report deals with public attitudes toward the death penalty.

U.S. Congress, House Committee on the Judiciary. Subcommittee on Crime. **Federal Death Penalty Legislation: Hearing, 101st Congress, 2nd Session on H.R. 2102....** 24 March–23 May 1990. Washington, D.C.: Government Printing Office, 1990. 671p.

The subcommittee's hearings on expanding the application of the death penalty for federal crimes provide an exhaustive examination of what could turn out to be an increasingly important aspect of the capital punishment question.

U.S. General Accounting Office. **"Death Penalty Sentencing: Research Indicates Pattern of Racial Disparities; Report to Senate and House Committee on the Judiciary."** 26 February 1990. Washington, D.C.: General Accounting Office, 1990. 13p.

This important report, which concerns several different studies of racial disparities in sentencing since the U.S. Supreme Court's *Furman* decision, concludes that there has, in fact, been a significant imbalance in the way death sentences have been handed out to whites and other races.

U.S. Senate, Committee on the Judiciary. **"Establishing Constitutional Procedures for the Imposition of Capital Punishment...."** Washington, D.C.: U.S. Government Printing Office, 1986.

Report of the committee that heard evidence on death penalty guidelines.

Pamphlets and Monographs

Amnesty International. **USA: Death Penalty and Juvenile Offenders.** New York: Amnesty International, October 1991. 83p.

A discussion of the death penalty as it is applied to juveniles, including a brief overall history and a somewhat more detailed account of 23 young people currently under sentence of death. Also available in Spanish.

Bedau, Hugo Adam. **The Case against the Death Penalty.** New York: American Civil Liberties Union, Capital Punishment Project, 1984.

A brief 24-page summary of the arguments of perhaps the most prolific American opponent of the death penalty.

Lincoln Institute for Research and Education. **"Capital Punishment: An Idea Whose Time Has Come Again."** Washington, D.C.: Lincoln Institute for Research and Education, 1986. 22p.

Makes a case for the death penalty, based on the rising incidence of violent crime and the "intellectual and moral bankruptcy of the arguments of those who have opposed the execution of murderers. . . ."

National Coalition to Abolish the Death Penalty. **"The Death Penalty: The Religious Community Calls for Abolition."** Washington, D.C.: National Coalition to Abolish the Death Penalty, undated.

The positions of several denominations calling for an end to the death penalty.

Smith, George C. **Capital Punishment 1986: Last Lines of Defense.** Washington Legal Foundation, 1986.

Contains six pro-death-penalty essays on various aspects of the subject. Foreword by Congressman Dick Armey.

Directory of Organizations

Abolitionist Directory. National Coalition to Abolish the Death Penalty.

An annual listing of all NCADP affiliates, as well as other organizations that work against the death penalty.

Bibliographies

Bedau, Hugo Adam. **"A Bibliography on Capital Punishment and Related Topics, 1948–1958."** *Prison Journal* (October 1958): 41–45.

Beman, Lemar T., ed. **Selected Articles on Capital Punishment.** New York: H.W. Wilson, 1925, xxxi–lxvii.

Fanning, Clara E., ed. **Selected Articles on Capital Punishment.** Minneapolis: H.W. Wilson, 1913, xiii–xxvi.

Flanders, Stephen A. **Capital Punishment.** New York: Facts on File, 1991, 102–168.

Lyons, Douglas B., and William J. Bowers, **"Selected Bibliography and References on Capital Punishment,"** in Bowers, *Executions in America.* Lexington, Mass.: D.C. Heath, 1974, 403–452.

Mackey, Philip English. **Voices against Death: American Opposition to Capital Punishment, 1787–1975.** New York: Burt Franklin & Co., 1976.

Radelet, Michael L., and Margaret Vandiver. **Capital Punishment in America: An Annotated Bibliography.** New York: Garland Publishing Company, 1988. 256p.

Roe, Tengela G. **Capital Punishment: Selected References, 1986–1991.** Revised March 1991. Washington, D.C.: Congressional Research Service, 1991.

United Nations. **The Death Penalty: A Bibliographical Research.** New York: United Nations, no date.

Periodicals Specializing in Capital Punishment Issues

Bureau of Justice Statistics Bulletin, Capital Punishment 19—
U.S. Department of Justice
Office of Justice Programs
Bureau of Justice Statistics
Washington, DC
Annual. No charge.

Since 1930, the Justice Department has published this yearly summary of facts and statistics related to the imposition and administration of the death penalty in the United States.

Capital Punishment for Female Offenders: Present Female Death Row Inmates and Death Sentences and Executions of Female Offenders
Victor L. Streib
Cleveland Marshall College of Law
Cleveland State University
1801 Euclid Avenue
Cleveland, Ohio 44115
(216) 687-2344
Unpriced.

Periodic reports on "the current implementation of the death penalty for female offenders."

Capital Report
National Legal Aid & Defender Association
Death Penalty Litigation Section
1625 K Street NW
Eighth Floor
Washington, DC 20006
(202) 452-0620

Bi-monthly. Yearly subscription: $18 for members of the NLADA; $15 for death penalty litigators. Availability limited.

Published specifically "for the education and assistance of individuals or programs engaged in death penalty defense." Available by subscription, but not "to individuals or programs engaged in death penalty prosecution."

Death Penalty Bulletin (North Carolina Prison and Jail Project Bulletin)
North Carolina Prison and Jail Project
Box 309
Durham, NC 27702-0309

Strongly opposed to the death penalty, this newsletter focuses on prison developments in North Carolina and the South.

The Death Penalty Exchange
National Coalition to Abolish the Death Penalty
1419 V Street NW
Washington, DC 20009
Periodic report.

Provides current information.

Death Row U.S.A.
NAACP Legal Defense and Educational Fund
Suite 1600
99 Hudson Street
New York, NY 10001-2897
Various dates. Unpriced.

Periodic update on death penalty developments in the United States. Includes summaries of court cases involving capital punishment, defines the issues they raise, both pending and decided, and provides names and races of all condemned prisoners in the United States.

Execution Alert
National Coalition to Abolish the Death Penalty
1419 V Street NW
Washington, DC 20009
(202) 347-2411

Irregular bulletins on upcoming executions.

Execution Update
NAACP Legal Defense and Educational Fund
Suite 1600
99 Hudson Street
New York, NY 10001-2897
Various dates. Unpriced.

Periodic statistical update on death sentences and executions in the United States. Includes names and dates of death of everyone executed since the *Gregg* decision, with information on their sex and race and that of their victim(s).

The Juvenile Death Penalty Today: Present Death Row Inmates under Juvenile Death Sentences and Death Sentences and Executions for Juvenile Crimes
Victor L. Streib
Cleveland Marshall College of Law
Cleveland State University
1801 Euclid Avenue
Cleveland, Ohio 44115
(216) 687-2344
Various dates. Unpriced.

Irregular reports "on the current implementation of the juvenile death penalty."

Supreme Court of the United States Individual Slip Opinions
Superintendent of Documents
Government Printing Office
Washington, DC 20402-0001
Annual subscription: $161.

Opinions of the Supreme Court on individual cases, as announced from the bench.

Law Journals and Reviews

The following periodicals do not specialize in capital punishment issues, but are among the many similar publications that occasionally publish notable articles on the subject:

American Criminal Law Review. American Bar Association, Chicago, IL. Four times a year.

American Journal of Criminal Law. University of Texas, Austin, TX. Three times a year.

Columbia Law Review. Columbia University School of Law, New York, NY. Twelve times a year.

Harvard Law Review. Harvard Law Review Association, Gannett House, Cambridge, MA. Eight times a year.

Journal of Criminal Law, Criminology and Police Science. Northwestern University School of Law, Chicago, IL. Four times a year.

Stanford Law Review. Stanford University, Stanford, CA. Six times a year.

Stetson Law Review. Stetson University College of Law, St. Petersburg, FL. Irregular.

University of Chicago Law Review. University of Chicago, Chicago, IL. Four times a year.

Woodrow Wilson Journal of Law. Woodrow Wilson Journal of Law, Atlanta, GA. Irregular.

Yale Law Journal. Yale Law Journal, New Haven, CT. Eight times a year.

Selected Nonprint Resources

INCLUDED ON THIS LIST, along with a selection of educational films, videotapes, and filmstrips, are notable feature motion pictures that deal with executions. They are included either for the special perspectives they present, or because of the influence they have had on public attitudes toward capital punishment.

Capital Punishment (Bill of Rights in Action Series)
Type: VHS
Length: 23 min.
Date: 1982 (revised edition)
Cost: $79 (plus $4 shipping)
Source: Encyclopedia Britannica Educational Corporation
6th Floor
310 S. Michigan Avenue
Chicago, IL 60604
(800) 554-9862

The key questions of deterrence, retribution, and Eighth Amendment rights are framed as arguments presented by prosecuting and defense attorneys in a trial.

Death and the Mistress of Delay
Type: VHS
Length: 30 min.
Date: 1986
Cost: $60 (rent), $149 (purchase)

Source: Journal Films, Inc.
130 Pitner Avenue
Evanston, IL 60202
(800) 323-5448

Explores the issues surrounding the death penalty from the perspective of convicts on Florida's death row and a small group of attorneys battling to postpone their executions, if not to spare their lives.

Death Penalty (Crime File Series)
Type: VHS
Length: 28 min.
Date: 1985
Cost: $17 (plus $4.30 shipping and handling)
Source: National Institute of Justice   Box 6000
Rockville, MD 20850
(800) 851-3420

Explores the modern capital punishment debate in light of the international decline in the use of the death penalty.

Death Penalty
Type: 3/4″ U-matic cassette
Length: 29 min.
Date: 1979
Cost: $35 (rent)
Source: Dallas County Community College District Center for
Telecommunications
4343 North Highway 67
Mesquite, TX 75150-2095
(214) 746-2135

This winner of the Silver Award at the 1980 International Film and TV Festival explores the controversies surrounding the death penalty.

The Death Penalty: What Is Fair?
Type: Filmstrip (color)
Length: 81 frames, approximately 18 min.
Date: 1984
Cost: $28 (purchase)
Source: Contemporary Media Productions
Random House School Division
201 E. 5th
New York, NY 10022

This well-received filmstrip presents arguments for and against capital punishment, with a brief history of the practice.

Death Row and the Death Penalty

Type: VHS
Length: 14 min.
Cost: $50 (rent), $110 (purchase)
Source: Journal Films, Inc.
130 Pitner Avenue
Evanston, IL 60202
(800) 323-5448

This UPI film features scenes of an execution taking place, along with interviews with people on opposing sides of the death penalty issue.

Death Watch

Type: VHS, Beta
Length: 53 min.
Date: 1981
Cost: $150
Source: Dave Bell Associates
3211 Cahuenga Boulevard
West Hollywood, CA 90068
(213) 851-7801

A documentary view of life on the death row of Arizona State Prison, featuring interviews with six of the condemned residents.

The Executioner's Song

Type: VHS, Beta
Length: 157 min.
Date: 1982
Cost: $14.95 (purchase)
Source: International Video Entertainment (IVE)
15400 Sherman Way   Suite 500
Van Nuys, CA
(800) 423-7455

A made-for-television adaptation of Norman Mailer's book about Gary Gilmore, starring Tommy Lee Jones in an impressive performance as the killer who demanded his own execution. The videotaped version was edited for the European market and contains some material originally deemed unsuitable for American television.

The Expert

Type: VHS, 16mm (color)
Length: 30 min.
Date: 1984
Cost: $550 (16mm purchase), $400 (videotape purchase),
$50 (16mm rental)

Source: American Film Institute
501 Doheny Road
Beverly Hills, CA 90210

This dramatization, concerning a doctor preparing a gas chamber for an execution, is designed to spark group discussion about the pros and cons of capital punishment.

48 Hours: Death by Midnight
Type: VHS
Length: 60 min.
Date: 1992
Cost: $33.45
Source: CBS News
(800) 338-4847

This powerful documentary looks at the controversies surrounding last-minute death sentence appeals by focussing on the desperate efforts of an energetic lawyer to postpone the execution of a condemned Nebraska prisoner named Willie Otey. It raises such questions as the following, expressed by correspondent Richard Schlesinger: "When do appeals stop being safeguards and become delaying tactics that only postpone the inevitable? How easy should it be to execute someone?"

I Want To Live!
Type: VHS, Beta (black and white)
Length: 120 min.
Date: 1958
Cost: $24.98 (purchase)
Source: MGM/UA Home Video
8670 Wilshire Blvd.
Beverly Hills, CA 90211
(213) 967-2296

Based on the true case of Barbara Graham, a prostitute and convicted murderer gassed to death in California in 1955. Susan Hayward won an Academy Award for her sympathetic portrayal of Graham as a victim of misfortune and circumstance, who ended up in the San Quentin gas chamber by mistake. The film ends with a long, detailed—and, for the 1950s, extremely graphic—depiction of Graham's long wait in the death cell, her walk next door to the little death chamber, and finally, her death by asphyxiation. No less a figure than the Nobel Prize winner, author Albert Camus, used *I Want To Live!* to illustrate his opposition to the death penalty. Referring to its portrayal of death in the gas chamber as "the reality of our time," he predicted that "[t]he day will come when such documents will seem to us to refer to prehistoric times, and we shall consider them as unbelievable as we now find it unbelievable that in earlier centuries witches were burned or thieves had their right hands cut off."

License To Kill
Type: VHS, 16mm film (color)
Length: 28 min.
Date: 1984
Cost: $425 (16mm purchase), $350 (videotape purchase), $55 (16mm rental)
Source: The Cinema Guild
           1697 Broadway
           Room 802
           New York, NY 10019
           (800) 422-0423

An introductory discussion of capital punishment, past and present, with opinions from abolitionists, judges, lawyers, death row convicts, and the mother of a murder victim.

Nightline (15 April 1992)
Type: VHS
Length: 30 min.
Date: 1992
Cost: $18.93 (purchase, including shipping and handling)
Source: MPI Home Video
           (800) 222-9420

Host Ted Koppel leads a discussion of the (then) upcoming execution of Robert Alton Harris, featuring Harris's attorney, who was trying to block the execution; the California Attorney General, whose office had prosecuted Harris and was asking for the execution to proceed; and a former California Supreme Court justice who had voted to uphold Harris's death sentence, but who believed that clemency should be granted in his case.

The Ox-Bow Incident
Type: VHS, Beta (black and white)
Length: 75 min.
Date: 1943
Cost: $19.98 (purchase)
Source: Discount Video Tapes, Inc.
           833 "A" North Hollywood
           P.O. Box 7122
           Burbank, CA 91510

Three innocent cowboys are mistaken for criminals and hung by a self-righteous mob in this famous cautionary tale, starring Henry Fonda.

Although the story is fictional, the film is a powerful indictment of the lynch mob mentality. It was named best picture of 1943 by the National Board of Review, and was nominated for Academy Awards for Best Picture and Best Director (William Wellman).

The Thin Blue Line
Type: VHS, Beta
Length: 101 min.
Date: 1988
Cost: $89.99
Source: HBO Video
            1100 Avenue of the Americas
            New York, NY 10036
            (212) 512-7400

This excellent documentary chronicles the case of Randall Adams, an innocent man convicted and sentenced to death for the murder of a Dallas policeman in 1977. At the time *The Thin Blue Line* was made, Adams was still in prison in Texas. The film was so persuasive that the case was reopened, and Adams was ultimately released.

U.S. Campaign against the Death Penalty
Type: VHS
Length: 28 min.
Date: 1987
Cost: $20
Source: Amnesty International
            Publications Department
            322 Eighth Avenue
            New York, NY 10001
            (212) 807-8400

Produced and directed by Paul Stern. An attack on the death penalty in the United States, arguing that it is "arbitrary, racially discriminatory and a violation of human rights" that "should be unconditionally abolished."

Appendix:
Furman v. Georgia and *Gregg v. Georgia*

Included here are extracts from *Furman v. Georgia,* 408 U.S. 238, 92 S.Ct. 2726 (1972), and *Gregg v. Georgia,* 428 U.S. 153, 96 S.Ct. 2909 (1976).

Justice Thurgood Marshall: Concurring Opinion, *Furman v. Georgia*

The criminal acts with which we are confronted are ugly, vicious, reprehensible acts. Their sheer brutality cannot and should not be minimized. But, we are not called upon to condone the penalized conduct; we are asked only to examine the penalty imposed on each of the petitioners and to determine whether or not it violates the Eighth Amendment. The question then is not whether we condone rape or murder, for surely we do not; it is whether capital punishment is "a punishment no longer consistent with our own self-respect" and, therefore, violative of the Eighth Amendment. . . .

Candor compels me to confess that I am not oblivious to the fact that this is truly a matter of life and death. Not only does it involve the lives of these three petitioners, but those of the almost 600 other condemned men and women in this country currently awaiting execution. While this fact cannot affect our ultimate decision, it necessitates that the decision be free from any possibility of error. . . .

In order to assess whether or not death is an excessive or unnecessary penalty, it is necessary to consider the reasons why a legislature might select it as punishment for one or more offenses, and examine whether less severe penalties would satisfy the legitimate legislative wants as well as capital punishment. If they would, then the death penalty is unnecessarily cruel, and, therefore, unconstitutional.

There are six purposes conceivably served by capital punishment: retribution, deterrence, prevention of repetitive criminal acts, encouragement of guilty pleas and confessions, eugenics, and economy. These are considered *seriatim* below.

A. The concept of retribution is one of the most misunderstood in all of our criminal jurisprudence. The principal source of confusion derives from the fact that, in dealing with the concept, most people confuse the question "why do men in fact punish?" with the question "what justifies men in punishing?" Men may punish for any number of reasons, but the reason that punishment is morally good or morally justifiable is that someone has broken the law. Thus, it can correctly be said that breaking the law is the *sine qua non* of punishment, or, in other words, that we only tolerate punishment as it is imposed on one who deviates from the norm established by the criminal law.

The fact that the State may seek retribution against those who have broken its laws does not mean that retribution may then become the State's sole end in punishing. Our jurisprudence has always accepted deterrence in general, deterrence of individual recidivism, isolation of dangerous persons, and rehabilitation as proper goals of punishment. . . . Retaliation, vengeance, and retribution have been roundly condemned as intolerable aspirations for a government in a free society. Punishment as retribution has been condemned by scholars for centuries, and the Eighth Amendment itself was adopted to prevent punishment from becoming synonymous with vengeance.

In *Weems v. United States* . . . the Court, in the course of holding that Weems' punishment violated the Eighth Amendment, contrasted it with penalties provided for other offenses and concluded: "[T]his contrast shows more than different exercises of legislative judgment. It is greater than that. It condemns the sentence in this case as cruel and unusual. It exhibits a difference between unrestrained power and that which is exercised under the spirit of constitutional limitations formed to establish justice. The State thereby suffers nothing and loses no power. *The purpose of punishment is fulfilled, crime is* repressed *by penalties of just, not tormenting, severity, its repetition is prevented, and hope is given for the reformation of the criminal.*" [Emphasis added.]

It is plain that the view of the *Weems* Court was that punishment for the sake of retribution was not permissible under the Eighth Amendment. This is the only view that the Court could have taken if the "cruel and unusual" language were to be given any meaning. Retribution surely underlies the imposition of some punishment on one who commits a criminal act. But, the fact that *some* punishment may be imposed does not mean that *any* punishment is permissible. If retribution alone could serve as a justification for any particular penalty, then all penalties selected by the legislature would by definition be acceptable means for designating society's moral approbation of a particular act. The "cruel and unusual" language would thus be read out of the Constitution and the fears of Patrick Henry and the other Founding Fathers would become realities.

To preserve the integrity of the Eighth Amendment, the Court has consistently denigrated retribution as a permissible goal of punishment. It is undoubtedly correct that there is a demand for vengeance on the part of many persons in a community against one who is convicted of a particularly offensive act. At times a cry is heard that morality requires vengeance to evidence society's abhorrence of the act. But the Eighth Amendment is our insulation from our baser selves. The "cruel and unusual" language limits the avenues through which vengeance can be channeled. Were this not so, the language would be empty and a return to the rack and other tortures would be possible in a given case.

Mr. Justice Story wrote that the Eighth Amendment's limitation on punishment "would seem to be wholly unnecessary in a free government, since it is scarcely possible that any department of such a government should authorize or justify such atrocious conduct."

The history of the Eighth Amendment supports only the conclusion that retribution for its own sake is improper.

B. The most hotly contested issue regarding capital punishment is whether it is better than life imprisonment as a deterrent to crime.

While the contrary position has been argued, it is my firm opinion that the death penalty is a more severe sanction than life imprisonment. Admittedly, there are some persons who would rather die than languish in prison for a lifetime. But, whether or not they should be able to choose death as an alternative is a far different question from that presented here—i.e., whether the State can impose death as a punishment. Death is irrevocable; life imprisonment is not. Death, of course makes rehabilitation impossible; life imprisonment does not. In short, death has always been viewed as the ultimate sanction, and it seems to be perfectly reasonable to continue to view it as such.

It must be kept in mind, then, that the question to be considered is not simply whether capital punishment is a deterrent, but whether it is a better deterrent than life imprisonment.

There is no more complex problem than determining the deterrent efficacy of the death penalty. "Capital punishment has obviously failed as a deterrent when a murder is committed. We can number its failures. But we can not number its successes. No one can ever know how many people have refrained from murder because of the fear of being hanged." This is the nub of the problem and it is exacerbated by the paucity of useful data. The United States is more fortunate than most countries, however, in that it has what are generally considered to be the world's most reliable statistics.

The two strongest arguments in favor of capital punishment as a deterrent are both logical hypotheses devoid of evidentiary support, but persuasive nonetheless. The first proposition was best stated by Sir

James Stephen in 1864: "No other punishment deters men so effectually from committing crime as the punishment of death. This is one of those propositions which is difficult to prove, simply because they are in themselves more obvious than any proof can make them. It is possible to display ingenuity in arguing against it, but that is all. The whole experience of mankind is in the other direction. The threat of instant death is one to which resort has always been made when there was an absolute necessity for producing some result. . . . No one goes to certain inevitable death except by compulsion. Put the matter the other way. Was there ever yet a criminal who, when sentenced to death and brought out to die, would refuse the offer of a commutation of his sentence for the severest secondary punishment? Surely not. Why is this? It can only be because 'All that a man has will he give for his life.' In any secondary punishment, however terrible, there is hope; but death is death; its terrors cannot be described more forcibly."

This hypothesis relates to the use of capital punishment as a deterrent for any crime. The second proposition is that "if life imprisonment is the maximum penalty for a crime such as murder, an offender who is serving a life sentence cannot then be deterred from murdering a fellow inmate or a prison officer." This hypothesis advocates a limited deterrent effect under particular circumstances.

Abolitionists attempt to disprove these hypotheses by amassing statistical evidence to demonstrate that there is no correlation between criminal activity and the existence or nonexistence of a capital sanction. Almost all of the evidence involves the crime of murder, since murder is punishable by death in more jurisdictions than are other offenses, and almost 90% of all executions since 1930 have been pursuant to murder convictions.

Thorsten Sellin, one of the leading authorities on capital punishment, has urged that if the death penalty deters prospective murderers, the following hypotheses should be true:

"(a) Murders should be less frequent in states that have the death penalty than in those states that have abolished it, other factors being equal. Comparisons of this nature must be made among states that are as alike as possible in all other respects—character of population, social and economic condition, etc.—in order not to introduce factors known to influence murder rates in a serious manner but present in only one of these states."

"(b) Murders should increase when the death penalty is abolished and should decline when it is restored."

"(c) The deterrent effect should be greatest and therefore affect murder rates most powerfully in those communities where

the crime occurred and its consequences are most strongly
brought home to the population."

"(d) Law enforcement officers would be safer from murderous
attacks in states that have the death penalty than in those
without it."

Sellin's evidence indicates that not one of these propositions is
true. This evidence has its problems, however. One is that there
are no accurate figures for capital murders; there are only figures on
homicides and they, of course, include noncapital killings. A second
problem is that certain murders undoubtedly are misinterpreted as
accidental deaths or suicides, and there is no way of estimating the
number of such undetected crimes. A third problem is that not all
homicides are reported. Despite these difficulties, most authorities
have assumed that the proportion of capital murders in a State's or
nation's homicide statistics remains reasonably constant, and that the
homicide statistics are therefore useful.

Sellin's statistics demonstrate that there is no correlation between
the murder rate and the presence or absence of the capital sanction.
He compares States that have similar characteristics and finds that
irrespective of their position on capital punishment, they have similar
murder rates. In the New England States, for example, there is no
correlation between executions and homicide rates. The same is true
for Midwestern States and for all others studied. Both the United
Nations and Great Britain have acknowledged the validity of Sellin's
statistics.

Sellin also concludes that abolition and/or reintroduction of the
death penalty had no effect on the homicide rates of the various
States involved. This conclusion is borne out by others who have
made similar inquiries and by the experience of other countries.
Despite problems with the statistics, Sellin's evidence has been relied
upon in international studies of capital punishment.

Statistics also show that the deterrent effect of capital punishment
is no greater in those communities where executions take place than in
other communities. In fact, there is some evidence that imposition of
capital punishment may actually encourage crime, rather than deter it.
And, while police and law enforcement officers are the strongest
advocates of capital punishment, the evidence is overwhelming that
police are no safer in communities that retain the sanction than in
those that have abolished it.

There is also a substantial body of data showing that the existence
of the death penalty has virtually no effect on the homicide rate in
prisons. Most of the persons sentenced to death are murderers, and
murderers tend to be model prisoners.

In sum, the only support for the theory that capital punishment is an effective deterrent is found in the hypotheses with which we began and the occasional stories about a specific individual being deterred from doing a contemplated criminal act. These claims of specific deterrence are often spurious, however, and may be more than counter-balanced by the tendency of capital punishment to incite certain crimes.

The United Nations Committee that studied capital punishment found that "[i]t is generally agreed between the retentionists and abolitionists, whatever their opinions about the validity of comparative studies of deterrence, that the data which now exist show no correlation between the existence of capital punishment and lower rates of capital crime."

Despite the fact that abolitionists have not proved non-deterrence beyond a reasonable doubt, they have succeeded in showing by clear and convincing evidence that capital punishment is not necessary as a deterrent to crime in our society. This is all that they must do. We would shirk our judicial responsibilities if we failed to accept the presently existing statistics and demanded more proof. It may be that we now possess all the proof that anyone could ever hope to assemble on the subject. But, even if further proof were to be forthcoming, I believe there is more than enough evidence presently available for a decision in this case.

In 1793 William Bradford studied the utility of the death penalty in Pennsylvania and found that it probably had no deterrent effect but that more evidence was needed. Edward Livingston reached a similar conclusion with respect to deterrence in 1833 upon completion of his study for Louisiana. Virtually every study that has since been undertaken has reached the same result.

In light of the massive amount of evidence before us, I see no alternative but to conclude that capital punishment cannot be justified on the basis of its deterrent effect.

C. Much of what must be said about the death penalty as a device to prevent recidivism is obvious—if a murderer is executed, he cannot possibly commit another offense. The fact is, however, that murderers are extremely unlikely to commit other crimes either in prison or upon their release. For the most part, they are first offenders, and when released from prison they are known to become model citizens. Furthermore, most persons who commit capital crimes are not executed. With respect to those who are sentenced to die, it is critical to note that the jury is never asked to determine whether they are likely to be recidivists. In light of these facts, if capital punishment were justified purely on the basis of preventing recidivism, it would have to be considered to be excessive; no general need to obliterate all capital offenders could have been demonstrated, nor any specific need in individual cases.

D. The three final purposes which may underlie utilization of a capital sanction—encouraging guilty pleas and confessions, eugenics, and reducing state expenditure—may be dealt with quickly. If the death penalty is used to encourage guilty pleas and thus to deter suspects from exercising their rights under the Sixth Amendment to jury trials, it is unconstitutional. *United States v. Jackson*, 390 U.S. 570 (1968). Its elimination would do little to impair the State's bargaining position in criminal cases, since life imprisonment remains a severe sanction which can be used as leverage for bargaining for pleas or confessions in exchange either for charges of lesser offenses or recommendations of leniency.

Moreover, to the extent that capital punishment is used to encourage confessions and guilty pleas, it is not being used for punishment purposes. A State that justifies capital punishment on its utility as part of the conviction process could not profess to rely on capital punishment as a deterrent. Such a State's system would be structured with twin goals only: obtaining guilty pleas and confessions and imposing *imprisonment* as the maximum sanction. Since life imprisonment is sufficient for bargaining purposes, the death penalty is excessive if used for the same purposes.

In light of the previous discussion on deterrence, any suggestions concerning the benefits of capital punishment are obviously meritless. As I pointed out above, there is not even any attempt made to discover which capital offenders are likely to be recidivists, let alone which are positively incurable. No test or procedure presently exists by which incurables can be screened from those who would benefit from treatment. On the one hand, due process would seem to require that we have some procedure to demonstrate incurability before execution; and, on the other hand, equal protection would then seemingly require that all incurables be executed. . . . In addition, the "cruel and unusual" language would require that life imprisonment, treatment, and sterilization be inadequate for eugenic purposes. More importantly, this Nation has never formally professed eugenic goals, and the history of the world does not look kindly on them. If eugenics is one of our purposes, then the legislatures should say so forthrightly and design procedures to serve this goal. Until such time, I can only conclude, as has virtually everyone else who has looked at the problem, that capital punishment cannot be defended on the basis of any eugenic purposes.

As for the argument that it is cheaper to execute a capital offender than to imprison him for life, even assuming that such an argument, if true, would support a capital sanction, it is simply incorrect. A disproportionate amount of money spent on prisons is attributable to death row. Condemned men are not productive members of the prison community, although they could be, and executions are expensive. Appeals are often automatic, and courts admittedly spend more time with death cases.

At trial, the selection of jurors is likely to become a costly, time-consuming problem in a capital case, and defense counsel will reasonably exhaust every possible means to save his client from execution, no matter how long the trial takes.

During the period between conviction and execution, there are an inordinate number of collateral attacks on the conviction and attempts to obtain executive clemency, all of which exhaust the time, money, and effort of the State. There are also continual assertions that the condemned prisoner has gone insane. Because there is a formally established policy of not executing insane persons, great sums of money may be spent on detecting and curing mental illness in order to perform the execution. Since no one wants the responsibility for the execution, the condemned man is likely to be passed back and forth from doctors to custodial officials to courts like a ping-pong ball. The entire process is very costly.

When all is said and done, there can be no doubt that it costs more to execute a man than to keep him in prison for life.

E. There is but one conclusion that can be drawn from all of this — i.e., the death penalty is an excessive and unnecessary punishment that violates the Eighth Amendment. The statistical evidence is not convincing beyond all doubt, but it is persuasive. It is not improper at this point to take judicial notice of the fact that for more than 200 years men have labored to demonstrate that capital punishment serves no purpose that life imprisonment could not serve equally well. And they have done so with great success. Little, if any, evidence has been abduced to prove the contrary. The point has now been reached at which deference to the legislatures is tantamount to abdication of our judicial roles as factfinders, judges, and ultimate arbiters of the Constitution. We know that at some point the presumption of constitutionality accorded legislative acts gives way to a realistic assessment of those acts. This point comes when there is sufficient evidence available so that judges can determine, not whether the legislature acted wisely, but whether it had any rational basis whatsoever for acting. We have this evidence before us now. There is no rational basis for concluding that capital punishment is not excessive. It therefore violates the Eighth Amendment.

In addition, even if capital punishment is not excessive, it nonetheless violates the Eighth Amendment because it is morally unacceptable to the people of the United States at this time in their history.

In judging whether or not a given penalty is morally acceptable, most courts have said that the punishment is valid unless "it shocks the conscience and sense of justice of the people."

Judge Frank once noted the problems inherent in the use of such a measuring stick: "[The court,] before it reduces a sentence as 'cruel and unusual,' must have reasonably good assurances that the sentence offends the 'common conscience.' And, in any context, such a standard—the community's attitude—is usually an unknowable. It resembles a slithery shadow, since one can seldom learn, at all accurately, what the community, or a majority, actually feels. Even a carefully-taken 'public opinion poll' would be inconclusive in a case like this."

While a public opinion poll obviously is of some assistance in indicating public acceptance or rejection of a specific penalty, its utility cannot be very great. This is because whether or not a punishment is cruel and unusual depends, not on whether its mere mention "shocks the conscience and sense of justice of the people," but on whether people who were fully informed as to the purposes of the penalty and its liabilities would find the penalty shocking, unjust, and unacceptable.

In other words, the question with which we must deal is not whether a substantial portion of American citizens would today, if polled, opine that capital punishment is barbarously cruel, but whether they would find it to be so in the light of all the information presently available.

This is not to suggest that with respect to this test of unconstitutionality people are required to act rationally; they are not. With respect to this judgement, a violation of the Eighth Amendment is totally dependent on the predictable subjective, emotional reactions of informed citizens.

It has often been noted that American citizens know almost nothing about capital punishment. Some of the conclusions arrived at in the preceding section and the supporting evidence would be critical to an informed judgement on the morality of the death penalty: e.g., that the death penalty is no more effective a deterrent than life imprisonment, that convicted murderers are rarely executed, but are usually sentenced to a term in prison; that convicted murderers usually are model prisoners, and that they almost always become law-abiding citizens upon their release from prison; that the costs of executing a capital offender exceed the costs of imprisoning him for life; that while in prison, a convict under sentence of death performs none of the useful functions that life prisoners perform; that no attempt is made in the sentencing process to ferret out likely recidivists for execution; and that the death penalty may actually stimulate criminal activity.

This information would almost surely convince the average citizen that the death penalty was unwise, but a problem arises as to whether it would convince him that the penalty was morally reprehensible.

This problem arises from the fact that the public's desire for retribution, even though this is a goal that the legislature cannot constitutionally pursue as its sole justification for capital punishment, might influence the citizenry's view of the morality of capital punishment. The solution to the problem lies in the fact that no one has ever seriously advanced retribution as a legitimate goal of our society. Defenses of capital punishment are always mounted on deterrent or other similar theories. This should not be surprising. It is the people of this country who have urged in the past that prisons rehabilitate as well as isolate offenders, and it is the people who have injected a sense of purpose into our penology. I cannot believe that at this stage in our history, the American people would ever knowingly support purposeless vengeance. Thus, I believe that the great mass of citizens would conclude on the basis of the material already considered that the death penalty is immoral and therefore unconstitutional.

But, if this information needs supplementing, I believe that the following facts would serve to convince even the most hesitant of citizens to condemn death as a sanction: capital punishment is imposed discriminatorily against certain identifiable classes of people; there is evidence that innocent people have been executed before their innocence can be proved; and the death penalty wreaks havoc with our entire criminal justice system. Each of these facts is considered briefly below.

Regarding discrimination, it has been said that "[i]t is usually the poor, the illiterate, the underprivileged, the member of the minority group—the man who, because he is without means, and is defended by a court appointed attorney—who becomes society's sacrificial lamb. . . ." Indeed, a look at the bare statistics regarding executions is enough to betray much of the discrimination. A total 3,859 persons have been executed since 1930, of whom 1,751 were white and 2,066 were Negro; 455 persons, including 48 whites and 405 Negroes, were executed for rape. It is immediately apparent that Negroes were executed far more often than whites in proportion to their percentage of the population. Studies indicate that while the higher rate of execution among Negroes is partially due to a higher rate of crime, there is evidence of racial discrimination. Racial or other discriminations should not be surprising. In *McGautha v. California,* 402 U.S., at 207, this Court held "that committing to the untrammeled discretion of the jury the power to pronounce life or death in capital cases is [not] offensive to anything in the Constitution." This was an open invitation to discrimination.

There is also overwhelming evidence that the death penalty is employed against men and not women. Only 32 women have been executed since 1930, while 3,827 men have met a similar fate. It is difficult to understand why women have received such favored treatment since the purposes allegedly served by capital punishment seemingly are equally applicable to both sexes.

It also is evident that the burden of capital punishment falls upon the poor, the ignorant, and the underprivileged members of society. It is the poor, and the members of minority groups who are least able to voice their complaints against capital punishment. Their impotence leaves them victims of a sanction that the wealthier, better-represented, just-as-guilty person can escape. So long as the capital sanction is used only against the forlorn, easily forgotten members of society, legislators are content to maintain the status quo, because change would draw attention to the problem and concern might develop. Ignorance is perpetuated and apathy soon becomes its mate, and we have today's situation.

Just as Americans know little about who is executed and why, they are unaware of the potential dangers of executing an innocent man. Our "beyond a reasonable doubt" burden of proof in criminal cases is intended to protect the innocent, but we know it is not foolproof. Various studies have shown that people whose innocence is later convincingly established are convicted and sentenced to death.

Proving one's innocence after a jury finding of guilt is almost impossible. While reviewing courts are willing to entertain all kinds of collateral attacks where a sentence of death is involved, they very rarely dispute the jury's interpretation of the evidence. This is, perhaps, as it should be. But, if an innocent man has been found guilty, he must then depend on the good faith of the prosecutor's office to help him establish his innocence. There is evidence, however, that prosecutors do not welcome the idea of having convictions, which they labored hard to secure, overturned, and that their cooperation is highly unlikely.

No matter how careful the courts are, the possibility of perjured testimony, mistaken honest testimony, and human error are all too real. We have no way of judging how many innocent persons have been executed but we can be certain that there were some. Whether there were many is an open question made difficult by the loss of those who were most knowledgeable about the crime for which they were convicted. Surely there will be more as long as capital punishment remains part of our penal law.

While it is difficult to ascertain with certainty the degree to which the death penalty is discriminatorily imposed or the number of innocent persons sentenced to die, there is one conclusion about the penalty that is universally accepted—i.e., it "tends to distort the course of criminal law." As Mr. Justice Frankfurter said: "I am strongly against capital punishment. . . . When life is at hazard in a trial, it sensationalizes the whole thing almost unwittingly; the effect on juries, the Bar, the public, the Judiciary, I regard as very bad. I think scientifically the claim of deterrence is not worth much. Whatever proof there may be in my judgement does not outweigh the social loss due to the inherent sensationalism of a trial for life."

The deleterious effects of the death penalty are also felt otherwise than at trial. For example, its very existence "inevitably sabotages a social or institutional program of reformation." In short "[t]he presence of the death penalty as the keystone of our penal system bedevils the administration of criminal justice all the way down the line and is the stumbling block in the path of general reform and of the treatment of crime and criminals."

Assuming knowledge of all the facts presently available regarding capital punishment, the average citizen would, in my opinion, find it shocking to his conscience and sense of justice. For this reason alone capital punishment cannot stand.

To arrive at the conclusion that the death penalty violates the Eighth Amendment, we have had to engage in a long and tedious journey. The amount of information that we have assembled and sorted is enormous. Yet, I firmly believe that we have not deviated in the slightest from the principles with which we began.

At a time in our history when the streets of the Nation's cities inspire fear and despair, rather than pride and hope, it is difficult to maintain objectivity and concern for our fellow citizens. But, the measure of a country's greatness is its ability to retain compassion in times of crisis. No nation in the recorded history of man has a greater tradition of revering justice and fair treatment for all its citizens in times of turmoil, confusion, and tension than ours. This is a country which stands tallest in troubled times, a country that clings to fundamental principles, cherishes its constitutional heritage, and rejects simple solutions that compromise the values that lie at the roots of our democratic system.

In striking down capital punishment, this Court does not malign our system of government. On the contrary, it pays homage to it. Only in a free society could right triumph in difficult times, and could civilization record its magnificent advancement. In recognizing the humanity of our fellow beings, we pay ourselves the highest tribute. We achieve "a major milestone in the long road up from barbarianism" and join the approximately 70 other jurisdictions in the world which celebrate their regard for civilization and humanity by shunning capital punishment.

I concur in the judgments of the Court.

Justices Potter Stewart, Lewis Powell, and John Paul Stevens: Plurality Opinion, *Gregg v. Georgia*

The petitioner, Troy *Gregg,* was charged with committing armed robbery and murder. In accordance with Georgia procedure in capital cases, the trial was in two stages, a guilt stage and a sentencing stage. The evidence at the guilt trial established that on November 21, 1973, the petitioner and a traveling companion, Floyd Allen, while hitchhiking north in Florida were picked up by Fred Simmons and Bob Moore. Their car broke down, but they continued north after Simmons purchased another vehicle with some of the cash he was carrying. While still in Florida, they picked up another hitchhiker, Dennis Weaver, who rode with them to Atlanta, where he was let out about 11 p.m. A short time later the four men interrupted their journey for a rest stop along the highway. The next morning the bodies of Simmons and Moore were discovered in a ditch nearby.

On November 23, after reading about the shootings in an Atlanta newspaper, Weaver communicated with the Gwinnett County police and related information concerning the journey with the victims, including a description of the car. The next afternoon, the petitioner and Allen, while in Simmons' car, were arrested in Asheville, N.C. In the search incident to the arrest a .25-caliber pistol, later shown to be that used to kill Simmons and Moore, was found in the petitioner's pocket. After receiving the warnings required by *Miranda v. Arizona,* and signing a written waiver of his rights, the petitioner signed a written statement in which he admitted shooting, then robbing Simmons and Moore. He justified the slayings on grounds of self-defense. The next day, while being transferred to Lawrenceville, Ga., the petitioner and Allen were taken to the scene of the shootings. Upon arriving there, Allen recounted the events leading to the slayings. His version of these events was as follows: After Simmons and Moore left the car, the petitioner stated that he intended to rob them. The petitioner then took his pistol in hand and positioned himself on the car to improve his aim. As Simmons and Moore came up an embankment toward the car, the petitioner fired three shots and the two men fell near a ditch. The petitioner, at close range, then fired a shot into the head of each. He robbed them of valuables and drove away with Allen. The jury found the petitioner guilty of two counts of armed robbery and two counts of murder.

At the penalty stage, which took place before the same jury, neither the prosecutor nor the petitioner's lawyer offered any additional evidence. Both counsel, however, made lengthy arguments dealing generally with the propriety of capital punishment under the circumstances and with the weight of the evidence of guilt. The trial judge instructed the jury that it recommend either a death sentence or a life prison sentence on each count. The judge further charged the jury that in determining what sentence was appropriate the jury was free to consider the facts and circumstances, if any, presented by the parties in mitigation or aggravation.

Finally, the judge instructed the jury that it "would not be authorized to consider [imposing] the penalty of death" unless it first found beyond a reasonable doubt one of these aggravating circumstances:

> "One—That the offense of murder was committed while the offender was engaged in the commission of two other capital felonies, to-wit the armed robbery of [Simmons and Moore]"

> "Two—That the offender committed the offense of murder for the purpose of receiving money and the automobile described in the indictment"

> "Three—The offense of murder was outrageously and wantonly vile, horrible and inhuman, in that they [sic] involved the depravity of [the] mind of the defendant."

Finding the first and second of these circumstances, the jury returned verdicts of death on each count.

The Supreme Court of Georgia affirmed the convictions and the imposition of the death sentences for murder. . . .

We address initially the basic contention that the punishment of death for the crime of murder is, under all circumstances, "cruel and unusual" in violation of the *Eighth and Fourteenth Amendments of the Constitution.* In Part IV of this opinion, we will consider the sentence of death imposed under the Georgia statutes at issue in this case.

The Court on a number of occasions has both assumed and asserted the constitutionality of capital punishment. In several cases that assumption provided a necessary foundation for the decision, as the Court was asked to decide whether a particular method of carrying out a capital sentence would be allowed to stand under the Eighth Amendment. But until *Furman v. Georgia* the Court never confronted squarely the fundamental claim that the punishment of death always, regardless of the enormity of the offense or the procedure followed in imposing the sentence, is cruel and unusual punishment in violation of the Constitution. Although this issue was presented and addressed in *Furman*, it was not resolved by the Court. Four Justices would have held that capital punishment is not unconstitutional *per se;* two Justices would have reached the opposite conclusion; and three Justices, while agreeing that the statutes then before the Court were invalid as applied, left open the question whether such punishment may ever be imposed. We now hold that the punishment of death does not invariably violate the Constitution. . . .

The history of the prohibition of "cruel and unusual" punishment already has been reviewed at length. The phrase first appeared in the English Bill of Rights of 1689, which was drafted by Parliament at the accession of William and Mary. The English version appears to have been directed against punishments unauthorized by statute and beyond the jurisdiction of the sentencing court, as well as those disproportionate to the offense involved. The American draftsmen, who adopted the English phrasing in drafting the Eighth Amendment, were primarily concerned, however, with proscribing "tortures" and other "barbarous" methods of punishment.

In the earliest cases raising Eighth Amendment claims, the Court focused on particular methods of execution to determine whether they were too cruel to pass constitutional muster. The constitutionality of the sentence of death itself was not at issue, and the criterion used to evaluate the mode of execution was its similarity to "torture" and other "barbarous" methods. ("[I]t is safe to affirm that punishments of torture . . . and all others in the same line of unnecessary cruelty, are forbidden by that amendment. . . ."). . . .

But the Court has not confined the prohibition embodied in the Eighth Amendment to "barbarous" methods that were generally outlawed in the 18th century. Instead, the Amendment has been interpreted in a flexible and dynamic manner. The Court early recognized that "a principle to be vital must be capable of wider application than the mischief which gave it birth." Thus the Clause forbidding "cruel and unusual" punishments is not fastened to the obsolete but may acquire meaning as public opinion becomes enlightened by humane justice.

It is clear . . . that the Eighth Amendment has not been regarded as a static concept. As Mr. Chief Justice Warren said, in an oftquoted phrase, "[t]he Amendment must draw its meaning from the evolving standards of decency that mark the progress of a maturing society." Thus, an assessment of contemporary values concerning the infliction of a challenged sanction is relevant to the application of the Eighth Amendment. As we develop below more fully, this assessment does not call for a subjective judgement. It requires, rather, that we look to objective indicia that reflect the public attitude toward a given sanction.

But our cases also make clear that public perceptions of standards of decency with respect to criminal sanctions are not conclusive. A penalty also must accord with "the dignity of man," which is the "basic concept underlying the Eighth Amendment." This means, at least, that the punishment not be "excessive." When a form of punishment in the abstract (in this case, whether capital punishment may ever be imposed as a sanction for murder) rather than in the particular (the propriety of death as a penalty to be applied to a specific defendant for a specific crime) is under consideration, the inquiry into "excessiveness" has two aspects. First, the punishment must not involve the unnecessary and wanton infliction of pain. Second, the punishment must not be grossly out of proportion to the severity of the crime. . . .

Of course, the requirements of the Eighth Amendment must be applied with an awareness of the limited role to be played by the courts. This does not mean that judges have no role to play, for the Eighth Amendment is a restraint upon the exercise of legislative power.

"Judicial review, by definition, often involves a conflict between judicial and legislative judgement as to what the Constitution means or requires. In this respect, Eighth Amendment cases come to us in no different posture. It seems conceded by all that the Amendment imposes some obligations on the judiciary to judge the constitutionality of punishment and that there are punishments that the Amendment would bar whether legislatively approved or not."

But, while we have an obligation to insure that constitutional bounds are not overreached, we may not act as judges as we might as legislators. . . .

Therefore, in assessing a punishment selected by a democratically elected legislature against the constitutional measure, we presume its validity. We may not require the legislature to select the least severe penalty possible so long as the penalty selected is not cruelly inhumane or disproportionate to the crime involved. And a heavy burden rests on those who would attack the judgement of the representatives of the people.

This is true in part because the constitutional test is intertwined with an assessment of contemporary standards and the legislative judgement weighs heavily in ascertaining such standards. "[I]n a democratic society legislatures, not courts, are constituted to respond to the will and consequently the moral values of the people." The deference we owe to the decisions of the state legislatures under our federal system, is enhanced where the specification of punishments is concerned, for "these are peculiarly questions of legislative policy." Caution is necessary lest this Court become, "under the aegis of the Cruel and Unusual Punishment Clause, the ultimate arbiter of the standards of criminal responsibility . . . throughout the country." A decision that a given punishment is impermissible under the Eighth Amendment cannot be reversed short of a constitutional amendment. The ability of the people to express their preference through the normal democratic processes, as well as through ballot referenda, is shut off. Revisions cannot be made in the light of further experience. . . .

In the discussion to this point we have sought to identify the principles and considerations that guide a court in addressing an Eighth Amendment claim. We now consider specifically whether the sentence of death for the crime of murder is a *per se* violation of the Eighth and Fourteenth Amendments to the Constitution. We note first that history and precedent strongly support a negative answer to this question.

The imposition of the death penalty for the crime of murder has a long history of acceptance both in the United States and in England. The common-law rule imposed a mandatory death sentence on all convicted murderers. And the penalty continued to be used into the 20th century by most American States, although the breadth of the common-law rule was diminished, initially by narrowing the class of murderers to be punished by death and subsequently by widespread adoption of laws expressly granting juries the discretion to recommend mercy.

It is apparent from the text of the Constitution itself that the existence of capital punishment was accepted by the Framers. At the time the Eighth Amendment was ratified, capital punishment was a common sanction in every State. Indeed, the First Congress of the United States enacted legislation providing death as the penalty for specified crimes. The Fifth Amendment, adopted at the same time as the Eighth, contemplated the continued existence of the capital sanction by imposing certain limits on the prosecution of capital cases: "No person shall be held to answer for a capital or otherwise infamous crime, unless on a presentment or indictment of a Grand Jury . . . ; nor shall any person be subject for the same offense to be twice put in jeopardy of life or limb; . . . nor be deprived of life, liberty, or property, without due process of law. . . ."

And the Fourteenth Amendment adopted over three-quarters of a century later, similarly contemplates the existence of the capital sanction in providing that no State shall deprive any person of "life, liberty, or property" without due process of law.

For nearly two centuries, this Court, repeatedly and often expressly, has recognized that capital punishment is not invalid *per se*. . . .

Four years ago, the petitioners in *Furman* and its companion cases predicated their argument primarily upon the asserted proposition that standards of decency have evolved to the point where capital punishment no longer could be tolerated. The petitioners in those cases said, in effect, that the evolutionary process had come to an end, and that standards of decency required that the Eighth Amendment be construed finally as prohibiting capital punishment for any crime regardless of its depravity and impact on society. This view was accepted by two Justices. Three other Justices were unwilling to go so far; focusing on the procedures by which convicted defendants were selected for the death penalty rather than on the actual punishment inflicted, they joined in the conclusion that the statutes before the Court were constitutionally invalid.

The petitioners in the capital cases before the Court today renew the "standards of decency" argument, but developments during the four years since *Furman* have undercut substantially the assumptions upon which their argument rested. Despite the continuing debate, dating back to the 19th century, over the morality and utility of capital punishment, it is now evident that a large proportion of American society continues to regard it as an appropriate and necessary criminal sanction.

The most marked indication of society's endorsement of the death penalty for murder is the legislative response to *Furman*. The legislatures of at least 35 States have enacted new statutes that provide for the death penalty for at least some crimes that result in the death of another person. And the Congress of the United States, in 1974, enacted a statute providing the death penalty for aircraft piracy that results in death. These recently adopted statutes have attempted to address the concerns expressed by the Court in *Furman* primarily (i) by specifying the factors to be weighed and the procedures to be followed in deciding when to impose a capital sentence, or (ii) by making the death penalty mandatory for specified crimes. But all of the post-*Furman* statutes make clear that capital punishment itself has not been rejected by the elected representatives of the people.

In the only statewide referendum occurring since *Furman* and brought to our attention, the people of California adopted a constitutional amendment that authorized capital punishment, in effect negating a prior ruling by the Supreme Court of California that the death penalty violated the California Constitution.

The jury also is a significant and reliable objective index of contemporary values because it is so directly involved. The Court has said that "one of the most important functions any jury can perform in making . . . a selection [between life imprisonment and death for a defendant convicted in a capital case] is to maintain a link between the contemporary community's values and the penal system." It may be true that evolving standards have influenced juries in recent decades to be more discriminating in imposing the sentence of death. But the relative infrequency of jury verdicts imposing the death sentence does not indicate rejection of capital punishment *per se*. Rather, the reluctance of juries in many cases to impose the sentence may well reflect the humane feeling that this most irrevocable of sanctions should be reserved for a small number of extreme cases. Indeed, the actions of juries in many States since *Furman* are fully compatible with the legislative judgements, reflected in the new statutes, as to the continued utility and necessity of capital punishment in appropriate cases. At the close of 1974 at least 254 persons had been sentenced to death since *Furman,* and by the end of March 1976, more than 460 persons were subject to death sentences.

As we have seen, however, the Eighth Amendment demands more than that a challenged punishment be acceptable to contemporary society. The Court also must ask whether it comports with the basic concept of human dignity at the core of the Amendment. Although we cannot "invalidate a category of penalties because we deem less severe penalties adequate to serve the ends of penology," the sanction imposed cannot be so totally without penological justification that it results in the gratuitous infliction of suffering.

The death penalty is said to serve two principal social purposes: retribution and deterrence of capital crimes by prospective offenders.

In part, capital punishment is an expression of society's moral outrage at particularly offensive conduct. This function may be unappealing to many, but it is essential in an ordered society that asks its citizens to rely on legal processes rather than self-help to vindicate their wrongs.

"The instinct for retribution is part of the nature of man, and channeling that instinct in the administration of criminal justice serves an important purpose in promoting the stability of a society governed by law. When people begin to believe that organized society is unwilling or unable to impose upon criminal offenders the punishment they 'deserve,' then there are sown the seeds of anarchy—of self-help, vigilante justice, and lynch law."

"Retribution is no longer the dominant objective of the criminal law," but neither is it forbidden objective nor one inconsistent with our respect for the dignity of men. Indeed, the decision that capital punishment may be the appropriate sanction in extreme cases is an expression of the community belief that certain crimes are themselves so grievous an affront to humanity that the only adequate response may be the penalty of death.

Statistical attempts to evaluate the worth of the death penalty as a deterrent to crimes by potential offenders have occasioned a great deal of debate. The results simply have been inconclusive. As one opponent of capital punishment has said: "[A]fter all possible inquiry, including the probing of all possible methods of inquiry, we do not know, and for systematic and easily visible reasons cannot know, what the truth about this 'deterrent' effect may be. . . ."

"The inescapable flaw is . . . that social conditions in any state are not constant through time, and that social conditions are not the same in any two states. If an effect were observed (and the observed effects, one way or another, are not large) then one could not at all tell whether any of this effect is attributable to the presence or absence of capital punishment. A 'scientific'—that is to say, a soundly based—conclusion is simply impossible, and no methodological path out of this tangle suggests itself."

Although some of the studies suggest that the death penalty may not function as a significantly greater deterrent than lesser penalties, there is no convincing empirical evidence either supporting or refuting this view. We may nevertheless assume safely that there are murderers, such as those who act in passion, for whom the threat of death has little or no deterrent effect. But for many others, the death penalty undoubtedly is a significant deterrent. There are carefully contemplated murders, such as murder for hire, where the possible penalty of death may well enter into the cold calculus that precedes the decision to act. And there are some categories of murder, such as murder by a life prisoner, where other sanctions may not be adequate.

The value of capital punishment as a deterrent of crime is a complex factual issue the resolution of which properly rests with the legislatures, which can evaluate the results of statistical studies in terms of their own local conditions and with a flexibility of approach that is not available to the courts. Indeed, many of the post-*Furman* statutes reflect just such a responsible effort to define those crimes and those criminals for which capital punishment is most probably an effective deterrent.

In sum, we cannot say that the judgement of the Georgia Legislature that capital punishment may be necessary in some cases is clearly wrong. Considerations of federalism, as well as respect for the ability of a legislature to evaluate, in terms of its particular State, the moral consensus concerning the death penalty and its social utility as a sanction, require us to conclude, in the absence of more convincing evidence, that the infliction of death as a punishment for murder is not without justification and thus is not unconstitutionally severe.

Finally, we must consider whether the punishment of death is disproportionate in relation to the crime for which it is imposed. There is no question that death as a punishment is unique in its severity and irrevocability. When a defendant's life is at stake, the Court has been particularly sensitive to insure that every safeguard is observed. But we are concerned here only with the imposition of capital punishment for the crime of murder, and when a life has been taken deliberately by the offender, we cannot say that the punishment is invariably disproportionate to the crime. It is an extreme sanction, suitable to the most extreme of crimes.

We hold that the death penalty is not a form of punishment that may never be imposed, regardless of the circumstances of the offense, regardless of the character of the offender, and regardless of the procedure followed in reaching the decision to impose it. . . .

We now consider whether Georgia may impose the death penalty on the petitioner in this case.

While *Furman* did not hold that the infliction of the death penalty *per se* violates the Constitution's ban on cruel and unusual punishments, it did recognize that the penalty of death is different in kind from any other punishment imposed under our system of criminal justice. Because of the uniqueness of the death penalty, *Furman* held that it could not be imposed under sentencing procedures that created a substantial risk that it would be inflicted in an arbitrary and capricious manner. Mr. Justice White concluded that "the death penalty is exacted with great infrequency even for the most atrocious crimes and . . . there is no meaningful basis for distinguishing the few cases in which it is imposed from the many cases in which it is not." Indeed, the death sentences examined by the Court in *Furman* were "cruel and unusual in the same way that being struck by lightning is cruel and unusual. For, of all the people convicted of [capital crimes], many just as reprehensible as these, the petitioners [in *Furman* were] among a capriciously selected random handful upon whom the sentence of death has in fact been imposed. . . . [T]he Eighth and Fourteenth Amendments cannot tolerate the infliction of a sentence of death under legal systems that permit this unique penalty to be so wantonly and so freakishly imposed."

Furman mandates that where discretion is afforded a sentencing body on a matter so grave as the determination of whether a human life should be taken or spared, that discretion must be suitably directed and limited so as to minimize the risk of wholly arbitrary and capricious action.

It is certainly not a novel proposition that discretion in the area of sentencing be exercised in an informed manner. We have long recognized that "[f]or the determination of sentences, justice generally requires . . . that there be taken into account the circumstances of the offense together with the character and propensities of the offender." Otherwise, "the system cannot function in a consistent and a rational manner."

The cited studies assumed that the trial judge would be the sentencing authority. If an experienced trial judge, who daily faces the difficult task of imposing sentences, has a vital need for accurate information about a defendant and the crime he committed in order to be able to impose a rational sentence in the typical criminal case, then accurate sentencing information is an indispensable prerequisite to a reasoned determination of whether a defendant shall live or die by a jury of people who may never before have made a sentencing decision.

Jury sentencing has been considered desirable in capital cases in order "to maintain a link between contemporary community values and the penal system—a link without which the determination of punishment could hardly reflect 'the evolving standards of decency that mark the progress of a maturing society.'" But it creates special problems. Much of the information that is relevant to the sentencing decision may have no relevance to the question of guilt, or may even be extremely prejudicial to a fair determination of that question. This problem, however, is scarcely insurmountable. Those who have studied the question suggest that a bifurcated procedure—one in which the question of sentence is not considered until the determination of guilt has been made—is the best answer. . . .

When a human life is at stake and when the jury must have information prejudicial to the question of guilt but relevant to the question of penalty in order to impose a rational sentence, a bifurcated system is more likely to ensure elimination of the constitutional deficiencies identified in *Furman.*

But the provision of relevant information under fair procedural rules is not alone sufficient to guarantee that the information will be properly used in the imposition of punishment, especially if sentencing is performed by a jury. Since the members of a jury have had little, if any, previous experience in sentencing, they are unlikely to be skilled in dealing with the information they are given. To the extent that this problem is inherent in jury sentencing, it may not be totally correctable. It seems clear, however, that the problem will be alleviated if the jury is given guidance regarding the factors about the crime and the defendant that the State, representing organized society, deems particularly relevant to the sentencing decision.

The idea that a jury should be given guidance in its decision making is also hardly a novel proposition. Juries are invariably given careful instructions on the law and how to apply it before they are authorized to decide the merits of a lawsuit. It would be virtually unthinkable to follow any other course in a legal system that has traditionally operated by following prior precedents and fixed rules of law. When erroneous instructions are given, retrial is often required. It is quite simply a hallmark of our legal system that juries be carefully and adequately guided in their deliberations.

While some have suggested that standards to guide a capital jury's sentencing deliberations are impossible to formulate, the fact is that such standards have been developed. When the drafters of the Model Penal Code faced this problem, they concluded "that it is within the realm of possibility to point to the main circumstances of aggravation and of mitigation that should be weighed *and weighed against each other* when they are presented in a concrete case." While such standards are by necessity somewhat general, they do provide guidance to the sentencing authority and thereby reduce the likelihood that it will impose a sentence that fairly can be called capricious or arbitrary.

Where the sentencing authority is required to specify the factors it relied upon in reaching its decision, the further safeguard of meaningful appellate review is available to ensure that death sentences are not imposed capriciously or in a freakish manner.

In summary, the concerns expressed in *Furman* that the penalty of death not be imposed in an arbitrary or capricious manner can be met by a carefully drafted statute that ensures that the sentencing authority is given adequate information and guidance. As a general proposition these concerns are best met by a system that provides for a bifurcated proceeding at which the sentencing authority is apprised of the information relevant to the imposition of sentence and provided with standards to guide its use of the information.

We do not intend to suggest that only the above-described procedures would be permissible under *Furman* or that any sentencing system constructed along these general lines would inevitably satisfy the concerns of *Furman*, for each distinct system must be examined on an individual basis. Rather, we have embarked upon this general exposition to make clear that it is possible to construct capital-sentencing systems capable of meeting *Furman's* constitutional concerns. . . .

We now turn to consideration of the constitutionality of Georgia's capital-sentencing procedures. . . .

Georgia's new sentencing procedures require as a prerequisite to the imposition of the death penalty, specific jury findings as to the circumstances of the crime or the character of the defendant. Moreover, to guard further against a situation comparable to that presented in *Furman*, the Supreme Court of Georgia compares each death sentence with the sentences imposed on similarly situated defendants to ensure that the sentence of death in a particular case is not disproportionate. On their face these procedures seem to satisfy the concerns of *Furman*. No longer should there be "no meaningful basis for distinguishing the few cases in which [the death penalty] is imposed from the many cases in which it is not." . . .

The petitioner further contends that the capital-sentencing procedures adopted by Georgia in response to *Furman* do not eliminate the dangers of arbitrariness and caprice in jury sentencing that were held in *Furman* to be violative of the Eighth and Fourteenth Amendments. He claims that the statute is so broad and vague as to leave juries free to act as arbitrarily and capriciously as they wish in deciding whether to impose the death penalty. . . .

The petitioner attacks the seventh statutory aggravating circumstance, which authorizes imposition of the death penalty if the murder was "outrageously or wantonly vile, horrible or inhuman in that it involved torture, depravity of mind, or an aggravated battery to the victim," contending that it is so broad that capital punishment could be imposed in any murder case. It is, of course, arguable that any murder involves depravity of mind or an aggravated battery. But this language need not be construed in this way, and there is no reason to assume that the Supreme Court of Georgia will adopt such an open-ended construction. In only one case has it upheld a jury's decision to sentence a defendant to death when the only statutory aggravating circumstance found was that of the seventh, and homicide was a horrifying torture-murder. . . .

The petitioner objects, finally, to the wide open scope of evidence and argument allowed at presentence hearings. We think that the Georgia court wisely has chosen not to impose unnecessary restrictions on the evidence that can be offered at such a hearing and to approve open and far-ranging argument. So long as the evidence introduced and the arguments made at the presentence hearing do not prejudice a defendant, it is preferable not to impose restrictions. We think it desirable for the jury to have as much information before it as possible when it makes the sentencing decision. . . .

Finally, the Georgia statute has an additional provision designed to assure that the death penalty will not be imposed on a capriciously selected group of convicted defendants. The new sentencing procedures require that the State Supreme Court review every death sentence to determine whether it was imposed under the influence of passion, prejudice, or any other arbitrary factor, whether the evidence supports the findings of a statutory aggravating circumstance, and "[w]hether the sentence of death is excessive or disproportionate to the penalty imposed in similar cases, considering both the crime and the defendant." In performing its sentence-review function, the Georgia court has held that "if the death penalty is only rarely imposed for an act or it is substantially out of line with sentences imposed for other acts it will be set aside as excessive." *Coley v. State.* . . .

It is apparent that the Supreme Court of Georgia has taken its review responsibilities seriously. . . .

The provision for appellate review in the Georgia capital-sentencing system serves as a check against the random or arbitrary imposition of the death penalty. In particular, the proportionality review substantially eliminates the possibility that a person will be sentenced to die by the action of an aberrant jury. If a time does come when juries generally do not impose the death sentence in a certain kind of murder case, the appellate review procedures assure that no defendant convicted under such circumstances will suffer a sentence of death. . . .

The basic concern of *Furman* centered on those defendants who were being condemned to death capriciously and arbitrarily. Under the procedures before the Court in that case, sentencing authorities were not directed to give attention to the nature or circumstances of the crime committed or to the character or record of the defendant. Left unguided, juries imposed the death sentence in a way that could only be called freakish. The new Georgia sentencing procedures, by contrast, focus the jury's attention on the particularized nature of the crime and the particularized characteristics of the individual defendant. While the jury is permitted to consider any aggravating or mitigating circumstances, it must find and identify at least one statutory aggravating factor before it may impose a penalty of death. In this way the jury's discretion is channeled. No longer can a jury wantonly and freakishly impose the death sentence; it is always circumscribed by the legislative guidelines. In addition, the review function of the Supreme Court of Georgia affords additional assurance that the concerns that prompted our decision in *Furman* are not present to any significant degree in the Georgia procedure applied here.

For the reasons expressed in this opinion, we hold that the statutory system under which Gregg was sentenced to death does not violate the Constitution. Accordingly, the judgment of the Georgia Supreme Court is affirmed.

It is so ordered.

Glossary

abolitionist   One who opposes capital punishment and wants to see it abolished.

actual innocence   A claim that a defendant, or convicted person, did not commit the crime. Actual innocence can be distinguished from the mere legal innocence of someone found not guilty because of lack of proof, or whose conviction may be overturned on technical grounds.

appeals court   See court of appeals.

beheading   A once-common form of execution in which the head is severed from the body by use of a sword, axe, guillotine, or other device. It is currently in use only in Saudi Arabia, a handful of smaller Middle Eastern countries, the Congo, Mauritania, and Belgium.

capital case   A criminal case in which the life of the defendant is at risk.

capital crime   An offense legally punishable by death.

capital punishment   The use of death as a legally sanctioned punishment.

capricious   Tending to change abruptly, or without good reason; freakish, unpredictable. Critics complain that the death penalty is often applied capriciously.

chief justice   The presiding justice of the Supreme Court of the United States.

code   The written law; the entire law on any subject.

commutation   Altering the length or severity of a sentence. State governors may sometimes commute a death sentence into life imprisonment or some lesser penalty.

concurring opinion   In the U.S. Supreme Court, a written opinion that agrees with the overall conclusion of the Court, but goes beyond it to make certain points with which the entire majority may not agree.

court-appointed attorney   A lawyer assigned by a judge to represent a defendant, usually because the defendant cannot afford to hire one him- or herself. Court appointed attorneys are not well paid, and defendants often complain that they do not represent them with the same care and skill they devote to private clients.

court of appeals   A higher level court that hears appeals from decisions of lower courts and has the power to overturn those decisions. Each state has its own appeals court or courts. The federal court system has ten district courts of appeals.

crime   An act forbidden by the criminal law; an offense against the public order.

criminal   A person who has broken the law or who has been convicted of a crime.

decapitation   See beheading.

deter (deterrence, deterrent)   To prevent or discourage someone from doing something. Retentionists argue that capital punishment is needed in order to deter potential criminals from committing crimes.

dissent or dissenting opinion   In the U.S. Supreme Court, a written opinion disagreeing with a specific decision of the Court.

drawing and quartering   A process, no longer used, in which the body of a condemned criminal was torn apart—usually, although not always, after death.

drop   The fall of the body in a hanging, the distance and force of which determines whether death comes by asphyxiation or broken neck.

Eighth Amendment   The Eighth Amendment to the U.S. Constitution states: "Excessive bail shall not be required, nor excessive fines imposed, nor cruel and unusual punishments inflicted." Abolitionists argue that both specific methods of execution and capital punishment by its very nature are cruel and unusual and therefore forbidden by this amendment.

electric chair   The device used for carrying out electrocutions.

electrocution   The form of execution that causes death by running a charge of electricity through the body. It is employed by 15 states of the United States, which is the only country where it is used.

federal   Appertaining to the United States as a whole or to the national government.

federal courts   One of two court systems in the United States, the other being the state courts. It deals with cases involving federal laws, as well as cases involving interpretation of the U.S. Constitution.

federal crime   An offense forbidden by the laws of the United States, as opposed to a particular state or states. Some offenses can be both federal and state crimes.

first degree murder   The most serious degree of murder, and the one for which death is usually reserved. Each state law may define it differently.

garotte   Any of several devices for executing someone by strangulation; garotting is execution by strangulation.

gas   A form of execution in which death is produced by the release of toxic gas. It is used only in the United States, where it is employed by seven states.

gas chamber   A small room used to execute prisoners by the release of deadly gas.

gibbet   A gallows. Also, a structure from which hanged criminals are left to dangle as an example to others.

"Great Writ"   The writ of habeus corpus.

habeus corpus   (Latin for "you have the body.") A writ, or order of a court, ordering the authorities holding someone in custody to produce the prisoner and justify his or her imprisonment or other punishment. In essence, an appeal to the courts on behalf of a prisoner who claims to be being punished unjustly.

hanging   A form of execution in which the condemned prisoner is dropped at the end of a rope. Death is produced either by a broken neck or asphyxiation. Used in four states in the United States.

homicide   One person killing another. Homicides can be divided into three main categories: accidental homicides, justifiable homicides (such as killing in self-defense), and murders.

impalement A form of execution, no longer used, in which the victim is killed by being pierced with a spear, stake, or other sharp device.

judge A public official, elected or appointed, to officiate at trials and render legal decisions. Judges serve either in the federal or state court system.

juror A member of a jury.

jury A body of citizens legally impaneled to examine the facts of a case and make a decision.

jury nullification The refusal of a jury to convict a defendant they believe to be guilty, because they feel that he or she will be given too harsh a punishment.

justice The quality of righteousness. In criminal matters, the notion that legal procedures need to be fair, court decisions accurate, and any punishment both appropriate and deserved.

lethal injection A form of execution that produces death by the effects of a toxic chemical injected into the veins of the condemned man or woman. It is currently used only in the United States, where it is the most popular of all methods, being prescribed by 17 states.

lex talionis Latin term for the principle of retribution: "an eye for an eye and a tooth for a tooth."

lynching A murder committed by a vigilante group or other mob, often considered a kind of unofficial execution by those who carry it out. Historically lynching has been used to terrorize unpopular minorities, as well as to punish suspected criminals. The practice was once widespread in the southern United States, where it was used by whites to frighten and control the black population.

majority opinion In the Supreme Court, an opinion that has received the votes of more than half of the nine justices.

murder The unlawful and deliberate killing of a human being, with malice aforethought. There are various degrees of murder, with different punishments for each. In general, only first degree murder is punishable by death.

ordinary crimes Civilian criminal offenses, as opposed to crimes like treason or desertion from the military in times of war.

pardon   A release from punishment. The president has the power to pardon anyone accused or convicted of a federal crime. Many state governors have a similar power to cancel the punishment of anyone convicted of a state crime.

penal   Having to do with punishments, particularly legal punishments.

penology   The study of prisons and of methods of controlling and/or rehabilitating criminals.

plurality opinion   In the U.S. Supreme Court, a plurality opinion is the one that receives more votes than any other, although less than an absolute majority.

prosecutor   A legal officer of the state or federal government who has the job of presenting the government's case in court against a criminal defendant.

recidivist   A criminal who repeats his or her crime.

retentionist   One who favors capital punishment and wants to see it retained in the United States.

retribution   A deserved punishment.

sanction   Official approval of a punishment or reward; that which gives standing to a particular penalty and makes it binding. Also, a specific penalty designed to force people or institutions to behave in a certain way.

sentencing phase   Following a guilty verdict, that portion of a trial that determines what the punishment is to be. In certain death penalty states, the sentencing phase in a capital case amounts almost to a second trial, which is sometimes heard by different jurors than those who sat in judgment during the guilt phase of the trial.

shooting   A form of execution in which the death penalty is carried out by firing squad. Used by only two states.

state courts   The courts of the individual states, which deal with possible violations of state laws and constitutions.

state crime   An offense forbidden by the law of a particular state or states, as opposed to the laws of the federal government. Some offenses can be both state and federal crimes.

statute   A law or formal regulation.

stoning A form of execution in which stones are showered on the victim until death is produced by brain damage or asphyxiation. It is traditional in several Islamic countries and is currently in use in Iran and Pakistan, as well as five largely Arab nations.

Supreme Court of the United States The highest court in the country. It is charged, among other duties, with making the final decision in disputes over the meaning and application of the U.S. Constitution. It is the court of final appeal for condemned criminals claiming their constitutional rights are being violated.

vigilante A person who takes the law into his or her own hands. Vigilante groups—or vigilance committees—appear where there is a general feeling that the legal system is not working to protect the public and keep order. They take it upon themselves to violently abuse those they consider enemies of society, and sometimes to lynch them. Vigilante activity is illegal.

warrant A written order of a court.

writ A warrant in a criminal case.

writ of certiorari A writ from a higher court, ordering the record of a legal proceeding to be brought to the court. When a writ of certiorari is granted, it means that the higher court is accepting the case for review.

Index